With much love

David

A-Servin' of 'Er Majesty the Queen
An account of my Service career

Group Captain David Greenway OBE

A-Servin' of 'Er Majesty the Queen
An account of my Service career

Vanguard Press

A CIP catalogue record for this title is
available from the British Library.

ISBN 978 1 83794 113 1

*Vanguard Press is an imprint of
Pegasus Elliot Mackenzie Publishers Ltd.*
www.pegasuspublishers.com

First Published in 2024

**Vanguard Press
Sheraton House Castle Park
Cambridge England**

Printed & Bound in Great Britain

The title of this book is taken from Rudyard Kipling's *Gunga Din*. It is what I have done all my life.

Chapter 1

A Child of the Raj

From 1932 to 1947, my father served with the 8th Gurkha Rifles as part of the Indian Army and, until we, his family, left the country in 1945, we followed the flag around India. My mother, who married him in 1934, joined him out there and had the usual welcome to the Officers' Wives' Club. "Do you play Mah-jong?" was the first question they asked. My mother had never heard of it, so was told, "Oh, don't worry. It is very easy. We'll teach you." At the end of the afternoon, she discovered that she had lost that month's housekeeping! She learnt very quickly and became an exceedingly good player.

We spent much of the time in the North West Frontier Province – in what is now Pakistan. We four children were all born out there, so I guess you might now consider us immigrants. It was a fascinating life for a small boy, and I vividly remember much of it even now – all those wonderful colours and smells.

As children, we were often under the care of the ayah, and sometimes my father's bearer, a lovely man called Minnah, who stayed with my father throughout his time in India. I remember only a happy childhood as we went from place to place across India, often by incredibly long train journeys. We travelled in reserved carriages, but whenever the train stopped, there was a great press of people trying to get into our compartment, shoving their *bistra*s (or bedding rolls) through the window in an effort to board the train. They never succeeded, but I remember feeling sad for them as they were pushed away – but I cannot remember by whom.

Amongst other places, we lived on the Afghan border, where we saw wonderful birds and were bombarded by hailstones the size of tennis balls. If nothing else, the incredible cacophony on the corrugated iron roof stopped any conversation, and we just had to wait for the storm to blow over. Often, sentry boxes were blown away, such was the severity of the wind. The drive up to Fort Lockhart was a feat of genius, because we climbed some six thousand feet in trucks, virtually straight up. The driver had to negotiate sickening hairpin bends, each of which needed two or three manoeuvres to get round, with the tail of the vehicle terrifyingly hanging over the edge with sheer drops behind us. On the lawn on Sundays, the Gurkha pipe major would march up and down, regaling us with that wonderful sound. We had picnics just over the Afghan border, but were always accompanied by a *bedruggah*, an ancient man who was supposed to guard us and keep the enemy at bay. He carried a very ancient firing piece, but whether he would have been any good, thankfully we never had to find out.

As soon as we got to the picnic spot, he usually went fast asleep.

As a side note, when I visited Pakistan with the Princess of Wales in 1991, I was talking to a brigadier and asked him if Fort Lockhart was still going strong. He denied all knowledge of it, but it eventually slipped out that any information about the fort was Top Secret! I imagine it is currently primed against any Afghan incursion, but it is still a beautiful place.

In the summer, we moved from the heat of Delhi up to the cool of the foothills of the Himalaya. We lived in a bungalow at Kasauli and looked across the valleys to Simla, now strangely called Shimla. It was all a part of the adventure, and my brother and I would often go down the hill to see great wrestling matches (called *kushti*s), which were very exciting. There were snake charmers and all sorts of creepy crawlies – enough to make one shudder. Once, when tucking in the cover on the sofa, the bearer removed his hand with a scorpion dangling from his finger. It just seemed to be a part of life.

I was first stung by a bee in the starter's box at the Rawalpindi racecourse – a very painful place to be stung. I have vivid recollections of that wonderful dehydrated milk called Klim which had a lovely flavour; I can taste it even now, almost eighty years later. It was a cream-coloured powder to which you added boiling water. And why was it called Klim? Milk re-constituted (or backwards) – brilliant!

At one stage, I remember being put in the care of the cook while my mother went out. It all seemed to be going well, when a man turned up and started chatting to the cook. I wasn't too much aware of what was going on, but, as I told my mother later, they did some sort of a dance which led to them dancing on a bed while lying down. I was obviously quite an innocent four-year-old, because I was saddened to hear that the cook had left. It's a funny old life, growing up.

I remember the first film I saw, but it wasn't in a cinema. Because my father was relatively senior, we lived in a big house in a fort and the cinema (or *bioscope* as it was called) came to us. Chairs were taken off the veranda for us to sit on and sheets were hung on a line across the lawn. When it got dark, the film started and we watched enthralled at some of Tom Mix's (or someone similar) capers. The wonderful thing, though, was that the servants were watching from the other side of the sheets, squatting on the ground and just as entranced as we were, watching it in reverse. Two for the price of one, which was excellent value!

Occasionally, my father's bearer, Minnah, would take my brother and me to school on his bicycle, with John usually on the crossbar and me in a wicker chair behind him. Launching off was quite a trick, but the return home was something else. We would get back to our bungalow in Delhi and Minnah would then cycle round and round, ringing his bell in an effort to summon help. He couldn't dismount in the usually accepted manner because he would have knocked me flying from the chair behind him. Thus, round and round we went. Eventually, when no help came, Minnah reverted to Plan B and, of necessity, he drove the bicycle into the hedge as the only means of stopping safely so that we could fall off gently. Magic memories.

Before we set off for England in January 1945, a man came and sat on the veranda and painted all the cabin trunks with our address. It was all done in immaculate script which you would be hard-pressed to produce on your computer; a master craftsman if ever I saw one. Another long train journey and we arrived at Bombay (now Mumbai), where we were put in a holding camp at Deolali before we were sent to our ship. And it was in Deolali that I had my first rude awakening. Only in retrospect did I realise that I had lived an entirely protected life. My father was a Gurkha officer, and thus we lived among the other officers. Indeed, the Gurkhas, who were Nepalese, lived in the Nepalese lines along with their NCOs. Only their officers were British. Deolali was thus my first encounter with the children of British 'other ranks'. Naturally, I was duffed up almost immediately, presumably because I was a rather poncy, precious little six-year-old boy; it was quite a sharp learning experience, and probably very good for the soul.

We boarded the *Île de France*, which was packed with soldiers returning home – as well as with returning families. The ship was too big to go through the Suez Canal as she was then the third largest liner afloat, so we set off for the Cape, calling at Durban, Cape Town and Freetown en route. Quite how my mother managed to keep us all under control I know not. We must have been a fearful handful with my brother John (eight), me (six) and my two sisters – Buffy (four) and Susan (two).

At one stage on the voyage, we started doing boat drills and, because I was now more confident, I often wandered off on my own. One day, the boat drill was called and, having collected my lifejacket, I lined up with a number of other people in the accepted manner. Eventually, this tall figure progressed towards us with a lot of gold braid on his arm, so I stopped him and asked why we were doing this. He very kindly explained, "It's in case we hit a mine."

"What's a mine?" I asked.

Patiently, he explained that it was something nasty that the Germans had dropped in the sea during the war. If you hit one, they tended to go bang and possibly make a hole in the ship – so we had to practise our lifeboat drills in case they were needed.

"Oh," I said. "There's been a war, has there?" Amazingly, I did not know that there had been a war, so I rushed off to tell my mother. "Do you know that there's been a war?"

Alas, she knew only too well, having lost two brothers killed in action, one who was a Spitfire pilot in the Battle of Britain and the other who was a Wellington pilot. That knowledge stuck in my head and, from then on, I somehow resolved to join the Royal Air Force to avenge them.

My Uncle John had been a Wellington bomber pilot during the war and was sadly posted 'missing, believed killed'. He had, however, successfully bombed the German battleships *Scharnhorst* and the *Gneisenau* in Brest harbour and, as my grandmother said, "He put his mark on those two ships." Uncle Mike was a Spitfire pilot during the Battle of Britain. He was shot down over Cap Griz Nez near Calais, and lay wounded on the ground. A German officer just walked up to him and murdered him. Mike is buried in the tiny village of Basinghen and it is the only Commonwealth War Grave in their cemetery. He is still referred to as 'our airman', which is lovely.

The voyage home was great fun for a small boy and I had a lovely time exploring this huge ship. I frequently accompanied a rather wild renegade boy called Drick, who was more adventurous than I, but I enjoyed being led astray. We often found ourselves down on the waterline, watching the sea go past just outside an open hatch, with the soldiers hanging their legs out over the side. Drick spent quite a bit of time down there gambling with the troops, and was often the subject of frequent Tannoy broadcasts by his mother: "Lost, a small boy, answers to the name of Drick. If anyone…," etc.

The other great memory I have of the *Île de France* was the delicious smell of fresh bread which permeated the dining room each day at breakfast. I have smelt it over the years, but nothing compares to that original French stuff.

Chapter 2

England

We arrived at Southampton having had, to me, a fascinating time. When we came back from India as quite young children, naturally we carried a number of the infections which we had acquired out there. We arrived in England to find a very different sort of life. For instance, we couldn't understand why no one else could speak Hindustani, since that was what we had spoken to our ayah. But other things were strange as well.

My two sisters went to the ladies' lavatory in South Street in Farnham one day, wearing very smart red handkerchiefs on their heads. A rather stuffy lady turned round and said, "Little boys aren't allowed in here!"

"We are not little boys," said my sister. "We are little girls with ringworm!" It was a very effective way of clearing the place. Alas, the lavatories in South Street have been removed, so where do ladies in difficulty go nowadays? I suppose they call it progress, but so much has changed from those halcyon days of the late 1940s. There was a truly wonderful ice cream shop with gloriously rich ices which I can still taste. There was an excellent jeweller, toy shops and the Elphicks department store, which had those amazing spring-loaded containers which fired money from all over the shop, back and forth to the central kiosk. It was a young boy's dream to watch these things whizzing around above our heads seemingly on long rubber bands.

My father remained in India until Partition in 1947, so we lived with my two grandmothers on either side of Farnham. To me, they were somewhat distant figures and quite fierce, which was hardly surprising. Both had been widowed for many years and both had brought up large families, so many uncles and aunts visited to see these strangers from India.

My mother's father had been a much-loved Royal Air Force chaplain during the First World War, spending most of his time with our fighter squadrons on the front line. It must have been a very difficult time for all of them with such a high loss rate among the young pilots. After the war, he went to RAF Cranwell and was chaplain there when it became the Royal Air Force College. He made the first cross for their chapel when he cut down a four-bladed propeller, which seemed very appropriate. They have replaced it with a huge silver cross and, when I visited the College, they were unable to find the original. I guess they call it progress. Sadly, my grandfather died in 1925, so quite how my grandmother managed to bring up seven children on her own is amazing, but they all turned out very nicely, so she must have done a wonderful job. My father's father had been

Governor of both Bristol Prison and of Wormwood Scrubs, and he, too, died relatively young, so we only knew our grandmothers, who were incredibly strong ladies – so living with them was quite an introduction. We must have run them ragged, four children from a far country being introduced to smooth-running households.

As an illustration of how sharp they were, Granny Keymer (my mother's mother), at the end of her life and in her nineties, was getting quite frail and was thus expected to pop off at any stage. Her family was gathered around her while she lay comatose on her bed. Eventually, the youngest of her daughters (who herself later died of Alzheimer's) said, "Well, there's obviously not much going on here. I think I'll nip into Alresford and do some shopping."

Whereupon, the voice from the bed said, "Don't be silly, Lucy. You know Thursdays is early closing!" And she was right! An amazing generation.

Initially, I went to a day school in Farnham while my brother John went off to Prep School in Sussex. I didn't much care for the day school, and nor, I think, did they care much for me, but we had great fun in the holidays. We played exciting games of cricket with all the local boys joining in, and we had amazing paper chases over miles of country, which makes me seem very old-fashioned. When did you last hear of a paper chase? Do they still have them, or are the young nowadays just staring at their hand-held devices? I'm afraid that there is going to be quite a bit of grumpy old man in this story, so you had better get used to it. We went happily on our own on buses and walked for miles without supervision in the woods and far afield, seemingly without a care in the world; but I wonder if my parents were concerned about our whereabouts.

Chapter 3

Prep School

Eventually, when I was seven, I was taken away from the day school and went to join my brother at Cumnor House School (CHS, as we called it), near Haywards Heath. I wasn't 'sent away' to boarding school as the modern generations seem to think. It was just the expected norm, so I didn't worry about it, or, indeed, feel bad about it. It was all going to be a bit of an adventure. Perhaps it was easier because a bunch of us boys from Farnham went there in the same coach, all chatting away with no concerns. But quite how my parents afforded this schooling defeats me. Apparently, my Great Aunt Mabel had heard that I was unhappy in Farnham, so she paid for me to go to CHS a term early, so that was a very generous gift and a great relief to me.

We had an outstanding Headmaster who was always known by his initials – LHMG – but Mr Gulland to his face. He was a real father-figure and we had excellent staff. There must have been about eighty of us in the school and we all got on extremely well. One of the great joys of being at Cumnor was Mr Gulland reading to us in the evenings as we sat at his feet. Nevil Shute was one of his favourite authors, and I was spell-bound by his stories, beautifully read. We listened to the six o'clock news and we were sitting at his feet when he told us that the King had died. We all burst into floods of tears.

For my first two years at the school, we lived in Birch Grove, which was Harold MacMillan's home, a lovely large house set in beautiful grounds. When he went up in the Government, MacMillan wanted it back, so the school moved about five miles to near Danehill.

Naturally, we boys got up to mischief quite often, with the result that a number of us were beaten with a slipper by the Headmaster. I must have been beaten about six times during my stay at CHS, several times in MacMillan's study, which was quite a notch on my CV, so I was obviously quite troublesome. But I don't think I set out to be naughty; I was just a weak follower. Brother John, who everyone thought was God's gift, never got into trouble, so he wasn't beaten at all, the creep. But did being beaten turn me into a raving danger in later life? Of course not. It was just a part of growing up – and we probably deserved what we got anyway.

It is significant that, on one of my school reports, LHMG had written, 'Perhaps he takes too literally the text from St Matthew's Gospel, "Take no thought for the morrow, what ye shall eat, what ye shall drink or what ye shall put on."' He was probably right on the money.

CHS performed a Shakespeare play in an outdoor theatre every summer term and the whole school was involved. In fact, as soon as the school moved when MacMillan wanted his house back, the first thing we did was to build another outdoor theatre there so that the tradition could be maintained. What a first-class teaching aid; it was thoroughly enjoyed by us all and it was also very exciting. In fact, the teaching was excellent and I remember the staff with great affection. They were real characters and their individual habits were naturally picked on mercilessly by us boys. Miss May was a large and fairly elderly lady who taught English. She had obviously been a teacher for a number of years, because as soon as she turned her back on the class, she said, "Shhh!" She had a wonderful hand and wrote quite beautifully on the blackboard. Her only real failing was, because she was so strict, Nick (the Headmaster's son) and I thought she must have been a German spy. These concerns were highlighted by our discovering great trails of wire left over the heathland where we went for walks, presumably left behind by soldiers training before D-Day – but we knew otherwise. We spent ages looking for her radio transmitter, but we never found it, so presumably she was a successful spy – and cunning with it as well.

And while I was having fun at Prep School, my father had left the Indian Army and had gone to theological college to become a priest. Once qualified, his first parish in 1949 was at Stonham Aspal in Suffolk. It was a lovely village, full of real characters, but moving there must have been quite a shock for my mother. The Rectory into which we moved had fifty-six rooms and no central heating. There was an Aga in the kitchen and, initially, we went to bed carrying paraffin lights. Thankfully, we had no accidents, but I imagine my parents must have been on tenterhooks. After some time, my father had Calor Gas lighting installed so at last we could see ourselves in the evenings – and there was a degree of heating from the gas lights. But I remember those bitterly cold winters when the ice formed on the inside of the large windows and, almost inevitably, we had a burst pipe which allowed water to cascade down the stairs. How my parents managed I haven't a clue, but somehow they did.

The house was a huge Georgian pile with three storeys and acres of gardens and woods and an orchard with almost every known fruit growing in abundance. Jim, the village postman, came and looked after the kitchen garden. The top floor of the house (which we called the attic) had six bedrooms, all interconnected by individual doors with a corridor running down the centre. And it was there that we stored the masses of apples and pears after they had been picked. We never managed to eat them all, so, at the end of the season, the fruit started to go off, so John and I were sent up to the attic to clear the rooms out, in readiness for the next season. Can you imagine the fun we had? Armed with rotting apples, we stalked each other round the rooms in the best B-movie style, hurling bad apples at each other so that the door posts and walls were covered in splat marks.

Naturally, after that, we had to clean the place up, but it had been glorious fun.

Amazingly, in comparison to modern times, we used to go home and to school, to and from Suffolk and Sussex, by train, crossing London by Underground without a care in the world. It all seemed so easy to just get on the Tube and to get out at Liverpool Street or Victoria. It was just another adventure and we got on with it, occasionally being intercepted by my lovely godmother who introduced me to a Knickerbocker Glory, which I thought was a bit racy until I tasted it.

Chapter 4

Public School

Both my brother and I had been put down for the public school at Marlborough, but shortly before John left CHS, the Headmaster asked why we were going there. My mother said that they thought it was a good school, wasn't it? "Oh, yes," said LHMG. "But I think they would do better at St Edwards, Oxford." My parents had never heard of the school before, but entirely on the Headmaster's recommendation, we were switched to Teddies.

Before I set off on the next step, I had 'that conversation' with my mother, who was studiously sewing Cash's name tags onto my clothes – with her eyes firmly staring downwards. "You're off to public school tomorrow," she said. "You may find the boys a bit different there. Any problems, ask your father." Truly wonderful and not very enlightening, but most fortunately, the wonderful LHMG had already had very sensible chats with the boys leaving CHS, so we were well-equipped.

St Edwards in 1952 was under the care of the Warden who had been at the school since 1922, so it was much in need of new blood. The staff were also quite long in the tooth, and naturally they were all caricatures with really outstanding mannerisms of which they were apparently unaware. Some were brilliant, while others I disliked intensely – but isn't it always thus? We lived in one of seven houses and, in my intake, we had some dozen of us who all got on extremely well. Naturally, because we were of like minds and enjoyed each other's company, we were constantly accused of being in a gang, but this was far from the truth. We just enjoyed life and got on with it.

Again, at Teddies, I and many other boys were subjected to corporal punishment, usually being beaten by the Head of House – boys beating boys, which may sound strange in these enlightened times when the young seem not to be disciplined at all. It was anything between four and six of the best, administered with a cane, but it did us no lasting damage. We had transgressed and undoubtedly deserved a beating, so you knew fairly forcefully where the boundaries were. Yes, the beatings hurt, but they were soon over. Quite the worst part of it all was the waiting. You were interviewed in the Prefects' Study and, if the case against you was deemed proven, you were told to "Go Away". You knew, therefore, that at some time during the evening Prep, you would be called to the Senior Dormitory, where some prefects were standing as witnesses. You were told to bend over and hold on to the bottom bar of a steel bed. It was a matter of honour that you made no sound and, if you remained silent, the Head of House would say, "Well taken," to which you were supposed to reply, "Thank you!" Later that evening, there was usually a cluster of boys behind you in the communal bathroom to inspect the damage and to admire the handiwork, usually looking for a five-barred-gate.

If your supposed crime was more serious, you were beaten by either the Housemaster or the Warden – neither of whom could wield a vicious cane with any great skill, although Warden Kendall used quite a handy top spin back-hand.

We had wonderful sports facilities at St Edwards and we were so lucky to play sports most afternoons. We played cricket in the summer term, rugger in the winter term and hockey and athletics in the spring term. We were close to the Thames, so there were wonderful rowing facilities as well. Uniquely, I fancy, we ran a straight 220 yards for some reason, despite having a 440 yards running track, albeit on grass. The working hours were somewhat strange in that we had quite a bit of prep in the mornings and also in the evenings, but it was nothing unusual and we just got on with it.

After a short period, we had a new headmaster, Frank Fisher, who had come to us from Repton. He was evidently trying us out before he went on to take over Wellington. His father was Geoffrey Fisher, then the Archbishop of Canterbury, so he had something of an air about him. I didn't much care for him, but my brother liked him, which may say something about him – or me.

When I was still quite new at Teddies, one of the senior boys started 'making eyes' at me, which I found a bit disturbing. At a loss as to how I should handle this predicament, I asked my brother what I should do. His helpful comment was, "I should tell him where to get off!"

I found his caring attitude most helpful and, when next I saw the senior boy, I called to him and said, "Liverpool Street!" Ha! That told him all right, and I had no more trouble from him. It's a funny old life growing up.

In addition to playing lots of sport, we were also encouraged to go and watch Oxford University play rugby, notably against Stanley's XV, which always included a number of internationals. I remember seeing the England fly-half, Richard Sharp, Onllwyn Brace (the Welsh scrum half who had a fantastic reverse pass), Cliff Morgan and the Irish hero, Jackie Kyle. Brilliant days! And then, in 1954, I had the most wonderful experience. There was an athletics meeting between Oxford University and the Amateur Athletic Association (known as the 3As). I had never seen any of these great named athletes perform, and so I sought permission to go down to the Iffley Road to see what was going on. I particularly wanted to see the international, Mark Pharoah, put the shot, but Roger Bannister was also running. It was at the time of the great anticipation of the first sub-four-minute mile, but the weather was awful on 6th May. The master who gave me permission to go said that nothing would happen and that it would be a real waste of time. The wind was very strong and buffeting, but, shortly before the off in the 1-mile, it dropped to nothing; so, when the race started, the sense of anticipation was absolutely fantastic. There was an electric atmosphere around the track as the three took off: Roger Bannister, Chris Chataway and Chris Brasher – plus the Oxford University athletes, but who was looking at them? We were all incredibly excited as the race developed, and I vividly remember Norris McWhirter commentating and counting down the time as Bannister approached the finish line. It was going to be incredibly close. When the result was announced, they had the classic utterly British voice saying, "Here is the result of the 1-mile. First, R. G. Bannister... time three minutes..." and the whole place took off. We were charging all over the track, hooting and cheering until eventually, after what must have been about five minutes, we had another dry announcement. "Here is the result of the 1-mile. First, R. G. Bannister... time three minutes...," and off we went again. It really was an incredible moment and wonderful to have been there to experience that historic occasion.

I love the story of the meeting of the Oxford Union that evening when it was suggested that, in order to recognise this fantastic achievement, the meeting should be adjourned for 3 minutes and 59.4 seconds. Sadly, this was rejected by the Indian President, who did not know of the world record, "Because we have not been notified of this proposal!"

When I was fifteen, I was awarded an RAF scholarship to join the Royal Air Force. I had to go to RAF Hornchurch in Essex to undertake the various tests and, to my horror, I was awarded a scholarship to go to the RAF College at Cranwell *as a navigator*. I wasn't too keen on this, but, for fear of missing the whole scholarship, I pressed on. As soon as Frank Fisher, the headmaster, heard of my award, he interviewed me and said, "You must be crazy. The RAF will not like you and you will not like the RAF. Why don't you join the Army?" Not one word of congratulation or well done; absolutely nothing, but just this damning statement from a headmaster who should have known better. Guy Gibson and Douglas Bader had been old boys at Teddies, so that was another good reason to continue with joining the RAF. However, smarting under his damning comments about my scholarship, at a later date when we had a cricket match against the Masters, I had the great joy of hitting the headmaster over the Woodstock Road. All he said was, "Nice shot for a 4-iron."

I wasn't academically inclined and usually dragged along towards the bottom of the classes. I had to get two A-levels in order to fulfil the requirements of my scholarship. However, when it came to choosing my A-levels, I wanted to do French and Geography, but this seemed beyond the wit of the school. Thus, I was put in the History sixth form, which was completely hopeless.

While I was doing History, I was missing out on French; while I was doing French, I was missing out on Geography; and while I was doing Geography, I was missing out on History. It was a ridiculous position and I stood no chance at all of getting the required A-levels.

In the summer holidays, after I had had a bad round of golf, my mother said to me, "How do you feel about going back to St Edwards next term?"

I said I didn't want to because I was fed up with the way they were treating me. My mother said that that was fine, but she wanted to know what I was going to do instead. I said I would try to join the RAF on a Direct Commission, which was a great relief to my parents because having children with no idea what they want to do is a nightmare. Thus, I returned to RAF Hornchurch for the aircrew selection board to have another look at me.

I was most anxious not to join as a navigator, so I tried to think what went wrong or right with my last interview. Eventually, I decided that it was perhaps my choice of job. In my previous interview they had asked me what I wanted to fly and I had said, "Fighters." When asked why, I blundered around with no real thought at all, which clearly did not impress them, since it did not impress me either. This time, I thought I would use a different tactic. So, when the question came up again, I said, "Bombers." When asked why, I launched into a prepared statement which included words like crew co-operation, team spirit, morale, all getting on together and so on; and, lo and behold, I was awarded a Direct Commission as a pilot.

Actually, whether my change of tactics had any bearing on the case I have no idea. As I have moved on in the RAF, I am fairly certain it was a question of supply and demand. Thus, when I applied to join initially, we probably had a surplus of pilots in the training machine, so I was given the job of navigator. On my second visit, I think they had plenty of navigators in the system and were short of pilots – hence my success at getting what I wanted to do, for which I was eternally grateful. Thankfully, despite my not going to Cranwell, the RAF never asked for the scholarship money back, which must have been a relief to my parents.

We had a very good Combined Cadet Force (CCF) at school, where we all got into military uniforms and did drill and manoeuvres in the country on Field Days, carrying the old Lee Enfield .303 rifles and occasionally firing blank ammunition. We also had excellent camps with CCFs from other schools, so it was a good learning experience and great fun, living in tents for a week. I don't think we were brainwashed into the military mindset; it was just a part of the school syllabus.

Eventually, I graduated to the RAF Section of the CCF, so we could now turn our eyes to the sky. To gain some air experience, we visited RAF Little Rissington, in the Cotswolds, where we were given a flight in an Anson, which frightened the life out of me. The aircraft stank of fuel and, for reasons which escape me, the pilot delighted in showing us how the aircraft stalled. To me, it just fell out of the sky, which wasn't what flying was supposed to be like at all, so I was terrified and wondered if I had made the right career decision. Surely it had to be better than that?

In 1954, my parents moved to the village of Theberton, in the east of Suffolk, for my father's second parish. The rectory was relatively modern in that this time we had electricity; so, as soon as I got home for the holidays, I dug out the old radio we had in India and plugged it in, only to blow all the fuses in the house! But it was from Theberton that I set out in RAF uniform to go to our CCF camp at RAF Swanton Morley, in Norfolk. I had to change trains at Ipswich, so I took the precaution of asking a porter if this was the Norwich train. "Oh yes," he said, so in I got, horrified to see us disappear down a single-track line towards Felixstowe. Naturally, it transpired that the train had just *come* from Norwich! There was nothing to do but to ride all the way to Felixstowe, because it was going to be the same train that would take me back to Ipswich for another go. My life has been a bit like that.

At home, we all trooped to church on Sundays and were immediately recognised as the Rector's children. At the last parish we had been told to sit in the front pew, which we did not like, so this time we made for a more central position, which was much better. Of course, being away at school for most of the time it was difficult to remember names or people, so we were always on the back foot, particularly when everyone apparently knew who we were. We had lovely families in the village and Theberton was in a lovely part of Suffolk, so we were very lucky. It was fairly exposed and, in the freezing winters, you could almost smell the vodka coming across the North Sea.

Chapter 5

Joining the Royal Air Force

I joined the RAF on a Direct Commission on 1st April 1957 at RAF Kirton-in-Lindsay in Lincolnshire, and I found it great fun from the off. I was thworn in by a wet fish with a lithp and a limp handshake, before I was interviewed by the staff. At one stage, a very pompous Education Officer asked me to name three authors beginning with a vowel, so I said, "Austen, Orwell and Eliot."

On the basis of this, he then said, "I put it to you, Greenway, that you do not read enough!" Quite how he came to this conclusion I haven't a clue, since he then said, "That's the only chap we've had today who has managed three!"

We went straight into square-bashing, which I found easy because of the good grounding I had had in the CCF. Moreover, my boots were always immaculate, again having spent hours at Teddies bulling not only my boots, but also those of the prefects (including my brother's) as part of the now defunct fagging system. In fact, I spent quite a bit of time teaching my fellow cadets how to bull their boots and generally keep their kit clean. Who said the CCF was bad for you? We also had to keep our barrack block immaculately clean, and I have a photograph somewhere of me on my hands and knees, polishing the floor – with an excellent reflection of me on the polished floor!

We had a wonderful drill instructor who was also in charge of the station cinema; he was more proud of that than in turning us out as officer cadets and was constantly telling us that his cinema had tip-up seats! Funny things you remember over the years. Those of us heading for Direct Commissions were paid £4 10s a week, while the poor National Service chaps only got thirty bob. It is no use trying to convert that to modern-day prices, but suffice it to say that I have never been better off than I was in those days.

What was interesting was to see how my fellow cadets came across – and this applied right across my training. We were a complete cross-section of society, including chaps from the East End as well as those from different parts – plus a few of us from public schools. A number of them were super-confident with a brash manner, often telling you how good they were; and, indeed, some of them even had private pilot's licences. But, as we went through the various courses, these were the ones who fell by the wayside and failed to make it through the system. I was just grateful to have avoided the chop (as we called it) all the way through – on every course I have done!

Chapter 6

Basic Flying Training

After three months at the Initial Training School, we set off for RAF Tern Hill, in Shropshire, to learn to fly; and almost the first thing we discovered was that we were now going to get ten shillings a day flying pay! Wow! We were going to fly the Piston Provost, an aircraft with two seats side by side so you could see what your instructor was doing and vice versa. But first we had ground school to learn how the aircraft worked and, indeed, actually flew. We were taught engines on the basis that we knew how a car engine worked, which put me at a distinct disadvantage since I was totally ignorant. Thus, I had to learn the answers to some of the questions parrot-fashion in order to pass, and I really only discovered the real answers when I became a flying instructor and had to teach my own students! Our engines instructor doubled as a Scoutmaster, so we were often left to our own devices. One day, we looked for some instructional films on engines and stumbled across a selection of his definitely suspect films, which did nothing for the syllabus, but cheered us up enormously.

The Piston Provost was quite a large aircraft, certainly on initial acquaintance, and you had to clamber up to get in the cockpit. A fellow student on the course ahead of me, on seeing the aircraft close up for the first time, apparently turned to his instructor and said, "I say. Haven't you got anything smaller we can start on?"

Eventually, we started flying, and I found it all quite an adventure and surprisingly not that difficult. There seemed to be an over-emphasis on getting ready for a forced landing, such was aircraft reliability in those days, but fortunately I never had to see if the training worked. But after a relatively short time I was sent solo, which was a wonderful experience. The instructor who was checking my suitability to fly on my own was a superb Flight Sergeant Instructor who just turned to me and said, "I think I need a coffee. Why don't you go off on your own and see how you get on?" He unstrapped from his seat and left. What a lovely man.

The first time you fly on your own is like nothing else. Usually, you are talking to or listening to your instructor, but now there was just the empty seat beside me, with this great throbbing thing under me, under my sole control. I felt completely euphoric and as happy as a sand boy – whatever that is. It was the first major step to becoming a pilot, so it was also a great relief. In the meantime, a few of our course departed early, having failed to fly solo.

The Tern Hill course lasted nine months as we went through the various stages of training. This included general handling, which taught you how to fly the aircraft in various configurations, to fly in formation with other aircraft – as well as how to navigate. The latter was great fun, but the navigation exercises could be a bit of a test. One of my major failings was that I was always forgetting to start the clock at the beginning of a navigation leg, so that finding out when it was time to turn resorted to a bit of a lottery. Towards the end of the navigation phase, we did a landing-away exercise which sent you to the other side of England. We were to fly to RAF Feltwell, in Norfolk, and went off in line astern at about five-minute intervals. Ahead of me was a very capable chap called Win Harris, who eventually made three-star Air Marshal. He was evidently good and was probably going to make top student, so stupidly I followed him rather than navigating myself. As we flew east, I caught up with Win as the visibility gradually reduced. When we were almost there, Win dived, so I followed him down through the murk, horrified to see that we were now at low level over a town. Not knowing where I was, I now had great difficulty finding Feltwell in the very poor visibility. It later transpired that Win lived in King's Lynn and that he had gone down to wave to his parents and, unknowingly, he had led me astray. What a leader!

At that time, the RAF was training Iraqi pilots to fly, and our course comprised about fifty percent Iraqis. They were a law unto themselves and seemed not to care about anything else other than going up to London at weekends.

We took it in turns to be course leader during training, and that was when I fell foul of the system. I had to march our flight down to the airfield so that we could go flying in the afternoon. Naturally, the Iraqis were their usual shambles and kept us all waiting, thus making us late for flying. I therefore gave them both barrels and shouted at them to make an effort and get a grip. For reasons best known to themselves, the Iraqis then went on strike; so, as course leader, I was summoned for interview with the station commander. Everyone knew that I had been called to account and waited with trepidation to see what my punishment might be. But the station commander was very friendly and said to me, "I understand that you called the Iraqis 'fucking Iraqis'. Is that correct?"

"Yes, sir," I said.

He then replied, "Oh, dear, it does upset them so. I quite understand your predicament, but could you please do me a favour? In future, don't call the fucking Iraqis 'fucking Iraqis', there's a good chap." What a wonderful interview!

Chapter 7

Advanced Flying Training

In March 1958, we went on to the next stage of flying training. We were off to RAF Swinderby, near Lincoln, to learn to fly jets; and yes, you've guessed it, they gave us an increase in flying pay! It was only another 2/- a day, but it all helped. We were to fly the Vampire with its twin-boomed tail, which had been one of our front-line jet fighters in the early 1950s. But first we had ground school, again to learn about the aircraft and its ejection seats with which the training version was fitted. Once more we had excellent instructors and, even now, I can remember our Chief Technician, who was a de Havilland man through and through, always referring to Rolls-Royce as "that firm in the Midlands!"

Because we were going to be flying over or near the sea, we had to do dinghy drills, so we set off for Leconfield, in Yorkshire, where we were to practise in the sea and then be picked up by a helicopter and winched to safety. That was the plan, but when we got there the wind was howling and the sea far too rough, so they decided to make us do dry lifts over the airfield so that we knew the procedures for helicopter winching, etc. Strangely, I had had a dream the night before in which the strop, which goes around you and to which the winch cable is attached, had broken. Accordingly, I deliberately went number three in the queue behind the two biggest chaps on the course. They went up and down satisfactorily, so I stepped forward and was lifted up and into the helicopter. It was then time to let me down, so I was eased out of the door some forty foot off the ground – and the strop broke. It was a very strange feeling, because I had been through this procedure in my dreams the previous night, so I fell completely relaxed because I had done it before. Meanwhile, my stunned fellow students said, "Good grief. Why does David want to jump from that height?" Typical, and with no sympathy at all. I was knocked out as I hit the ground and only cut my eye where my knee had come up on impact, so I was very lucky. They did, however, do the decent thing and hauled me off to Sick Quarters, where I was told to lie down while the rest of the course carried on with the dinghy drills. When it was time to leave, I was ushered onto the coach and was then sick a number of times on the return journey. Nobody checked for concussion or broken bones; I was just got rid of at best speed. When we got back to Swinderby, I found that I was seeing double, which was a bit disturbing, but I didn't dare tell the doctors for fear of losing my flying category. Most fortunately, we were in the ground school phase at the time, so I didn't have to fly for a couple of weeks, by which time my eyes thankfully reverted to normal.

But why did the winching strop break? In those days, the strop was just a piece of canvas material, stitched together at the point where the grab handle was connected. There was no check on how many lifts any strop had undertaken and, more to the point, they just used them in the sea, dried them out and then used them again. Eventually, the stitching was bound to rot; and, of course, I was the first and only chap to discover this. As a result of my accident, they immediately changed the design to make the strop a continuous weave so there was no longer any stitching to rot. Sadly, my successful trial was never acknowledged, although, throughout my career, I had awful neck pains and headaches, as a result of which their Airships kindly gave me a small disability pension when I left the Service. Happily, as a result of having this small War Disability Pension, that nice Mr Boris Johnson, when he was Mayor of London, gave me a free Oyster Card, which was very nice of him. It isn't a lot of use in Hampshire, but it was a nice idea.

Flying the Vampire was very different to the Piston Provost. In the latter, we had the propeller and the engine in front of us; but now, with the Vampire, we were ahead of the jet engine and, indeed, ahead of the aircraft, sitting in the nose with very little side reference unless you craned your neck to look at the wings, which were some distance behind you. The aircraft did not vibrate, so it was a very new experience. We had different marks of

Vampire. The T11 was a two-seater (with side-by-side ejection seats), and we had the single-seat Mark 5 (without an ejection seat) and Mark 9 aircraft, which did have an ejection seat. To my great surprise, the noses of these sleek, silver-painted fighter aircraft were made of plywood. They were very light on the controls and fun to fly, although you had to work hard to achieve the necessary accuracy. Because we now flew to over thirty thousand feet, we had to be on oxygen, so it was a very different envelope in which we operated. The aircraft was much quicker and more slippery than the Provost, so it was also quite a handful, but the flying syllabus was quite similar to that which we went through on our first aircraft.

Despite almost incessantly preparing for all sorts of emergencies throughout our basic and advanced flying training, we only had one engine failure on our course and that was on Vampires. One of my fellow students was a chap called Doc Whittle – son of the famous Sir Frank Whittle, who invented the jet engine. Doc had a major problem when his engine failed at height. Most happily, he managed to bring his stricken aircraft back to base for a safe landing and, joy of joys, he was then able to tell his father that the damned thing didn't work!

Throughout our training, we were subject to almost incessant checks, so you were always on your mettle. You tended to fly with the same instructor, but check rides were usually undertaken with more experienced and feared senior pilots. The interesting thing was that, not only were you and your skills being checked, but by inference, so was your instructor. Thankfully, I survived the rigours and actually had only minor problems along the way.

I landed once in a single-seat Vampire and was certain that all was not well with the aircraft. I turned off the runway after landing and meticulously went through my after-landing checks three times, but I still had an uneasy feeling that there was something wrong. Eventually, I gave up and taxied back to dispersal, surprised to see many students emerge from their hangars to have a look at me. Had I been low-flying and brought some branches back with me? Had something fallen off the aircraft? I really had no clue, so, as I came to a stop in the dispersal, I was met by a lovely chief who said, "Well, sir. You've done it this time!"

"Done what?" I asked.

"You'd better get out and have a look!" was the cryptic reply.

I stepped out of the aircraft and was surprised to meet the ground much sooner than I had anticipated. I then turned round to see my aircraft with its tail high in the air and the nose only an inch or so off the ground. It transpired that the nosewheel oleo, which effectively gives you spring loading, had collapsed and I had taxied in with the aircraft tilted some thirty degrees nose down. It wasn't my fault, but I felt a bit of a twit nonetheless. Without any reference to the outside world, with the wings out of sight behind me, it was difficult to realise what the problem was – except that I knew something was wrong and couldn't put my finger on it.

At Swinderby, I bought my first set of wheels: a very much underpowered Piatti scooter which, if run for too long, just conked out on me. The only solution seemed to be to change the plug, so I was forced to carry several spares on longer journeys. My Piatti had a large windscreen in front, so, in the event of fog (quite usual in those days), in order to see more clearly, I just shoved the screen down and continued on my journey with better visibility. There was one quite amusing episode when I was returning from an evening out in Lincoln. On returning to the Officers' Mess, I was startled to see many cars just lined up behind me, wondering where to go. The drivers had simply just followed me because it was obvious that I could see the road better than they could. After some discussion, I was persuaded to lead them back to the Fosse Way so that they could continue their crawl towards Newark.

I also had an epic weekend going to stay with my parents in Suffolk. A mad Australian on my course, called Bluey Buckingham, came with me, so we decided to make the trip on his motorbike rather than chance my Piatti. Bluey was a bit cavalier and, as a result, we crashed five times over the weekend! We slid off the road a couple of times, once on a wet level crossing, and, unbelievably, in the last one, we drove straight into a cow which had elected to cross the road in front of us. How we survived that lot I know not, but at least Bluey broke his arm when we hit the cow. I managed to land with minimum damage, just piling into Bluey's back!

So, after nine months on the Vampire, we were awarded our 'wings', much to our great relief and, indeed, pride. My parents and lovely family friends came up to witness the moment when the wings were actually pinned on us. But, instead of going directly to the celebratory reception after the parade, we all rushed back to our rooms to sew brand new wings on to our uniforms – and we all felt elated.

Chapter 8

Operational

In wondering what to apply for after we had got our wings, I opted for large aircraft as my first choice. However, my flying instructor at Swinderby had a bee in his bonnet about the necessity of having a permanent commission. He said that the easiest way to get one was to join the V-Force – the fleet of Vulcan, Victor and Valiant aircraft which provided our nuclear deterrent at that time – so, to my concern, he recommended me for that role. Other lesser mortals were just posted there; but, because I had been recommended, I was called to Headquarters No 1 Group to be interviewed by the Air Officer Commanding (AOC).

In those days, those of any other persuasion looked down on the V-Force, not only because we didn't much care for the role and the almost incessant alerts the crews had to hold, but because there was a rather disparaging rumour that the basic requirement to join them was that you had to have a Dinner Jacket, you had to have a Mess Kit (for formal dinner nights) and you had to go to church. Of course, we had no real idea; but you may imagine my surprise to be faced by the great man, one Air Vice-Marshal Bing Cross, whose opening phrase to me was, "Have you got a DJ? Have you got Mess Kit? Do you go to church?"

Stunned, I replied, "Yes, yes and yes, sir – my father is a parson."

"Oh, I say, that's capital. How do you feel about joining the V-Force?"

So I told him I wasn't very happy about it since I had opted for long- or medium-range piston-engined aircraft when I left flying training. "I suppose that means Transport Command, does it?" he said disapprovingly.

"Well, yes, sir," I said. "But it is still an essential part of the Royal Air Force."

"Huh!" he said. "So is the Midland Red Bus Service!"

Thus, I was grateful to escape and, within three weeks I received my posting to Coastal Command and their Shackletons.

As a rider to my V-Force interview, a few years later the great man was himself posted to become AOC-in-C Transport Command. Needless to say, I was sorely tempted to send him a signal saying, 'Welcome to the Midland Red!'

As often happened in the late 1950s, the supply of pilots was out of kilter with the demand; so, for the first year after I got my wings, I did a few interesting courses to pass the time and was then sent to RAF St Mawgan, near Newquay in Cornwall, to join No 206 Squadron, while I waited for a conversion course to be taught formally to fly the four-engined Shackleton. It was frustrating to a certain extent because we really wanted to be gainfully employed as pilots once we had left the training machine, but at least I was now on a squadron and flying in big aircraft – and straight away I loved it.

The Shackleton first flew in 1949 and, while it may have been developed as a follow-on to the Lancaster and the Lincoln bombers (and, indeed, looked not unlike them), it was specifically designed for the anti-submarine role. For this, you needed to have the ability to loiter at low level over the sea for long periods, far from shore. As the years passed, several variations on the original design were made which improved the aircraft's capability. Thus, we had different Marks of aircraft, but they all sounded and smelt the same! All Marks were powered by four Rolls-Royce Griffon piston engines, which had contra-rotating propellers. This means that, on each engine, we had two three-bladed propellers, with the front set rotating one way and the rear set rotating the other. To achieve the same amount of power with one set of propellers, the blades would have had to be enormously long, thereby necessarily making the undercarriage legs much longer and therefore heavier.

Equipment in the aircraft was also updated over the years, but the role and capability of each type was much the same. The normal aircrew complement was two pilots, two navigators, one flight engineer and a five-man team of air electronic specialists. The latter operated the long-range HF radios, the radar (to look for surface contacts) and the sonics (to listen for submerged submarines) – as well as all the internal pyrotechnics which we either dropped or fired from the aircraft. They also operated the tiny galley from which they produced wonderful food to sustain us in the air – although the rest of us helped with the food and drinks when we could.

Internally, all Shackletons were incredibly noisy, although the Mark 3 had improved sound-proofing. The propellers were whistling round beside the cockpit and the airflow past all the hatches made a dreadful hissing noise, so we all eventually went deaf. Incidentally, if you hoped to sell someone your car, it was quite a good ruse to take them flying first before they did a test ride. The car sounded like silk!

Perhaps the one thing really common to all Shackletons was the dreaded Elsan, which lurked just aft of the rear door. No matter what you did or didn't do, it always stank. Flying for up to sixteen hours at a time, it was much-needed, but I always tried to organise my body to reduce use of it to a minimum. On the plus side, we had excellent lookout positions, which were extremely useful in the hunt for submarines. It was amazing how often the Mark 1 eyeball came into its own, often seeing a submarine periscope or other aerials before the equipment kicked in.

Whilst I was unqualified on the aircraft, I joined a crew and did everything that they did. We were employed in the anti-submarine role, flying long and tiring sorties over the Atlantic approaches, principally hunting for Soviet submarines for the most part. We also practised our role with allied NATO submarines and surface ships. It was often incredibly boring, incessantly staring at the grey seas while the team in the back of the aircraft searched with their radar screens and other equipment. But what was truly wonderful was the fact that it was actually great fun. Twelve or more of us, in a very noisy, vibrating environment which essentially had been designed in the late 1940s, all working together at our various roles and, thankfully, all getting on extremely well together. Roughly half the crew were officers and the other half Senior NCOs, and each of us was good at his job. We had to be, because everyone was watching each other. Thus, it was a matter of great pride to do your job well or someone would comment on it. And this was naturally one of the big differences between us and the fighter pilot fraternity. We had some hundred aircrew on a Shackleton squadron, plus a similar number of ground crew. On a fighter squadron, they may have had about fifteen pilots and fewer ground crew, with nobody actually watching how the pilots performed – while we were watched all the time. Of course, fighter pilots incessantly told you how good they were, talking mostly with their hands in formation and buying up the conversation, while flying perhaps forty-minute sorties.

Meanwhile, we flew for hours and hours and relied heavily on feeding the inner man. Our NCOs, who were mostly signallers or air electronics experts, did wonders by providing hot meals and drinks at regular intervals, and we simply could not have operated without them. They really were fantastic, not only at their specialist jobs, but also how they managed to produce amazing food from the tiny galley we had in the back of the aircraft. Their real specialisation was a dish we called 'Honkers Stew', which has no known recipe. It seems to have been a bit of this, a bit of that, tins of some obscure stuff and other stuff you recognised, and it was always excellent.

We flew sorties up to and beyond sixteen hours at a time and it was always exhausting. While we may have been airborne for all that time, the flying took very little notice of our body clocks. Moreover, we had to brief for a sortie some two hours before take-off and then debrief the trip afterwards. What was perhaps more difficult to take in as the new boy was the fact that we were supposed to remain awake and alert through all this time, so it was quite a struggle.

Because I wasn't qualified on type, I was occasionally allowed to fly the aircraft when it was quiet; but, when we were hunting submarines, I spent much of my time in one of the lookout positions, searching the grey seas. Strangely, I found that I saw ships and submarines before the rest of the crew. I also gave as much help as I could in the galley, so I managed to earn my keep.

Chapter 9

Operational Conversion

In the autumn of 1959, I went to RAF Kinloss on the Moray Firth. I was to join the Maritime Operational Training Unit (universally known as MOTU) to be taught how to fly and operate the Shackleton. Nowadays, they put student pilots through a multi-engined conversion course as a stepping stone to the big stuff, but whether this is necessary or whether it makes them better able to cope, I know not. We went straight from the very small Vampire jets to the huge Shackletons, and really did not have a problem with the conversion. But, once again as usual, we started with the ground school phase. My course comprised me plus some very experienced senior officers (some of whom were returning to fly the Shackleton), and it was all great fun. I worked like crazy and managed to achieve ninety-four percent across the board in the ground school exams, only to find myself bottom of the course. I can't help thinking that their ranks may have had something to do with the marking!

And then we started on the flying phase. At St Mawgan, I had been flying the much heavier Mark 3

Shackleton, but now I was to fly the original Mark 1 version, which was now used as a trainer. Both types had essentially the same engines, the famous Rolls-Royce Griffons, but because the Mark 1 was not as heavy, it was much friskier and felt much lighter on the controls. A lot of our flying was with a full crew plus instructors, with anything up to about fifteen of us on board; but to start with we concentrated on learning to fly the aircraft, mostly in the approach and landing phase. The aircraft had a tail wheel, so landing in a cross-wind was quite a challenge. However, the aircraft had large rudders, which meant that you could crab down the approach centre line and then kick off the drift to straighten the aircraft for landing. If you came in a bit faster than required, the aircraft often ballooned after touchdown, making the whole thing a bit dangerous. The trick was to be accurate in your flying and to control your speed so that the aircraft settled in a three-point attitude on the runway. You were always conscious of being watched by your crew, and this did wonders for your application and skill levels. You had to be good or you would get stick from the back-end team!

Having supposedly mastered landing the aircraft, we were then taught the operational business of hunting for submarines and effectively fighting the aircraft. It helped me enormously having been on a squadron beforehand so that I knew the jargon in what was a very complicated learning process. In an operational environment, the Shackleton carried homing torpedoes and depth charges in the bomb bay, plus a number of sonobuoys, which we dropped to listen for submarines beneath the surface. Within the aircraft we carried smoke markers, which we dropped in the water to mark a position, and we had flares to help us see a target at night as well as photo-flashes to take night photographs. It was quite a comprehensive package to understand, but thankfully we had wonderful teams of mostly NCOs in the back of the aircraft who did a tremendous job of work, not only with the flares, etc., but also operating the radar, the long-range radios (W/T in the jargon, meaning Wireless Telegraphy) and the sonics, interpreting the sounds and squawks from the sonobuoys. On top of that, they also ran the galley in any quieter moments. But flying the Shack was an enormous team effort and the greatest fun.

Training in Scotland was excellent, with fantastic visibility in the clean air, while any weather systems seemed to speed through without giving us too much trouble. During the course, we also did winter survival training in the Cairngorms, which necessitated stomping through the snow and learning about Arctic survival. We slept in a large tent and, as usual, we had one man who snored for Scotland. In the mornings, he was always surprised that his bed was covered in flying boots which we had all thrown at him in an attempt to get a decent night's sleep. It didn't seem to matter that he was a very senior officer!

Chapter 10

Qualified Shackleton Pilot

Happily, I passed the conversion course and then returned to RAF St Mawgan, now as a qualified Shackleton co-pilot, albeit on a different mark of Shackleton. I was assigned to the same crew with which I had previously worked, which was nice as I knew the team. There was always wonderful repartee, and you had to keep on your toes. I remember one day when the NCOs were laughing about some programme they had seen on TV and, when I asked which programme they were talking about, I was told it was something called *Morecambe and Wise*. They were surprised that I had never heard of them, probably because the box in the Officers' Mess seemed to be stuck on the BBC. I wonder what happened to them or if they were any good?

Retaining a sense of humour was essential on a Shackleton crew, and, with twelve men all connected by intercom, the situation was ripe for comments – particularly if someone stuffed up. Of course, the Captain of the aircraft was ultimately responsible for the efficiency and safety of his crew, but he, too, was not protected from caustic comments. At one stage, he turned to me and said, "F... you, Co-pilot. I make the funnies on this crew!" What an accolade!

Matters have obviously moved on from when I was in Coastal Command in the 1960s, but the job is still much the same. Flying in a Shackleton has been best described as long moments of boredom interspersed with blind moments of panic – and that just about sums it up. Often, it was tedious in the extreme, just staring at the grey seas for hours on end, looking for submarines; but we were not only looking. Usually, we also had the radar team in the radar compartment trying to find contacts, trying to get a radar return from a submarine if it showed anything above the surface of the sea. In those days, diesel-electric submarines had to charge their batteries, and to do this they had to put up a breathing tube (called a snort) to run their diesel engines. Nowadays, it is mostly nuclear submarines they are chasing, and these don't need to snort. They very rarely put anything above the surface, but the problems they face are similar.

Apart from the anti-submarine role, we also carried out Search and Rescue (S&R) duties. We carried a large multi-man dinghy and survival equipment in the bomb bay which could be dropped to survivors in the water, and we often practised this role. We also had a crew on S&R standby so that we could provide rapid response if someone was in difficulties. Indeed, we were called to look for downed aircraft on a number of occasions, and these were often sad times. On the other hand, we were called to help an American Super Constellation which was crossing the Atlantic. It was in serious difficulties having lost its No 3 engine. Indeed, the propeller had come off and had impaled itself in the fuselage, just behind the co-pilot's head. We thrashed out over the Atlantic, ready to escort the inbound aircraft to terra firma. The Shackleton was designed to fly low and slow, but it surprised us that we could not keep up with the distressed aircraft, which sped past us on three engines, on its way towards Shannon. In the event, things were going so well that the captain of the aircraft elected to overfly Ireland and landed quite happily at Heathrow. We, meanwhile, were still airborne, trying to get back to St Mawgan!

I had one perilously close shave on Shackletons. Because we had been developed from a 1940s design, our flight instruments were not the most modern. Without a reliable radio altimeter (which often gave random readings, so we did not have much faith in it), we had to rely on a Met man's guess as to what the barometric pressure would be way out over the Atlantic. Moreover, while our radar was quite good, it, too, could lull you into a sense of false security, so you had to keep on your toes. On this occasion, we took part in a 'No Light' exercise with the Royal Navy which was supposed to simulate wartime conditions. By that I mean that neither we nor our ships would show any lights at night, so it was quite realistic. During this night exercise, we got an intermittent radar contact at about six miles, which was a classic example of the contact you might have on a submarine charging its batteries. We went to Action Stations and, as we remained in contact on the radar, I descended to our minimum height at night of three hundred feet. With two pilots, one remained head down, flying the aircraft on instruments, while the other had his head up, looking out for the submarine which would be illuminated when we fired the flares we used at night. In our case, my aircraft captain was looking out while I remained on instruments. You may imagine my horror, when the first flare went off, to see the whole of my windscreen just full of HMS *Tiger*, eight thousand five hundred tons, beam on and very close. I just pulled back on the control column and we whizzed just over the ship, breathing more easily as we sped away. We must have been down at about fifty feet, so it was really too close for comfort. Every piece of our equipment had not been working as advertised. For instance, we should have picked up HMS *Tiger* at about thirty miles on our radar. If we had flown into the ship, unquestionably the crash would have been put down as 'pilot error'. There is a technical term for this sort of thing. It is called 'bloody dangerous!'

Apart from the flying, we also had other tasks, which included getting ready for our Annual Formal Inspection. On one occasion, the Inspecting Officer was Air Chief Marshal Sir Edward Chilton, the C-in-C of Coastal Command – affectionately known as Chillie. The Great Man inspected the assembled rows of airmen and stopped in front of a very junior chap who, unusually, was wearing a number of medals.

"How long have you been in the Air Force, Airman?" asked Chillie.

"Six months, sir," was the response.

"Well, where did you get all those medals?"

"I was in the Navy before, sir."

"Ah," said Chillie. "We don't get many sailors in the RAF."

"No, sir," said our intrepid airman. "They're mostly in the Navy!"

Truly wonderful, and I was on parade to witness it.

Chillie was an old Coastal Command man from way back, and he had some funny ideas. For instance, he wrote a pamphlet in an effort to inspire all his officers to greater things. The document was called *The Coastal Command Captain*. In it he spelt out how he expected these chaps to behave. He gave several examples, most of which fell on stony ground. He set out how he expected his aircraft captains to behave and gave an outline of a day in the life of one such super-star. Each day started with:

0600 Wake up; cold shower.

0615 Went for three-mile run with crew

0700 Breakfast with crew

0715 Attended briefing with crew, etc., etc.

I am afraid Chillie lost us at the 0600 requirements. However, not to be outdone, he then wrote to all officers along the following lines:

'You have all had a chance to see my thoughts on how a Coastal Command aircraft captain should behave. These men are the leaders of the Command and, as such, I believe they should be recognised as leaders. I am therefore going to introduce the Coastal Command Captain's tie, so that these fine men can be recognised in civilian clothes. To this end, I would like some suggestions as to the design of this tie.'

To my knowledge, I think Chillie got only one reply – and that from my own captain, who wrote, 'Sir, what a splendid suggestion. Could I suggest that we have the tie black so that we can also wear it with uniform?" Nothing more was heard of this scheme.

We had one epic moment in the early 1960s, when we had some American aircraft operating with us from RAF St Mawgan. At the end of the exercise, they had a couple of days spare, so we asked them what they would like to do. They told us that they had heard a lot about our British pubs and, if it wasn't too much trouble, they would very much like to visit one. Naturally, we agreed, but we made no mention of the fact that it was 1st May and that there was usually mayhem in Padstow as they celebrated ''Obby 'Oss Day'. The traditions of this are lost in the mists of time, but suffice it to say that the bottom line is the fact that the pubs are open all day. Thus, we set off with these innocent Yanks and, much as we expected, we had to park the cars about half a mile from Padstow before we descended into the town. At ten a.m., the place was crowded, with people pressing into the pubs, while the early risers were seen to be falling all over the place, with many comatose in their happiness. It was, as it always is, an amazing sight, but we made no mention of this abnormal riotous behaviour. We had a few beers, before setting off back to St Mawgan. At some point, one of the dazed Americans said, "Jeez. I've never seen anything like it. Is it always like that?"

Our Flight Commander said, "No. You ought to see it on Saturdays!"

We were flying in what is now termed The Cold War, and we were not interested in only anti-submarine warfare. During exercises and in areas of interest, there was a constant presence of Soviet intelligence-gathering ships and trawlers. They also exercised their potentially hostile surface warships, so we monitored these as well, photographing everything and helping to maintain our intelligence database. Indeed, we also monitored Soviet ships as they went on their way to deliver nuclear missiles to Cuba in what became known as the Cuban Missile Crisis of 1962.

On one occasion, we were sent to find a Soviet ice-breaker which NATO had lost touch with, so we set off for Norwegian waters in really dreadful weather. We were actually airborne for sixteen and a half hours, having spent most of our time flying in cloud at low level, so we were pretty much exhausted when we landed at Ørland on the coast of Norway. Naturally, the Norwegians did not have the requisite fuel or oil bowsers, so we spent much time teetering on the wings and the engines refuelling the aircraft. We then received a message which read, 'Return to St Mawgan when the crew is rested', so we went to the bar to get some rest, eventually falling into bed at some awful hour. Imagine my horror on being shaken awake at five a.m. by the Norwegian Duty Officer to be told that there was a signal for me. I pointed out that I wasn't the captain of the aircraft, but the man explained that he could not rouse him. Thus, I read the signal, which said, 'Take off first light and search area...' We should have refused, but anyway, we did as ordered and I flew the aircraft on my own for some five hours with my captain slumped comatose in the other seat. I was becoming more and more uncomfortable, desperate to go to the loo and flying cross-legged. Eventually, I could stand it no more and got someone to wake the captain, who was still far away in the land of nod. We searched all day and then landed exhausted back at St Mawgan. And no, we never did find that ice-breaker.

Apart from the routine flying, we also attended courses at the Joint Anti-Submarine School (JASS) in Londonderry. We were given lectures on the latest topics and, in particular, in the simulators we swapped roles with our Royal Naval counterparts to help us better understand each other's problems. It was fascinating stuff and always great fun with frequent laughter, which made it all very worthwhile. The RN, in particular, is riddled with acronyms, so everything seems to be in some sort of code. The Senior Naval Officer, Northern Ireland, was known as SNONI, while the Officer in Tactical Command of ships or a convoy is known at the OTC. There are many others ready to confuse the unwary, but it all seems to work. We flew JASSEX exercises with ships and submarines and did several exercises in the ground trainers. But what was wonderful, in the days before computers or electronic displays, was that all movements were plotted by lovely WRNS from behind a glass screen so that you could see the plan of the battle unfold in the operations room. They were quite brilliant, and their wonderfully clear writing was a joy to behold, particularly when you consider that they had to write in reverse so that we, on the other side of the glass, could read the right way round what they had written. I don't think that they do that nowadays, what with computers and such, but those girls did a wonderful job.

One epic simulated exercise I remember ended quite early in complete chaos, with ships colliding and aircraft crashing. Thus, we were summoned back to the operations room to be addressed by SNONI.

"I have never seen such a bloody shambles in all my life. What on earth was going on?" he asked.

One of our co-pilots, who went by the magic name of Ug Le Gras, said, "I'm very sorry, sir. I was the OTC and I was a bit confused by all these nautical expressions being bandied about, like, 'Easy on your mizzen hand down' and 'abaft the beam', and I didn't understand what was going on – so it was probably my fault."

"I'm not surprised at all, young man. You have my sympathy," was SNONI's kind response. "Now, who the hell was using these expressions?"

"Well," said Ug, "as a matter of fact, sir, I was!"

There was no answer to that, so we left and retired to the bar.

During my first tour, I had three different squadron commanders, one of whom was a real leader, Wing Commander John Bazalgette – sometimes known as the Bazcommander or Bazcommander Winklegette. He was a real star and I would have followed him anywhere and often did, if only to try to extricate him from some ridiculous situation. He needed looking after and he sort of adopted me as an unofficial ADC, which was always fun. Nell was Baz's placid wife who was the ideal foil for him, so she looked after him when I wasn't around. I had to go and help at his house whenever he had a function and was present when he did one of his party tricks. He used to drink a pint of beer while hanging upside down from a cross-beam in his house. Alas, on this occasion, his footing slipped and he crashed with a sickening thud, senseless, to the floor. All Nell said was, "Ah well, boys. I guess that's the end of the party!" A visiting Wing Commander, Bud Lewin, and I helped carry Baz off to bed and I then stayed to help tidy up.

Some months later, I was put forward for a Permanent Commission, and who should be President of the Board but Bud Lewin! No contest.

My final interview for this upgrade was with the AOC at our Group Headquarters at Mountbatten, near Plymouth. We had the usual sort of chat and, at one point, he asked me what I thought of the security situation. Amazingly, I had the cheek to say to him, "Well, I don't think much of the security around here!"

"Why not?" the big chief asked.

"Well," I said, "has anyone told you about the Russian Electronic Intelligence [ELINT] trawler, looking over your shoulder and moored behind you in the bay?" The short answer was, no they hadn't and yes, it was an ELINT trawler. Timing is all.

Chapter 11

South America

In 1960, our squadron was selected to send two Shackletons to take part in Argentina's XVIIth Aeronautical Week (the equivalent of our Farnborough Air Show), and, most happily, our crew was one of those chosen to go. We were all kitted out in white overalls for this special trip because we were to take our AOC with us. The intention was that we should all look smart on arrival at each airfield; but, incredibly, we had one airman, one Senior Aircraftman Handscombe, who had rendered his two white overalls black with oil before we even got to our first stop! He was an obvious liability, so he was banned from leaving the aircraft until the arrival procedures were over.

On arrival, we (the crew) were all supposed to leap down the ladder in the nose hatch at the front of the aircraft and line up looking very smart, awaiting the great man's somewhat more gentlemanly exit from the rear aircraft, down some steps which had to be wheeled up to the aircraft. Our first stop was at Gibraltar, so we all lined up in the expected manner, but there was no AOC. All we could hear were knocking and thumping noises coming from the back of the aircraft, but no progress. After fully five minutes, there was much cursing and shambling, before the AOC and his ADC crawled out through the nose hatch, together with their swords! Quite ridiculous, but very funny. Someone had locked the rear door after we had all loaded our kit on the aircraft the previous evening so that all we had to do was to clamber up the nose ladder to speed our departure. The rear door remained locked. What a cock-up.

Our next stop was at Dakar in Senegal, where we stopped for a day so that we could cross the Atlantic at night in the supposedly quieter and better weather. As one of the junior officers around, I was dispatched to the airfield to guard our two aircraft before we took off at midnight – on my own! I don't think I have ever felt so lonely. It was absolutely pitch black and all they had given me was a pretty useless torch. How was I supposed to guard Her Majesty's aircraft like that? Perhaps even more frightening was the fact that the locals all had very black skins so, in the event that they took exception to our presence, how was I to see them approaching? I did the only sensible thing, locking one aircraft and then climbing into ours and locking myself in. Whether anyone approached our aircraft was impossible to tell, but what a useless and pointless exercise it was. However, I was extremely grateful eventually to see my crew emerging through the night some five hours later. We then flew across the Atlantic to Recife, in the top right-hand corner of Brazil, before we set off for Rio de Janeiro.

Not to put too fine a point on it, Recife is one of the hell-holes of the world. It was incredibly hot and humid and we were hard-pressed to find anything to do, so a few of us went downtown in the evening to see what the place was like. It had nothing to recommend it, so we cut our losses and popped into a bar for a quick drink. We wore long trousers against the expected mosquito attacks, but Dick, our *very* British Air Electronics Officer, insisted on dressing like the Raj overseas and wore very short shorts. As we sat down at a table, there was a scurry of girls who made a bee-line for us and started chatting us up – without much success, since Portuguese was not one of our strong points. However, they obviously fancied Dick's naked legs, and he was much-embarrassed by their excessive attention as they stroked him at every available opportunity. We then discovered that we had unwittingly called in at a brothel, so we beat a hasty retreat, accompanied by jeers and cat-calls from the disappointed locals.

We managed to get back to our hotel and sat outside, the while being bombed by the biggest cicadas I have ever seen – at least three inches long and heavy with it. The noise they made was indescribable, and there were so many falling from the trees that the walk back inside was accompanied by the awful crunching of cicadas under your feet. Not the best place to stay, but we managed to save Dick for another day.

Before our departure from Recife, for reasons which escape me, the flight engineer managed to put more fuel on the aircraft than was needed for our flight. However, as things turned out, this proved to be an absolute boon. On the way south and beyond halfway to Rio, the aircraft compass system decided to pack up – as did our radar. This was followed by our navigation instruments failing, so we were now reduced to flying on a suspect magnetic compass and a very suspect radio compass which gave us rough bearings to or from a beacon. Matters were not helped by layered cloud now filling the sky ahead of us, and, with the very high ground around Rio very much in our thoughts, we sent out an emergency call to Air Traffic Control. Needless to say, it wasn't acknowledged. Thus, without clearance to descend, we loitered in the overhead for about an hour and a half until we had to resort to desperate measures.

Norman Pearson, our lovely flight sergeant 2nd navigator, took control of the situation and told us to descend on a southerly heading until we broke through the cloud base. This was a very hairy manoeuvre because we didn't really know exactly where we were. In the meantime, the other Shackleton which had carried the AOC had already landed at Rio. We were supposed to be following them, but, with no sign of our aircraft, the AOC went up to Air Traffic Control to find out what was happening. He heard our emergency calls and questioned why air traffic did not acknowledge us.

"But, señor, if I speak to heem, I am then responsible!" Not much help there, then.

Much to our relief, we broke cloud at one thousand five hundred feet over the sea and then turned back towards Rio. We had very poor maps, but Norman was the soul of calm. He told us to head for a radio beacon called Ilha Rasa, so we did. It was raining quite heavily, so we had to descend with the cloud base until we were down to about three hundred feet in very poor visibility with nothing in sight and the light fading. With five pilots on board, I was banished to a lookout position, so I lay in the tail of the aircraft, desperate to see something which would give us a clue as to where we were. I had gone through the 'concerned' phase and was convinced that we would have to put the aircraft down on Copacabana Beach – if we ever got there. Then, suddenly, from one of the pilots came the cry, "Jesus!" At that point, a lighthouse flashed between my legs and VERY close indeed. We worked out then that Ilha meant island.

Once more, Norman calmed the situation and gave us a course to steer, so we set off into the murk. The lights of Rio appeared in front of us and then the lights of an airfield. We flew over it a number of times, calling on the radio and firing red flares, but we got no response. I told the captain that I thought the runway looked very short and, since there was no other Shackleton on the ground, I thought that it was the wrong airfield. Once again, Norman gave us a new course to steer and we headed into the dark, still at low level, leaving the lights of Rio behind us. Incredibly, then, out of the night ahead of us, appeared the flashing beacon for Galeão, the International Airport for Rio. Without any assistance from Air Traffic, we just did a circuit and landed with precious little fuel left. Amazingly, while we were lurking in the dark to make our approach, the air traffic controller turned and said, "You had better get the Blood Wagon out." The AOC asked the reason for this dramatic language, to be told, "They don't often come out of that valley!" So we went to the bar.

We were supposed to have been thirty minutes behind the lead Shackleton and landing in daylight; but, in the event, we were nearly two hours behind them. You will know of the wonderful statue of Christ the Redeemer with his arms outspread which overlooks Rio from the Corcovado. One of our signallers swore blind that, as we lurked past the city in the darkness, he saw the statue with its hands clasped in prayer.

The next morning, we went back to the aircraft to see if we could rectify the snags on it, and asked to speak with the instruments ace. This turned out to be the aforementioned Handscombe, so our hearts fell.

"Can you fix the compass, please?"

"No, sir. I don't understand it!" Nice one. So we asked if he could let us peruse the necessary Air Publication so that we could all put our heads together to try to solve the problem. "No, sir," said Handscombe. "I don't understand that either, so I left it behind!"

There really was no answer to that, so we continued our epic journey with the bare minimum of navigation aids, and managed to complete the long detachment without further difficulty. In the daylight of the next morning, we saw that on our way inbound from Ilha Rasa we had flown through a narrow gap at three hundred feet with the rocks on either side as high as eight hundred feet.

We stopped in Rio for a couple of days before we set off for Buenos Aires, expecting to fly on to Cordoba in the west of Argentina to show the flag. On our arrival, we were met with the statement, "I do not theenk, señor, that you should be going there."

"But we are *supposed* to go there."

"I know, señor, but we do not advise it. You see, there has been a revolution!"

And so we spent ten days in Buenos Aires, being escorted by the Argentinian Air Force, who apparently had endless expense accounts so that we could be properly looked after. It all passed in a daze, invariably winding up in a nightclub and getting to bed at about three or four in the morning, accompanied by the cry, "OK, I peek you up at eight o'clock!"

We then had a signal to say that we were *not* to take part in the XVIIth Aeronautical Week, so, on the appointed day, we went to witness their Air Force at play. It was all to happen in the River Plate, so the banks were crowded with excited citizens. We were considered to be VIPs, so we were ushered on to a very plush jetty which stuck out from the shore, to give us the best possible view of the proceedings. But rather than being just a flying display, it turned out to be a firepower demonstration. Moored in front of us were many petrol-filled buoys; the plan was that aircraft would fly behind us, before turning in to attack these buoys. That seemed to be OK to start with, but the wind began to increase from behind us, blowing the aircraft out over the river. In turn, this meant that, if the aircraft were to hit their targets, unless they made suitable corrections for the wind, they would have to turn back and effectively point directly at us – not a very happy situation. And this was precisely what they did.

The first demonstrations were by their training aircraft, the Morane Saulnier, and they were to fire machine guns. One or two of the pilots were pretty good, managing to hit the buoys, but most of them were really poor. But, whenever a buoy was hit, there was a satisfactory petrol explosion accompanied by raucous cheers from the crowd. Next on the programme we had "Our fairst-line fighter, de Glostair Meteor. She will fire the sixty-pound rockets!" Now we were more concerned as, yet again, the pilots failed to allow for the cross-wind and made dangerous passes very close to the crowd. The final straw was when one over-confident young man continued his turn, lowered his nose and attempted to blast a buoy which was only some fifty yards away in direct line with us. To a man, as the Yanks would have it, we hit the dirt. Incredibly, the rockets overshot the buoy

74

and exploded on the water only some thirty yards in front of us. I had been chatting up the Air Attaché's daughter at the time, who said, "What are you doing down there. I thought you RAF chaps are supposed to be brave!"

"Yes," I said, "but we aren't stupid." We turned around to see many people holding their heads with their faces covered in blood, so it was a close call, but some nine people in the crowd were killed as a result of this stupidity.

Following this terrible error, I went off to find my boss, John Bazalgette. I showed him a piece of shrapnel which I had found on the ground some ten feet from our AOC. I said that I thought that it was lucky the great man hadn't been hit. All Baz could say was, "What a pity the AOC didn't get hit. If he had, it would have been everybody one step up the promotion ladder, go!"

The next entry in the flying programme was a demonstration by Argentinian Avro Lincoln bombers which were due to attack the same targets, this time with thousand-pound bombs! We could hear them circling above, but thankfully our prayers were answered and low cloud came over to blot out their targets. We were very lucky, of course, but we might well have been safer to go and join in the Cordoba revolution instead.

Thankfully, we made it back to the UK with no further problems and returned to the more normal daily grind and somewhat unglamorous flying which took place out of sight of the general population. However, I had many happy memories of a wonderful detachment, during which I fell in love with a really beautiful girl from the British Embassy in Rio – but that's another story.

Chapter 12

Shackleton Operations

A lot of our flying on Shackletons was training for our war roles. Perhaps the only real difference was that in peacetime, nobody was shooting at us, and secondly, we only used practice weapons against any targets. We might have been at peace, but we had to be ready for any eventuality. We spent many hours droning out over the grey and sometimes very rough seas, usually flying at around a thousand feet in the turbulence, looking for submarines. We had a fairly capable radar which could detect ships out to quite a distance, but it could also detect submarines when they put up their periscope or snort. The latter, which was a sort of breathing tube, was required so that they could run their diesel engines to charge their batteries. We also had lookouts posted all the time because, no matter what other equipment we were using, the Mark 1 eyeball was a really essential asset in any circumstances. Many times we made visual contact with a periscope before any other kit noticed it.

Submarines in the 1960s were by and large conventional boats, although the nuclear ones were just beginning to come on the scene. These were absolutely huge. For instance, being used to playing with conventional submarines, I once saw one and, calling my crew to 'Action Stations', I told them that we had a surface submarine three miles on the starboard bow. It was a rare incredibly clear day, so we had almost unlimited visibility. But the sub wasn't at three miles; twenty-two miles later we came upon the USS *Patrick Henry*, which was almost seven thousand tons, whereas our British conventional boats were about two thousand five hundred tons.

If we had visual contact with a submarine, we pilots would attack it with practice depth charges. We dropped down to a hundred feet and, using our experience, judged when to drop the weapons by eye. We had no bomb sight; we just used our judgement to straddle the target with hundred-yard-long stick practice bombs. Naturally, we had to practise these attacks so one built up one's expertise, and we were actually very accurate. I don't remember any pilots missing their target using the Mark 1 eyeball. Our flight instruments were not that accurate, so you judged the height visually and, after a time, it became almost second nature. If the sea surface was ruffled, height estimation was relatively easy; but, in a flat calm it could be quite tricky, and a few Shackletons actually bounced off the sea, which wasn't at all clever – also known as bloody dangerous. In those conditions, it was better to glance sideways to judge your height to see how much room you had beneath the wing.

If the submarine contact disappeared, we dropped sonobuoys into the water to track submerged objects. A sonobuoy had a floating canister from which hydrophones were lowered to listen for any noise a submarine might make – usually cavitation from the noises of their propellers. If the buoys heard anything from a sub, you got a signal displayed on the navigator's plotting table in the aircraft. With more than one of these *passive* buoys in the water, we could get a fix so we could track the sub's movements. This enabled the navigators and the sonics team to work out where the sub should be so that we could drop homing torpedoes onto the contact. These procedures required the complete concentration and cohesion of the crew, so it was very much a team effort. It was also very satisfying when it all worked out.

We also carried *active* sonobuoys which worked on the same principle, except that these buoys sent out a series of pings – similar to what you may have seen in the film *The Hunt for Red October*, except that Sean Connery only asked for "One ping only, Vasily!" The hydrophone of the active sonobuoy rotated so that you could ping through three hundred and sixty degrees, hoping to get an echo from a submarine. An echo gave you range and bearing to the contact and gave a more accurate fix on a submarine, although the detection range from an active buoy was somewhat reduced.

St Mawgan was a lovely place for my first operational tour. The flying was fun and I managed to play a lot of golf at Trevose Golf Club, which was quite a test in the wind. I often played with my great friend Mike Peaker. We played in the 1962 Coastal Command Championship and Mike and I had 2/6d on the result. I was in the group behind him and had no idea that I was playing with the current champion. All I did was concentrate on my and Mike's scores. After thirty-six holes, we met at the 18th to compare scores, and Mike said, "Well done. You've won."

"Good-oh," I said. "I'll have the half crown."

"No," he said, "you've won the Championship!"

I had no idea. I was simply trying to get half a crown off Mike, so there may be a lesson there for budding golfers.

Towards the end of my first tour, I was promoted to captain a crew, which was a great fillip for me. All decisions were ultimately mine and it was, naturally, quite a responsibility. Of course, you had your crew of specialists working with you, so you ignored their suggestions at your peril, but it was enormously satisfying. On one occasion, I had the new squadron commander flying with me as navigator and was horrified to hear that he had made an awful decision behind my back. Of course, he may have been trying me out, to see how I reacted, but he was very chastened when I took him aside after our sortie to give him an almighty rocket. Suffice it to say, he never did that again!

As a part of our training, we did various overseas detachments, principally to Malta and to Gibraltar, from where we flew on operational exercises in their local areas. The Malta detachment was particularly fun, enjoying three weeks in the sun. I hired a car and managed to see the whole island while we were there. Gib, too, was fun, but on a much more compressed scale. We were allowed over the Spanish border into La Linea and beyond, so it wasn't as claustrophobic as it might seem, but we played hard and we worked hard.

At the end of a three-week detachment in Gibraltar, under the command of the wonderful John Bazalgette, we threw a cocktail party on the Friday to thank the station for their hospitality. Naturally, we had to taste the cocktails some time before the party, so we were well ahead of the game before our guests arrived. For reasons which escape me, we continued the party through the night while I looked after Baz. At one stage I lost him, but was glad to find him sitting outside the Officers' Mess. He turned to me and said, "Isn't this a marvellous place? They've got this thing here where you can walk for ages and you aren't very far away!" He had been walking round and round the roundabout outside the Mess!

A further party continued through the Saturday night and, at breakfast on the Sunday morning, Baz suddenly remembered that he was supposed to have lunch with the AOC! We spent the rest of the morning pouring black coffee down him, before we put him in a taxi to the Great Man's house and then waited to see if the honour of the squadron was still intact. On arrival at Air House, Baz apparently told the AOC's wife that he wasn't feeling very well, whereupon she said, "Nonsense, John, you're pissed. I'll look after you!"

Baz returned to us after lunch to report that all was well and that he had upheld the honour of the squadron, which was a great relief to us waiting chaps. He then put his hand in his top pocket and said, "Look what I've got!" He produced all the AOC's silver coffee spoons, so a young officer was immediately dispatched to Air House to rectify the problem.

But you do meet some funny chaps. On one trip to Gibraltar, I took an elderly wing commander with us. He was currently employed at our headquarters, so I asked him why he was visiting Gibraltar. "Oh," he said, "I want to visit my brothel!" It transpired that, when he commanded a Shackleton squadron, he had been over the border in La Linea with his boys. As they were leaving quite late in the evening, there was a fearful ruckus going on down the road, so they went to investigate. It transpired that the police were having words with a madame. She had apparently not paid her dues for running this brothel and she had insufficient funds. This all seemed a bit unfair, so they asked what the fine was and, when they converted the sum from pesetas to sterling, they realised that it was a very small amount. Thus, they had a whip-round and paid the lady's fine for her, much to her relief and gratitude. The next day, they returned to the brothel and nailed a squadron plaque over the front door, because they reckoned they had either bought it or, at the very least, now had shares in the place. Shackleton people were very strange.

I have done some useless things in my time, but few match my epic in the winter of 1963 at St Mawgan. You may know that RAF St Mawgan, near Newquay in Cornwall, was one of a number of Master Diversion Airfields (MDA) in the UK and, as such, it was required to be open twenty-four hours a day to receive or assist any aircraft in an emergency. It never seemed to be a problem, and it was nice to know that, on those incredibly long sorties which we used to fly, usually looking for thirty degrees West, we had a guaranteed home base to return to – no matter at what time we were due to land.

You may remember that wonderful line from *Beyond the Fringe* in which a pilot is being briefed to do a sortie. "War's not going very well, I'm afraid. Take a crate, Perkins. Nip over to Bremen. Have a shufti. Don't come back. We need a futile gesture at this stage." Patently, in the winter of 1962-3, we needed such a gesture.

For reasons which escape me, the whole country was suddenly covered in snow and the world seemed to grind to a halt. Nothing seemed to be moving anywhere. Both RNAS Culdrose and RAF Chivenor (our nearest airfields) were out, and incredibly, St Mawgan had two to three feet of snow covering the whole airfield. It truly was amazing, because nobody could remember if this had ever happened before. It all looked very peaceful with everything white. And then the penny dropped. We were an MDA! We had to *do* something. Let's look at the Snowplan. Unfortunately, there didn't seem to be one, so panic set in. We must clear the runway.

As far as I could tell, I seemed to be the answer to the problem. I was called to the Ops Room and was told to take a coach-load of airmen up to the threshold of 31, the main runway. There we would be issued with shovels. Shovels! Have you ever stood on the end of a standard NATO runway? They are enormous. St Mawgan's was three thousand yards long and a hundred yards wide – lovely to land on, but impressive when covered with snow. "Don't worry, old boy. We'll send out some coffee in an hour or so."

And so we dug, all bleeding morning. The interesting problem was, where do you start? And, when you have some snow on your shovel, where do you put it? At a minimum, it is fifty yards to either side of you before you can chuck it off the concrete. There isn't really an answer, but we dug for ever and we never even got as far as the numbers. It was quite useless and all rather pointless. And no, we never did get our coffee. I think we were the only people moving on the airfield, so I imagine that the rest were looking for the Snowplan. Shortly thereafter, I was posted to RAF Luqa in Malta. They didn't have a Snowplan either, but they didn't seem to need one.

Chapter 13

Malta and Captain of my own crew

In the summer of 1963, at the end of my time in Cornwall, I was posted to Malta. Initially, I wasn't too pleased with this because I had already seen all the island and I had, in fact, asked to go to Gibraltar. The system couldn't work the change, so off I went to Malta – and what a fabulous posting it was. There is an enormous difference when you visit a place and see it from the outside looking in, compared to being stationed there and being on the inside looking out. And I had a ball. People often ask what life was like in those days, but I always tell them the weather was fantastic, we were all bronzed and handsome, the girls were beautiful, the money was right, the people were right, the flying was excellent and the fun we had was almost unbelievable.

We had some thirty-five bachelors living in the Officers' Mess, and we could not have had a better time. Incredibly, petrol was 4/3d a gallon, the same price as a Penguin paperback in those days. The most expensive bottle of local wine was also 4/3d, but we mostly drank much cheaper stuff which cost about 1/1d. Incredibly, you could get a barely palatable red for 9d a bottle, if you took your own bottle! What a life!

We bachelors had the most marvellous fun together. The mid-60s was the beginning of the time of the Beatles and, while we were beginning to get to grips with them, there was always Ray Charles and others of that ilk who kept us singing away and probably behaving badly at the same time. Thursday was reputed to be pay night for the WRNS who worked for the Navy, and we often headed down to the south-east bars – but sadly never saw one. Shortly after I arrived in Malta, on my first visit to one of these bars, I was given a lift by Ben, a rather strange navigator. We got there all right and parked on the waterfront, but for the return journey he had to ask me to reverse his car away from the sea because he wasn't sure which gear was reverse! It will not surprise you to know that Ben became one of my navigators.

During these evening escapades, someone would suddenly shout, "Last one down The Gut is a sissy!" There was then a mad rush for the cars as we headed for Valetta some ten miles or so away. I should point out that The Gut was a street of ill repute with many bars and heaven knows what else going on. The bars, etc., have long since been closed and the street has been tarted up with nice restaurants and, if you can believe it, Marks and Sparks as well! But I remember one epic evening when my friend Geoff happened to cannon off The Lion Fountain on his way to The Gut. Alas, he left his VW Beetle's wing clattering in the road. However, ever resourceful, he went to the nearby police station the next day to enquire whether anyone had handed in his car's wing because a friend of his had borrowed his car and returned it with the wing missing. Amazingly, he got it back!

I joined No 38 Squadron at RAF Luqa, this time flying the Mark 2 Shackleton. This was an older type of the aircraft and was not as nice inside or outside as the Mark 3 version which I had flown at St Mawgan. The main difference was that the Mark 3 Shack had a nosewheel undercarriage, while the Mark 2 had a tail wheel. When I did my conversion to the Mark 2, I honestly thought that the ailerons had jammed. In order to turn the aircraft, you needed a fairly hefty boot on the rudder to help the aircraft turn a corner. It was quite a change from the much heavier Mark 3, which was much lighter on the controls. But the role was the same, and perhaps the only thing different was the weather. It seemed to be almost incessant sunshine, and, of course, it was very hot in comparison to the UK. Often, when we went flying, such was the heat inside the cockpit that, when holding your arm out, sweat dripped off your forearm and your flying suit was absolutely soaked at the end of the sortie. At that time, we had many naval ships based in Malta, so, for much of the time, we exercised with both submarines and surface vessels, which was also great fun. After a fairly short time, I was given my own crew to captain, so that was also a great step forward.

Having your own crew is a big responsibility, but I was lucky that I had an excellent bunch of chaps with me. Our crews comprised two Pilots, two Navigators, one Flight Engineer and a five-man back-end team – an Air Electronics Officer and four Signallers; five officers and five NCOs, which was a nice mix. There was much mickey-taking and laughter, but when the job got serious, so did we.

It was always fascinating to meet Army officers who could not understand how we called our NCOs by their Christian names when they were all 'Sir' and 'Sar'-major', etc. They simply could not understand it. I pointed out that we fight a very different war and I would no more expect to tell them how to fight a war than I would like them to tell me how to fly an aeroplane. It worked for us and it worked for them.

It was a very happy time on the squadron, where we worked hard and we also played hard. Because of the heat, in the summer we worked from 0700 to 1300, except when you were flying – and this could be at any time during the day or night. It was just a fact of life, and we got on with it. But there were always moments of light relief.

A new flight commander joined us, having previously flown Sabre jet fighter aircraft, so this was a totally different world for him. Landing the Shackleton was quite an art which took him a long time to get to grips with, so when he was practising circuits and bumps, we got our chairs out to watch him making a considerable

Horlicks of it all. It surprised me when the squadron commander (a navigator) came and asked what we were doing, so I explained. He then said, "Well, I think I'll go and get my chair. You can't be had for the Board of Inquiry if you have witnessed the accident!"

Much of our flying was practising our war role of anti-submarine warfare, as well as watching and monitoring Soviet surface ships and submarines. There was thus much emphasis on searching for tiny contacts in the vast areas of the Mediterranean and co-operating with surface ships which we were trying to protect. Invariably, these searches resulted in our finding a submarine and then attacking it using practice weapons, so it was excellent training for us.

On one occasion, before we went flying, I was called in by the squadron CO, who said, "You are taking Charles Schembri flying with you today, so please look after him."

I had no idea what he was talking about, so he explained that it was squadron policy to keep on the good side of the Maltese police. Charles Schembri, a small, rotund man with a fierce reputation, was the No 1 speed cop! Would I please ensure that he had a good time? Well, what a challenge. It was one of those days when everything worked. He was thrilled to see us bombing a submarine, so I put him in the co-pilot's seat and gave him a stick of bombs, telling him when to press the bomb release. We all cried out, "A kill! A kill! Charles, you are fantastic!" And, of course, he was as pleased as punch.

When we had finished working with the Navy, we headed back to Malta. It was one of those very rare summer days when there was no haze and you could see the island laid out like a map. "Look at that, Charles. Isn't that amazing?"

He responded by saying, "I have never seen Sicily from the air."

"That's not Sicily," I said. "That's Malta!"

"But I have never seen Sicily from the air."

So, off we went to Sicily and showed him round it. He was, naturally, delighted; and, after we landed, he was profuse in his thanks. "Any problem, señor, you come and see me!" I thought no more about it, but I actually got a friend for life.

In early 1964, we were sent to Cyprus because the Turks and the Greeks were threatening to be at each other's throats. On arrival, we were tasked with flying between the Turkish mainland and the northern coast of Cyprus.

"I want three Shackletons airborne all the time to ensure that nothing is going on up there," the big chief said.

"We could do that with one aircraft," said our boss.

"No, I must insist on three aircraft."

He was somewhat surprised when our boss said, "We've got radar, you know."

Incredible really. All they seemed to think about over there was the aircraft they had flying from Cyprus, and they ignored all that we were doing in Malta – under their command. And so we started a long grind of fairly useless flying, doing two twelve-hour sorties a day, taking off at midday and midnight so regularly that we reckoned that the chaps at RAF Akrotiri could set their clocks by us. Very little happened, except that we all flew in excess of a hundred hours a month with little to show for it.

When I returned to Malta following my stint in Cyprus, I took many ground crew with us, so we had a pretty full aircraft. We flew at about two thousand feet at night and, as we approached the south of Greece, we had quite a bit of turbulence from the strong winds blowing down the Aegean Sea. I left my co-pilot at the controls and went down the back of the aircraft for a pee. There was an acrid smell when I was there and I turned to see one of our ground crew being sick down his front. I sped forward to the galley, where another chap went, "Whaaa!", and vomited all over his mate. Again, I rushed forward to see another miscreant hurling over the AEO's boots and, as I got towards the cockpit, a chap turned and grinned into the engineer's tool kit. As I got to the cockpit, I pulled the blackout curtain back, crying with laughter, and said to my co-pilot, "Paul, you've got to see it down the back. It is like fire spreading through the aircraft." Whereupon, a head appeared from the nose of the aircraft and barfed all over my feet! True, I promise you. The joys of flying in a smelly old aircraft!

We always had a crew on Search and Rescue standby, which was a bit of a drag, but we were always ready to go when the call came. In the mid-1960s, flying over the Mediterranean was quite a feat for the mainly piston-engined aircraft of the day, so we were sometimes called to monitor people in potential difficulties. But, when the Royal Family and VIPs overflew the Mediterranean, we were airborne while they were in our area. I remember one particular sortie which we covered when, I think, a senior member of the Government went to attend the funeral of India's Prime Minister, Lal Bahadur Shastri. Once we had completed our Search and Rescue coverage, we headed back to Malta, which must have been two hours away. Suddenly, and without warning, came the cry from the back of the aircraft, "Fire in the galley!"

I immediately initiated our drills and turned towards the nearest land, but all I heard down the back of the aircraft was the thumping of heavy feet as people rushed about. Eventually, having received no update from the team at the back, I said, "For crying out loud. Will someone please tell me what the hell is burning?"

After a short pause, a dark and serious voice said, "Lal Bahadur Shastri." Bloody Gunson! Bunny Gunson was one of my crew who had a wicked sense of humour and had persuaded the crew to join in this jolly jape. He was (and remains) an absolute star, and at one point during his career, he managed to get the very crusty AOC on the stage during the winter pantomime and made him sing, "I'm a pink toothbrush, you're a blue toothbrush…" I would have put money on nobody managing to do that.

92

Bunny went on to be an Air Traffic Controller in the Midlands. He also does brilliant talks. Look him up; he's now reverted to David Gunson, and he is very funny. It was great having him on my crew.

There were many wonderful restaurants all over Malta, but it was before the days of good fridges and freezers. One often saw the latest catch from the fishing fleet flung up on the quayside, just lying there in the baking hot sun – but we thought nothing of it. Everything was safe and good to eat, wasn't it? Well, not so, actually. Twice in my time I got some fearful lurgi and both times it was very nasty. When you get this sort of thing, you think back as to what might have caused it. Once, it followed my eating clam chowder, and once, after I had had a delicious swordfish meal. The lurgi was sufficient to almost lay me out and was so awful that I have since sworn off shellfish and have only recently gone back to the lovely swordfish. It just wasn't worth the risk.

The lurgi was exactly the same in both cases, and it started with my feeling dreadful, followed by the roof of my mouth going numb and then, some time later, my coming out in what I can only describe as bloody great Vesuvius spots. They were huge and always appeared in the same places, almost exclusively restricted to the sweaty areas of my body. Thus, I had these spots behind my knees, under my arms and around my crotch, with, if you can imagine it, three on my John Thomas. And, boy, did they itch! I tried all sorts of cures for them, but the only stuff which seemed to help was some powder called Sterzac, which I think is used to help heal the umbilical cord. Quite why this worked, I haven't a clue, but I was desperate for any sort of help.

Putting the powder on most of my spots was relatively straight forward, but my John Thomas presented a different problem. How do you keep powder on your chopper? Well, the Greenway mastermind went into overdrive and I devised a cunning plan. You cannot wrap a bandage round it, so I made a cottonwool bed for it, on which I sprinkled lots of Sterzac. This parcel was then wrapped round the wounded equipment and, to keep it in place, I wound cotton around it many times to keep the damned thing on. Most happily, the procedure seemed to work, and I was very grateful that the awful itching was now under some sort of control.

But I had forgotten the basics. Dear reader, what do cottonwool, powder and sweat make? Yes, you have probably guessed. The answer is Plaster of Paris – which sets rock hard! Naturally, it was difficult to remove, so I was now reduced to hitting my chopper with a heavy spoon or something similar until the beast shattered. What a palaver, but I trust you understand why I steer clear of shellfish.

We did detachments to Greece, to Aden and to Sharjah (in the Arabian Gulf), as well as to Idris in Libya and to Gibraltar, all of which was very good training and great fun. And, we did very realistic dinghy drills, where we were taken miles out to sea, out of sight of land, and chucked into the water to right our dinghy and to get on with survival procedures. The launch disappeared over the horizon, so we really were on our own. It is amazing how lonely it feels in the empty sea. After two hours, we erected our Search and Rescue beacon, at which point one of our Shackleton crews would take off to search for us. They had no idea where we were, so it was a very good exercise for them as well as for us. It is extremely difficult to see a tiny thing like a dinghy in the water, so it was very realistic. Eventually, we were found by our rescuers, and then the fun started as they bombed us with everything they had. At least that was what it felt like. From the air, it all seems very simple. The first thing you drop is an 8½lb flame float to mark the position, since it is much easier to see smoke than it is to see a dinghy. You aim to drop this thing about five yards downwind of the dinghy, but, when you are in the water, looking up with no other reference, it feels as if the aircraft is aiming directly at you – and it is terrifying. The next thing they will drop is a Marker Marine, which weighs about 500lb and is designed to burn for three hours, and, from underneath, it looks huge as it enters the water with a fearful bang. And then, once the crew had resolved their plans, the next thing they were to drop was the Lindholme Rescue Equipment. This consisted of three large containers which comprised survival equipment, with the central container holding a nine-man, multi-seat dinghy. The containers were joined together by flotation cord, so the whole thing stretched some four hundred yards. The aim was to drop this monstrous package some five yards downwind of you and, from underneath, it was very alarming. The joy of the exercise was that, the next day, the roles were reversed so that you could frighten the other crew!

At about that time, I was at a drinks party at Xemxija (pronounced Shemshia) in the north of Malta when I was introduced to a Pathé News man. He had heard that I was a pilot and wanted to know how he could hire an aircraft to take some air-to-ground film of Malta. I suggested to him that he need not bother with a little aircraft, but why didn't he come and fly with me since we were to have a practice flypast in readiness for Malta's Independence Ceremony. Gleefully, he leapt at my offer and the resultant Pathé newsreel coverage of the Ceremony proper was liberally interspersed with Shackletons in formation, Shackletons turning, Shackletons changing formation and so on, which was marvellous publicity for the squadron. The man had heavily overspent his film allowance, but we didn't care. A copy of the Pathé film is now played in the Malta War Museum at Senglea, overlooking Grand Harbour. So there it is; I am now officially a museum piece, flying an even older aircraft.

Shortly after that, two friends rang me up to demand what I had been doing. They were both hauled in by the speed cops along the same stretch of road and had been given the third degree, with all notes being laboriously hand-written. When it was discovered that they were members of the RAF, they were asked the question, "Do you know Flight Lieutenant Greenway?"

When they said they did, MP1, my new friend Charles Schembri, said, "What a waste of paper!" Amazing.

And when the policeman asked John why he was speeding, he explained that his son had fallen and banged his head and he needed to take him to Bighi Hospital. "Right, Señor. Follow us!" And off they went with lights flashing and sirens blaring! See – it pays to know me.

There were many functions leading up to Malta's Independence, when Prince Philip came to give the island away. I was hauled in to be one of his ADCs at Verdala Palace, where there was to be a huge reception for the great and the good. The whole Independence thing was organised by a retired colonel who had cornered the market by being the only chap who knew, so he had specialised in organising their independence for Commonwealth countries. Accordingly, he briefed some six of us who had been made ADCs for the night. We met in formal Mess Kit at three p.m. to be told that we had better have a drink, because it would be impossible to get another while the epic was going on. Indeed, he said, if anyone offered us a drink during the evening, we were to accept it, because it would be a long time before we got another. Clearly, he had his priorities right, so we got stuck into a few G&Ts. Our task was to shepherd Prince Philip from one group of select people to another through this great throng; and, believe it or not, at practically every turn, drinks were thrust into our hands. Thus, the evening passed with no pain at all and, much to our and Prince Philip's surprise, he was delivered to his car exactly on time. We were warmly congratulated by the colonel, who led us away for more drinks to celebrate a successful evening! So, *that's* how you give countries away.

When I arrived in Malta in high summer, the island, and particularly the golf course, was really parched and there were great cracks all over the ground. With no rain in summer, everything was brown, including the greens, so we had to wait for the rains to come in the autumn so that the grass could grow to make the course reasonably playable. We had a meeting in the Club House and wondered if we could get help from the Army. The Club Captain was asked to try to interest the head of the Army in Malta in golf. Accordingly, Peter Deedes managed to get the General Officer Commanding (GOC) playing. The GOC was General Johnnie Frost (of Arnhem Bridge fame), and he was a lovely chap. As we got to the end of winter and the golf course was beginning to dry up, Peter turned to Johnnie Frost (who had, by now, got the golf bug) and said, "I'm afraid we are going to have to stop playing soon. You see, the greens will not be fit for play with cracks all over them. If only we could get water on the greens."

"How do you do that?" asked the General.

"Well," said Peter, "we have the piping, but we cannot get it to the greens."

Johnnie Frost thought for a bit and then said, "Bloody good training for the Sappers!"

And, within three weeks, we had water on all the greens! And, when the summer came along, the island was brown except for eighteen nice green patches. Needless to say, the local people came and had their picnics on the greens, until we managed to persuade them that they were actually for a different purpose.

As I said earlier, the girls in Malta were all lovely, and I managed to persuade one of them to marry me. There were so many girls there that they all had nicknames to differentiate between them. Amongst others, we had a number of girls called Pat, so they were called Pat Mk1, Pat Mk2, Pat Naudi and, for something different, Pat Duus – Duus being her surname – and that was the one who kindly agreed to be mine. But, for simplicity, the boys just called her Duus, and the name stuck such that some fifty-eight years later, I still call her Duus – but she still doesn't come when I call her.

It just so happened that her parents came out to visit her in Malta before they went for a week's holiday in Sicily. At that time she had had a boyfriend called Bob. However, on their return to Malta, they were somewhat surprised to find me as the new boyfriend. They eventually got used to me and made me very welcome in the family, but for the first two years of our marriage, my father-in-law kept calling me Bob! Hmmm…

Chapter 14

ADC to the AOC

We got married in 1965 and I was then taken off the squadron to become ADC to the new incoming Air Officer Commanding (AOC) Malta. This was quite a surprise, because ADCs are normally bachelors on the basis that you really cannot serve two masters at once – as I discovered. On the other hand, it helped enormously that I knew Malta pretty well, although I did not really know the hierarchy. The island was like a little Ruritania, with everyone having an ambassador, together with the necessary supporting cast, so it was quite a social whirl.

My master, the AOC, was a very photogenic and slightly crusty man. He was shown in the Air Force List as E.G. Jones, but, when he wrote to me, he signed himself Gordon Jones. Thus, confusion reigned, so I asked his predecessor, a really lovely man called David McKinlay, what I should do. He said, "Why don't you box clever and get two different sets of headed writing paper, one with E. G. Jones and the other with E. Gordon Jones; then you've covered all the bases."

Naturally, when the great man arrived, he said that he wanted to be known as Gordon Jones, not E. Gordon Jones or E. G. Jones! Ah well, we tried. My wife and I referred to him as GJ, but he was quite a difficult man to serve, although I had quite a bit of fun during my time with him. He lived at Ariel House, which had a little duck pond with some half a dozen beautiful white ducks. During the handover, David McKinlay asked GJ if he liked ducks. We were a bit shaken to hear GJ say, "Oh yes. I am very partial to duck!" GJ was also called Tap by his friends, but I never discovered why.

My job, as ADC, was to look after my boss and his wife, mostly on the social side, and I spent quite a bit of my time heading to and from Ariel House. Over the year, I must have been up and down the five miles or so at least four hundred times. And yet, when we went back to Malta in 1999, when we drove up to find the house, I had the greatest difficulty in finding it. There had been many new buildings in the intervening thirty-four years, but I surely should have been able to find the big house. Eventually, I worked out that it must be behind this new high wall which surrounded a big compound. There appeared to be no means of access, but I noted a few secretary-type girls exiting through a doorway which was marked 'Russian Embassy'. On approaching this, I pressed a button and explained that I would like to see the AOC's house. A voice replied, "Other gate." So we drove round to find 'Other Gate', where I came across a large wrought-iron structure which was evidently the main way in. I left my wife and my daughter in the car and said to the wall, "OK, I am at other gate, what should I do now?"

And the wall said, "Come in." The gates then creaked open in the best *Hammer House of Horror*-style, so I entered.

The gates then creaked closed again behind me, so I said, "OK, I'm in, now what should I do?"

And a tree said, "Go up road."

At the top of the drive was a large office block, so I entered it and went to queue at a very large and high desk which was surrounded by a throng of foreigners. Eventually, I got to the desk and the chap wanted to know my business. I explained that I wondered if it was possible to see Ariel House, because my boss used to live there. There was much muttering before the man said, "Sit."

I must have waited twenty minutes or so before a very serious man with a clipboard and a briefcase appeared and escorted me to a silent booth. I feared the worst, because the walls were covered in egg boxes and I thought I could see blood on the floor where previous incumbents had had their knuckles dragging along. The man sat down and said, "What you want?" So I explained that I wanted to see Ariel House if it was possible, so that I could take a photograph for my boss who used to live there. And the man said, "What you do?" So I explained that I had been ADC to the AOC Malta, who had lived in Ariel House. Again, the man said, "What you do?" So I said that I had been Aide de Camp to the Air Officer

Commanding, etc. This did not impress him, so, yet again, he asked, "What you do?" He must have asked me the same question another four or five times, and each time I explained my quest in a different manner.

Eventually, I lost my cool and said, "Listen to me, you stupid sod; before I was ADC, I flew Shackleton aircraft from RAF Luqa, looking for bastards like you!"

"Why you not say so?" he said. "Do you want to see the house? Would you like to meet the Ambassador and have a tour of the house?" The swine could speak English perfectly. I must have been away from my family for over an hour and, not surprisingly, they were beginning to get a bit restive. Who says diplomacy is dead?

Shortly before David McKinlay left Malta as AOC, we had a visit by the Under Secretary of State for the RAF, one Bruce Millan MP, later a European Commissioner. A formal visit programme was organised and, throughout his week-long visit, he did nothing and said nothing apart from following the schedule. The final thing on his programme was a lunch in the Officers' Mess at RAF Luqa, after which the AOC asked him if he had enjoyed his visit.

"I think I'd like to look at a barrack block," he said.

"But it isn't on the programme; no one will be expecting you. They won't be ready for you."

"Never mind," he said. "I'd still like to look at a barrack block."

So this convoy of staff cars went to the domestic site and stopped outside US of S's choice. OC Admin Wing rushed ahead, threw the door open and said, "Gentlemen, the Under Secretary of State for the Royal Air Force."

There was stunned indifference from within while the entourage filed into the room. There were two airmen in there, one lying naked on his bed, reading a paperback, and the other in his Y-fronts at the window, cleaning out his goldfish bowl. Discretion being the better part of valour, OC Admin approached the man at the window and said, "Didn't you hear what I said? I said the Under Secretary of State for the Royal Air Force."

The airman didn't bother to turn round. After a short pause, he said, "I don't stand to attention for no fucken Under Secretary of State for the RAF; he's a fucken MP, and all fucken MPs talk out of their fucken arses!"

The AOC snorted and the entourage filed out again.

Priceless, but true! The airman was interviewed on the Monday morning and was asked to moderate his language. He was also warmly congratulated on knowing that US of S was an MP.

One of my jobs for the AOC was to organise his dinner parties, before which I had to go up to the house in Black Tie to ensure that his guests were nicely looked after. I was then supposed to disappear back to my wife. Quite early in my new job, my boss had what we called a First Eleven Dinner Party, which included the Governor-General, the other two Heads of the Services, and two ambassadors, all accompanied by their ladies. The Archbishop of Malta, Monsignor Gonzi, was also included, as was the British High Commissioner, whose wife was off the island. A nice dinner party for fourteen, you would think. However, during the pre-drinks, I was surprised to see the Archbishop – accompanied by a Catholic Priest. I sidled up to him and asked him if he, like me, would be leaving when the guests went in to dinner. "Oh no," he said. "I always dine with His Grace." Thus, I stepped smartly to my boss and said that he should probably get me to get another round of drinks in.

"Oh no, David. We are about to go in."

I explained the predicament and then told the kitchen staff the problem, which fazed them not at all. They always prepared a 'little extra' in case of emergencies (so that they, too, could eat well!), so the food was covered. But trying to fit fifteen people round a fourteen-seat table was quite a trick. Needless to say, I elicited an apology from the ADC to the Governor-General, who had briefed me on all the protocol of the island. But, from then on, the accompanying priest was always referred to as Mrs Gonzi.

One of the quirks of Malta was that, on 1st January, everyone had to renew their Driving Licence, their Road Tax and their permit to drive in Valletta. Naturally, each item required queueing at a different desk, and the whole of the main Police Station was absolutely crammed with people, pushing and shoving. It didn't help that I had both the AOC's and his wife's licences plus mine and my wife's, as well as that of the AOC's PA, so it was going to be a long day, which I could ill-afford. At that point, I suddenly remembered my friend Charles Schembri – the No 1 speed cop.

I made my way to the Police Headquarters, which backed on to the main Police Station, and he welcomed me with open arms. We chatted over a coffee about nothing in particular for some fifteen minutes, before he asked, "By the way, señor, why did you come to see me?" I showed him my handful of licences and all he said was, "No problem at all!" At that point, he rose from his seat and started shouting. He didn't bother with the handle, but kicked the door open to reveal this horde of people who parted like the Red Sea. Then, all I could hear was that 'bdm-bdm' sound when things are stamped in a hurry. The whole process took him less than five minutes and he reappeared with a grin on his face, saying, "Is fixed, señor!" What a star! He must have saved me at least a day's queueing.

The follow-up was even more fascinating, because he now knew that I was no longer just the captain of a Shackleton, but I was now ADC to the AOC. Each of the Heads of Service were driven round in their big staff cars with their pennants flapping on the bonnet, as, indeed, were all the ambassadors, etc. At all the public functions such as the big service at the cathedral and various parades throughout the year, protocol demanded that we arrived in the right order. However, this meant nothing to Charles, and he made mayhem with the programmes. I invariably accompanied the AOC, so, whenever he saw our car, all traffic was stopped while we were ushered to the front of everyone else – which pleased the AOC, but did nothing for the organisation of the day! Sadly, when the Labour Party won the next election, Charles was one of the first people to be fired.

The RAF in Malta came under the command of the AOC-in-C Near East Air Force, so he was effectively my AOC's boss. At one point, my boss went to attend the C-in-C's Conference, so I went with him to Cyprus. I wasn't included in the conference, so I hung about 'in case I was needed'. When the Great Men had concluded their doubtless important meeting, a few of the senior men retired to the C-in-C's house. They chatted for a bit while I, as very much the junior man and the youngest by some distance, lurked in attendance – looking like a spare whatnot with nothing to do. On a table beside me, a photograph frame had obviously fallen on its face, so I stepped over to pick it up. There was a great bellow from the C-in-C from the far end of the room, "DON'T TOUCH IT!" I leapt back as if electrocuted, whereupon he said, "No one is allowed to touch that. I had to put Harold Wilson up on his way to some conference and, when he left, he presented me with a photograph of himself, saying that that table would be a nice place to keep it. As soon as he left, I placed the damned thing face down, and there it has stayed!"

Also in the group of the top brass was the Senior Air Staff Officer, one Air Vice-Marshal Micky Martin – yes, he of the Dambuster Raid. He realised that I was just hanging around with nothing to do, so he turned to my boss and said, "Hey, Tap. You don't want your ADC for anything, do you? He can't go shopping for you because all the shops are closed on Saturday afternoon. He'll only get in the way here, so why don't I take him away?"

Eventually, my boss agreed, so Micky Martin put his arm round my shoulder and said, "Come on, David. Let's go and get pissed!" So we did. What a lovely man he was, absolutely charming and completely self-effacing.

The Deputy Leader of the Labour Party at that time, George Brown, also night-stopped with the C-in-C at one stage. After darkness descended, George Brown said, "I think I'll go down and see the chaps at RAF Akrotiri."

He was told that nothing had been laid on, nobody was expecting him and that his visit would be a complete waste of time, but he was adamant. So, ignoring this advice, the C-in-C's staff car was summoned and George was taken the twelve miles to Akrotiri. He walked into the bar in the Officers' Mess and said, "Hello, chaps. My name is George Brown."

The only response he got was from a laconic Australian sitting in the corner, who said, "Yeah? Well mine's a pint."

Chapter 15

Personal Staff Officer

I was ADC for only a year before my boss went off to Cyprus to become the new AOC-in-C of the Near East Air Force, under whose remit Malta sat. Thus, a new AOC appeared to take over Malta, accompanied by his own ADC. I became the new AOC's Personal Staff Officer in his NATO hat of Deputy C-in-C (Air) in the Headquarters Allied Forces (Mediterranean) – known generally as HAFMED. The NATO Headquarters was just across the road from the Air Headquarters, so the AOC wore two hats. But, before the AOCs switched roles, they had a two-day handover so he and his successor could presumably chat about current topics and so on. However, as soon as GJ departed, I was asked to go up to Ariel House to speak with the new AOC.

"Right, David," he said. "You know the local set-up. I want you to order me a Rover 2000; and, of course, I want it Duty Free."

I said, "You know that you have to keep a car overseas for a year before you can take it home Duty Free?"

"Yes, of course I know that. Why do you ask?"

So I said to him, "Have you read the Red file in your safe, sir?"

"What Red file?" he asked.

"Ah," I said. "Can I get you a drink?"

"It is only ten thirty; I don't need a bloody drink!"

"I know, sir," I said. "I'll just go and get you a drink."

So I went to his drinks cupboard and made him a huge Gin and Tonic. I invited him onto the balcony and said, "Sir, there is a Red file in your safe about which only the AOC, his Deputy, the PA and I know, which says not only you and I, but also all the Army, the Navy and the RAF will be off the island in three weeks. And you want me to order you a Duty Free car?"

Needless to say, he took a huge gulp of the G&T. I found it incredible that the subject had not come up during the handover. It was at the time of one of the many difficult political stand-offs with the Maltese Government, so plans had to be laid, but thankfully the order was rescinded and normal life resumed.

In my new job in HAFMED, almost the first thing that happened was the necessity of having various in-briefings as they called it in the NATO vernacular. The first, and presumably the most important, topic on the agenda was a briefing by the Disbursing Officer, who seemed to be a very serious American. He started by saying that since this was a NATO posting, he needed to explain the allowances. "You are restricted to only fifteen bottles of duty-free hard stuff a month!"

Only fifteen! Ye gods, how do they manage to get through that lot? What a way to start a new job.

My mad aunt had recently married a very smooth man (who we were convinced could possibly be M of James Bond fame). They came to Malta on their honeymoon and we thought it would be very useful if we invited my new boss, together with them, to dinner, since they must have contemporaries in common. We gave them a beef fondue to make it a convivial evening, but the whole thing turned into a disaster. Yes, they had mutual acquaintances, but they totally disagreed about their merits. Thus, we had statements like, "Old Freddie Snooks is a wonderful chap." "Nonsense, he's a bloody fool!" And while this was going on, they were literally fencing with their fondue forks across the flames! To cap it all, I dropped the Pavlova meringue all over the kitchen floor – so that just about summed up the evening! Surprisingly, nobody seemed to notice that I had pieced the meringue back together with judicious use of the cream. They were still arguing!

During my final few months in Malta, the last Commander-in-Chief Mediterranean retired, as the British fleet was gradually reduced in size. The post of C-in-C Med had been in existence since 1654, so it was quite a moment when Admiral Sir John Hamilton left the island. As I have said, all nations had ambassadors in Malta, so everyone needed to say goodbye. It was, therefore, an incredibly hectic last few months for him. Each week, David Jeans, his Flag Lieutenant (Naval ADC), went through the weekly diary with Sir John, and every time they went through the procedure, Sir John always asked, "And what is happening during my last week?" David explained that he was out to dinner with the Governor-General, the AOC and the GOC before he left on the Friday. "Good," said Sir John. "I want to keep the last Thursday free."

And the same conversation occurred every week for the last eight weeks or so. As the final week approached, Sir John said, "Is that last Thursday still clear?"

"Yes, sir," said David.

"Good," said Sir John. "Let's have a dinner party."

"You must be mad," said David.

"No," said the Admiral. "Lady Dorothy and I will be there, and I would like you and Sylvia to be there, so I would be grateful if you could please fill the rest of the places with your friends!"

Oh, what a lovely gesture! It was his way of thanking his Flag Lieutenant for all his hard work. It was a fabulous evening and it just underlined what a really lovely man Sir John Hamilton was. He was quite the nicest man you could meet, and he was a real gentleman.

Shortly before I finished my time in Malta, I was detailed to organise the RAF fly-past to coincide with the Queen's Birthday Parade. It is all to do with timing, of course, but it was nigh on impossible to get the Army to do any real practice from which I could glean any accurate timing. For instance, during the rehearsals, they would say, "Let's do that again," or "We'll assume that bit's been done," so any timing I might have been logging went out of the window.

Matters were not helped by my having a pretty useless VHF radio on which I tried to speak to the Canberra, which was also rehearsing for the great day, so it was all a bit of a shambles. Every so often a lone Canberra would whizz past, which had no bearing on what was happening on the parade ground, so this did nothing for anyone's peace of mind. We were supposed to coincide with the symbolic arrival of the Queen (when a General Salute was given), but we were nowhere near the mark.

At the end of the final rehearsal, the brigadier turned to me and said, "I imagine you RAF chaps will try to get it right on the day!"

I responded with the winning line, "If you can organise a parade, sir, I can organise a fly-past!" Not the most tactful comment, but I was incensed by the shambolic practices.

And so we came to the great day, with a huge crowd and all the VIPs in attendance. Our fly-past was now a formation of four Canberra PR9s, so we started the ceremony with a fair bit of tension in the air. Despite my careful checking of the timings during the parade rehearsals, they suddenly speeded up the proceedings, so that I was now screaming to the Canberras to come in as quickly as possible in order to coincide with the Royal

Salute. The parade duly presented arms, but, in the sky, nothing. There was a long pause before the brigadier shrugged his shoulders and ordered the advance in Review Order, which involved the troops marching forward fourteen paces before halting for a second Royal Salute. The parade ground was surrounded by high buildings, so I could neither hear nor see the incoming formation; but, at the exact moment of the second Present Arms, there was a truly shattering noise and four Canberras came over the saluting dais at full power and at very low level. It really was incredible and the brigadier completely lost the plot, so the Regimental Sergeant Major had to pick up the parade orders until he managed to get his brain reorganised.

At the subsequent drinks party in the Army Headquarters, I was talking with the Senior Air Staff Officer (SASO) when the Prime Minister's wife came over and asked who had organised the amazing fly-past. When she was told that I was the culprit, she said, "Well, that was fantastic. I know how you get the timing down to hours and minutes, but how do you get it down to seconds?"

And the SASO looked at me and said, "Don't tell her!" Quite. I don't think the brigadier ever forgave me.

While I was in Malta, I played lots of golf, which was both fun and a bit different. The standard was remarkably high and, most happily, despite being outnumbered, we beat the Army in the inter-Services matches. They even brought in from the UK a 'flanker' on detachment in the shape of the current Army Champion, but I managed to see him off – much to my satisfaction.

When we got married, many of my golf matches had to be postponed while I was off the island. Thus, my wife had a rude introduction to her expected married life while I caught up with the golfing diary and the competitions. I made the final of the handicap knockout competition and was drawn against a chap who most members thought was a bandit (playing off a false handicap), so feelings were running rather high. Many members came up to me and asked me to thrash him, if only for the good of the game. The final was played over thirty-six holes, the only time I have ever played a thirty-six-hole matchplay event, so I approached it in determined fashion. Thankfully, I had lunch 9-up and, in the early afternoon, I won 12-up with eleven holes to play. I don't think I have ever been so popular!

So, after five summers on the trot in Malta, it all had to end, and in 1967 I returned to the UK, to the real world – with my wife now significantly pregnant.

Chapter 16

Return to England

I did a two-month Junior Staff Course at RAF Tern Hill in Shropshire, which was a good mind-clearing exercise in all things which a young officer should know. There was much writing and public speaking involved, which was excellent training, but we all felt the pressure. However, we were certain that all work and no play would undoubtedly make us very dull, so we worked like crazy at the beginning of each week, which enabled us to take the Thursday nights off. Thus, with our minds cleared of all serious stuff, we let our hair down by visiting Mr Smith's in Hanley in the potteries. The fact that this turned out to be a strip club was neither here nor there, because, naturally, I only went to hear the comedians, some of whom were exceedingly funny. Oh yes, the girls were nice as well, and it was a real steal, because we got into the club for half a crown by flashing our RAF identity cards! It was worth joining the Service for that alone!

Now it was time to learn how to become a Qualified Flying Instructor (QFI).

I had not flown for some time and, more to the point, I had not flown the Jet Provost, so I was sent to do a Jet Refresher Course at RAF Manby in Lincolnshire. The course was only for two months and, with my wife now heavily pregnant, we had to find somewhere to live fairly rapidly. We settled on a boarding house in Mablethorpe which had some thirty beds in it. Thankfully, the holidaymakers had all gone home, so we had the place to ourselves. I commuted daily to Manby while my wife prepared to give birth, waiting patiently while overdue. Meanwhile, our next move was getting perilously close.

I struggled with learning about the new aircraft and the flying, and was thus not much help when my wife was taken into Louth General Hospital to give birth to Sally. We were thrilled with her arrival and were so grateful that she was fine. We were, however, horrified that she appeared to be almost the only 'normal' child in the maternity ward. Naturally, my family and others sent Patricia flowers, so, in true fashion, I said to her, "You've already got lots of flowers, so I haven't brought you any!" As you may imagine, this did not go down too well and, even after fifty-eight-plus years, I am still trying to live it down.

Such are the requirements of a life in the Services that, within a month, we were on the move again for me to attend the Central Flying School (CFS) at RAF Little Rissington in Gloucestershire. No accommodation was provided, so, at the last minute, we managed to rent a tiny cottage in Milton-under-Wychwood, again leaving my wife to cope with a month-old baby while I started the flying instructors' course. At that time, the large Hastings and Beverley aircraft had been retired from the RAF, so our course largely comprised multi-engined pilots looking for another role. I didn't fancy being an instructor on the Jet Provost, so I fervently hoped to be assigned to instructing on the twin-engined Varsity.

The first half of the course was learning to instruct on the Jet Provost, after which we were to be streamed to become instructors on possibly different aircraft. In those days, the course was regimented, and one had to give briefings in the correct manner with no deviations for one's own personality. Each briefing had to match the accepted template, which at least meant that you covered the salient points – although we were conscious of possibly becoming automatons.

Each aspect of the flying was taught to you by an instructor, and you then went off and flew with another student so that you could practise the lesson together. This was followed by you then giving the lesson back to your instructor before you went on to the next phase. I did not much enjoy that part of the course and I was oh so grateful to change to the twin-piston-engined Varsity; I found the instruction so much better and we were treated more like adults rather than mere students.

The teaching was similar with lessons being taught back and forth, but there were moments of light relief. For your first solo on the Varsity, you were given a student from the Jet Provost side, so, while you were never flying on your own, the chap in the other seat knew nothing about your aircraft. As I was finishing my trip, Air Traffic Control asked if I could nip over to RAF Gaydon to pick up an instructor who needed a lift back to base, so off we went. The instructor climbed aboard and casually sat behind us while I returned to Little Rissington. At the end of the sortie, I performed the run-down checks which involved moving various levers and switches in a pleasing and eye-catching fashion, when my 'co-pilot' asked why I was doing that. "I don't really know," I replied.

"WHY don't you know?" came the fierce voice from the back.

"Well," I said, "this may surprise you, but this is my first solo!"

The look on his face was priceless. It later transpired that he was a well-known hard man and was known throughout the Varsity fleet as 'Hitler's Henchman'!

Chapter 17

Flying Instructor

Having qualified as a QFI, in 1968 I was posted to RAF Oakington, near Cambridge. Once more, we had to find somewhere to live, so we rented an old and ramshackle house in Haddenham, near Ely. At that time, a number of my contemporaries were talking about buying houses, so I approached an insurance chap who had set up his stall in the Officers' Mess and said, "I have no idea what I am doing. Should I buy a house? Can I afford a house? How do you go about it?"

His eyes must have lit up, but the end result was our buying a brand new four-bedroomed detached house with central heating and garage for the princely sum of £5,100 – on a 100% mortgage! It was a stretch financially, but we had a foot in the market. Of course, price comparisons are hopeless, but, when we went to my next job in Germany, I had to sell the house because I could not afford the £45 a month mortgage, such was the perilous financial position of a junior officer in those days.

To put it into context, one day when we were driving, Sally threw half a crown out of the car window.

We had to stop by the roadside and search for the coin in the long grass because that was all we had to see us to the end of the week! Every single thing we bought for the house was second-hand, at which the young of today now seem to sneer. Our bed, which was one of those amazing, creaky things with a wind-up tensioner to stretch the springs, I got for 30/-. It made strange sproinging noises when you turned over, but it was very comfortable. Our dining table cost 30/-, as did the set of six chairs, which we still use now. We bought a portable black-and-white television and watched the moon landing through a snowstorm. Our washing machine was a second-hand Hoover Keymatic; we splashed out and bought it for £11.

The Varsity was a wonderful aeroplane to instruct on. It was about the size of a Vickers Wellington and big enough to be something of a handful. It was an excellent stepping stone for the students to get them ready for much larger aircraft. It had, thankfully, a large cockpit, with the two pilots sitting side by side, and it was easy to see what your student was doing so that you could help him with the various aspects of flying the aircraft. Whilst it may have looked a bit ponderous, it had enough vices to keep you on your toes.

Naturally, as soon as I met my first students as a QFI, the first thing I had to teach them was instrument flying, the one thing which had not been covered on the CFS course! My students and I were both learning as we went along, but the one thing that sticks in my mind is how much instructing improved your own flying accuracy. If you were demonstrating something, it really had to be spot on, so speeds and heights were more accurately flown than I had ever done in the past. One of the judgements was how far to let a student wander off before it was time to call a halt and demonstrate how something should be done – the while, of course, remembering how I had blundered through my flying training when I went through the system. Some students struggled, while a very few were quite simply outstanding. In the latter case, my reports were often questioned, and the only way to resolve any dispute was to invite another instructor to fly with my exceptional young men. I was delighted when they agreed with my assessment.

Teaching young men to fly multi-engined aircraft was great fun and also very rewarding. We had a good bunch of instructors and we all got on well, each of us sharing our experiences, so we also learned quite a bit from the lessons of others. As you grew in confidence and, indeed, in competence, so you advanced up the assessment ladder, and eventually I became an A2 instructor, which was shorthand for Above Average.

As in all my flying jobs, we were constantly checked to make sure we were up to snuff and that we were not letting our standards slide. To this end, we had annual visits from the CFS staff (known throughout the land as 'The Trappers' because we thought that they were trying to trap you). They not only flew with you, but they also asked all sorts of questions to assess your ability as an instructor. In preparation for these visits, we used to sit around discussing the technicalities of the aircraft and the various parts of the flying syllabus. At one point, the subject of the wing fences came up. On the Varsity, these were strips of metal on top of the wing (aligned with the direction of travel), and there are many reasons why they are (or were) fitted to aircraft; usually, it was to correct some slight problem with the airflow. We could not agree the answer, so we thought we ought to ask Vickers, who had made the aircraft in the first place. We rang Weybridge and the following conversation ensued.

"Good morning. I am a flying instructor at RAF Oakington, and I wonder if I could ask a technical question?"

"Yes, of course," said the nice receptionist lady. "Which aircraft are you interested in?" On being told we wanted to know about the Varsity, she said, "Oh yes, just a minute, I'll put you through to one of the designers."

A voice then said, "Wallis."

"Oh, good morning, sir. I'm sorry to trouble you, but a bunch of instructors are sitting around discussing the Varsity and we cannot agree the function of the wing fences on the aircraft. I wonder if you could please give us the party line?"

"Give me a moment," came the response. And then the great man said, "Do you know, I cannot remember why I put them there!"

Oh, what a wonderful exchange, but from then on we were longing for the Trappers to ask about the wing

123

fences, because they would have had the answer, "If Sir Barnes Wallis doesn't know, why should we know?"

After a few months of waiting while our house was being built, we eventually moved in to what was effectively a building site. With Sally now running around, I had to lay turf to make an instant lawn. This was fine, but all the neighbouring children came to play on it while their parents raked and smoothed and titivated their gardens to get immaculate lawns, all the while destroying mine! Meanwhile, with my wife now pregnant with Daniel, we had much fun learning to be new parents, while filling the house with second-hand stuff. We started making home-brewed beer and wine (most of which was awful), but we drank it anyway. We had a squadron party for about thirty people and it cost us the princely sum of £9.00. It was a roaring success, with the wives driving the chaps home, thank goodness – but all the home brew went.

We had a Ford Anglia Estate, but, with my having to drive the twelve miles to Oakington each day, I could not leave my wife without a car – so I bought a three-wheeler Messerschmitt, which was close to lethal. It was quite fun to drive, but it did not travel at any great speed. On the way to and from work, I cowered in the nearside lane while these thundering monster trucks hammered past me, blowing me aside without a care in the world.

When the time came, my wife went off to Ely Hospital for Daniel's arrival, so I was left in charge of Sally. I wanted to Ronseal the parquet floor in our sitting room, so I put Sally in her playpen and got on with the sanding and applying this powerful substance. But what was lovely was that I had not a peep out of Sally as she was fast asleep in her cage. It was only much later that we wondered whether I might have knocked her out with all the fumes, but she seemed undamaged. Oh yes, the floor looked smashing, and we were delighted with Daniel's arrival.

Flying a multi-engined aircraft is quite a step up from whistling around the sky in a Jet Provost, so the Varsity was an excellent vehicle for teaching young men the difference of flying with a crew and, indeed, with a co-pilot. We practised engine failures so that the students could get used to controlling the aircraft and, if necessary, bringing it home on one engine. As the first pilot, the engine failure drill comprised you identifying which engine had failed. You then shut the engine down by doing the first three actions of closing the throttle of the offending engine, lowering the propeller pitch lever and pressing the engine feathering button. These actions stopped the engine and turned the blades into the airflow to reduce the drag on the aircraft. You then asked your co-pilot to carry out the remaining shut-down drills while you concentrated on maintaining control of the aircraft. Initially, one of the problems of having an engine failure invariably gave rise to a fair rush of adrenaline, so there was a tendency for hands to flash all over the cockpit, reaching for levers and switches. The situation was, therefore, ripe for a cock-up, so it was essential to stop your students panicking. As the instructor, I sat in the right-hand seat and acted as co-pilot for the student captain. As a very good learning point, I used to foul-up the engine shut-down drills by switching off the ignition switches on the live engine so that we effectively had both engines switched off. This often resulted in a bit of a panic by my student, so I took control and pointed out that nothing had seriously gone wrong. All I had done was click off a set of switches on the live engine, but we were not falling out of the sky. I had simply cocked-up the drills because, unless you were very lucky, someone was bound to do that to you in later life. The whole point of this was to stop any panicking. The aircraft was now gliding with the live propeller being turned by the airflow. All one had to do was maintain airspeed and thus keep control over the aircraft, albeit descending all the while. The last possible thing you should do was just to put the switches back where they were without thinking, because this was likely to cause the engine to explode into life and very likely give you a runaway propeller. This is called an overspeed and is exceedingly dangerous. The most important thing to do was to close both engine throttles so that nothing untoward could happen. Then, now that the situation was under control, you could investigate what had actually happened and rectify the problem. It was an excellent teaching process and, once the adrenaline had died down, all my students appreciated the lesson. I was surprised, however, not to see this as part of the formal syllabus to prevent any future disasters.

We only had one serious incident during my tour at Oakington, when one of our aircraft was involved in a mid-air collision with a small aircraft from Cambridge. The Varsity was flown by my great friend Harry Thomson, who, without exception, was the best pilot I ever flew with. Harry had just taken off from Oakington and, on climbing away from the airfield in cloud and under radar control, he was demonstrating to his student how to maintain tracking the centreline by checking various instruments. At about three hundred feet there was a bang on his port side and his aircraft was knocked left wing low by about forty-five degrees. Completely unfazed, Harry recovered the situation and continued his explanations to his student. He suggested that they had a major snag, so he continued climbing in cloud and then, still in cloud, he positioned himself for an instrument landing. He sent out an emergency call on his radio, but, for some reason, Air Traffic Control did not react. Harry was given clearance for his instrument approach, still chatting quietly to his student, who was completely unaware that they were in serious trouble. They landed back at Oakington and the student was horrified to see that they had lost some seven feet of their left wing in the collision. Incredibly, the first Air Traffic realised that there had been a problem was when someone asked, "What is that glider doing landing on the grass?" It wasn't a glider; it was a Cessna without its undercarriage.

We had the usual Board of Inquiry to investigate the incident, and, such are the strange workings of the RAF,

Harry was warned that he might be held culpable for the collision. He was in cloud, under the direction of Air Traffic Control and he was flying on instruments. The Board noted that Harry had said he had not been looking out; they pointed out that the flying rules stipulated that the captain of the aircraft is responsible for look-out at all times – *ergo*, he must be guilty. The Cessna had flown from Cambridge and was in our prohibited area, but what incensed me was that the system seemed to want to make out that it was Harry's fault.

At that time, Prince Charles was learning to fly from Oakington, and he came to a formal Dinner Night in the Officers' Mess. Harry and I were introduced to him after the meal and we had a nice chat, before Harry wandered off. I then asked Prince Charles if he knew who he had been speaking to, and I rather rudely pinned him in a corner and went through Harry's epic flight with him, explaining what a brilliant piece of flying it had been. After some five minutes, I concluded by saying, "If he is not awarded an Air Force Cross for that exemplary display, there is something seriously wrong with the RAF."

The stigma hung over Harry for some time, and he left for a posting in Germany while we continued to wonder what was happening. After a few months, Harry was summoned to HQ RAF Germany for interview with the C-in-C. Thinking that he had committed some misdemeanour, Harry was kept waiting for some time before he was ushered into the inner sanctum. There was no preamble, just a statement. "I thought you ought to read that." The C-in-C passed over a copy of the *London Gazette*, which announced the award of an AFC. The C-in-C then went on, "I can give it to you, or you can opt to go to Buckingham Palace to have it presented to you by the Queen."

"Well," said Harry, "I don't get many chances to meet the Queen, so I think I'd like to do that."

"Right," said the C-in-C. "You have to take annual leave and you have to pay your own fare!" So that is how we treat our heroes!

I was involved with one epic incident in which I was thankfully blameless. We taught the students how to fly on airways overseas, so, in the summer, we took them to Malta. With the aircraft's fairly short range, we had to stop to refuel at Nice in the South of France. I was captaining the lead Varsity, while Mike, another QFI, was captain of the second. As planned, we set off from Nice about thirty minutes ahead of Mike's aircraft, and, much to my surprise, as we approached Rome, we were given a mandatory diversion back to Nice. We had no idea of the reason, so there was much muttering on the return journey.

It transpired that, when they did the pre-flight checks on Mike's aircraft, the pilots were unable to move the cross-feed cock. The latter allowed you to transfer fuel from one side of the aircraft to the other, and it was essential that you could open and close it in flight. Inability to open the thing was definitely a no-go situation. Mark, another QFI with Mike, offered to go and see if he could release the jammed cock manually by jiggling the offending lever. Thus, he went into the nosewheel compartment (underneath the cockpit) through which travel any number of different linkages. Mark shook one, but Mike in the cockpit said, "No. That's no good. Try another one." So Mark shook another lever and got the same response. He tried two more, when there was a desperate fart from the port wing root, and the very large emergency dayglo multi-seat dinghy emerged into the daylight, looking like some sort of awful wart on top of the wing. Matters were not helped by their being parked in front of the civil terminal, so this was all going on in full view of the public, to the huge embarrassment of the crew. Indeed, a Boeing 707 taxied past them with the pilots waving and crying with laughter.

Of course, the crew's reaction was quite naturally, "Quick, get it inside!" Incredibly, they were unable to deflate the thing with any degree of normality, so they stabbed it to death with their aircrew knives! The back of the aircraft was thus filled with this rubberised disaster which did nothing to help the situation.

When the dinghy inflated, it bent the hatch in which it was stored. Alas, the crew was unable to bend the thing back into shape so that they could continue to Malta. The problem was exacerbated by my having the airframes expert on my aircraft while Mike had the engineering whizz. A bent hatch was an airframe problem, which is why I was recalled to Nice to help solve the problem. I'm afraid I never saw the dayglo wart, but it must have been very funny to watch.

It is funny how things work out. You fly with both good and not so good student pilots and you wonder what will happen to them in the future. A number of them really struggled, but some were excellent. Ian Dow was a quite delightful young man and an outstanding pilot. To show you what sort of a chap he was, he was the only student I left at the controls so that I could go down the back of the aircraft to have a pee. It did not surprise me in the least that Ian went on to be a VIP pilot, eventually becoming a brilliant and much-loved aircraft captain on The Queen's Flight. Nigel Beresford was another excellent young man who had undoubted potential. He finished his RAF career as CO of The Queen's Flight, while Martin Withers was another young man who impressed me with his flying skills and his calm attitude. Martin, of course, was the captain of the first Vulcan to bomb Stanley in the Falklands War. I guess I did all right as a QFI.

Chapter 18

Germany

After my tour as a QFI, in June 1971, to my surprise, I was posted to a ground job in Germany. I rang my postings officer to ask what I had done wrong, to be told that, on my last report, I had requested, 'Anywhere Overseas.' Hmm. No further comment. I also asked the questions, "What chance being short-toured; what chance promotion; and what chance Staff College?"

The answers I got were, "No, no and no way."

Duly chastened, I went to RAF Laarbruch on the German/Dutch border to become OC General Duties Flight (OC GD Flight) – a sort of Station Adjutant, but with lots of extra bits added on.

There was no married quarter on the station for us, but we managed to get a house some ten miles to the south, which was nice. There were lovely woods nearby, but the real problem was that we only had one car. With Sally going to Nursery School, we all had to be up and off by seven thirty, with everyone in the car. I was dropped at the office and then my wife had to sit around with the children, waiting for the school to open. She then went home with Daniel, before returning to collect Sally and me for the return journey so that I could have the car for the rest of the day, invariably finishing work after seven p.m. It was a dreadful performance, but thankfully we managed to move on to the base after six months, so life became easier.

We arrived in the summer, so everyone was wearing what we called shirt-sleeve order, i.e. no sweater or jacket. I was working in the station headquarters as part of the Administration Wing, so, to all intents and purposes, I was 'only' an admin chap. As such, I was given stick by these steely young aircrew who thought that they were the bee's knees, and eventually I had had enough. I turned to this obnoxious little prat and said, "Two things amaze me about you aircrew lot. First of all, how you justify all that flying pay, and secondly, how you manage to spend it all!" I left him gawping on his bar stool, and it was only some months later, when we got towards autumn and I put my tunic on again, that he noted that I, too, was a pilot – and probably better than him!

The job was absolutely fascinating, and I had fingers in so many different pies. I was incredibly busy, but I had a really wonderful boss called Ron Alison, who, having checked me out, just let me get on with it. We clicked immediately, so it was always great fun, although there were parts of my job which were a real grind. For instance, I was the bank manager for the Service Institute Fund (SIF) and I had to juggle two sterling accounts and two deutsche mark (DM) accounts. These accounts had to be laboriously hand-written into ledgers and had to be balanced every day. I took over the job from a navigator who added huge columns of figures in his head. He totalled the lot while I was still working on the tens column! The only way round this predicament was to borrow an adding machine from the Accounts Section, but only after they had finished their day. I was thus stuck to working in the evenings. The monthly reconciliation usually culminated in festoons of adding machine tape draped all round my office, but it had to be done. We were audited by a fearsome lady called Dr Leopold, who could have starred in *From Russia With Love*, and I looked forward to her visits in trepidation. My predecessor used to argue ferociously with her, but, since I did not really understand what she was saying, I dutifully said, "Yes, Dr Leopold" a number of times as she went through her report. This pleased her no end, and she turned to my boss and said that I obviously had a grip on the situation and that I was very good! Little did she know.

The fascinating thing about the SIF was that it could be used to provide facilities to support the airmen and airwomen, so we had a pretty free rein. The one thing you could not do was make a loss, so as soon as anything looked like turning bad, we knocked it on the head immediately. For instance, the SIF had originally provided washing machines for the airmen and airwomen to use in their barrack blocks, which may sound perfectly reasonable. However, there were the usual squabbles, with people removing other's clothing from the machines, and, as often happened, when the machines failed to work as advertised, a degree of DIY came in, which rendered the whole operation useless. We therefore decided to remove the machines from the barrack blocks and to install a launderette. We got Miele to come and design the thing and spent some DM30,000 (approximately £4,000) on fixing it up. The machines used specially shaped Miele coins, so you could charge whatever you needed for use of the machines (and there was no point in breaking in to steal these worthless pieces of metal). We employed wives to run the place and gave a discount if you wanted to do your own washing. However, airmen being airmen, they soon gave up on this and got the girls to do their dhobi for an additional fee (extra for ironing!), so everyone was satisfied. We made so much money that we used the profit to start a very nice coffee bar, again employing some of the wives to run it.

With the Munich Olympics coming up in 1972, I thought we should try to raise some money for the British Olympic Appeal Fund. I wanted to raffle a car and, having discussed this with my boss, we ended up raffling three cars! It was all about where car salesmen could have their pitch on the station, so I approached the Fiat rep. He had the key slot beside the station headquarters, so I was able to get some leverage on him. The three different models cost about DM20,000 in total, so I suggested that we could buy the three of them for

DM15,000. Naturally, this fell on stony ground, until we mentioned that the BMW rep was keen to take over the best pitch, so he caved in. We raffled each car in turn, selling six hundred tickets at DM10 a go. The first car took only a week to sell, the second took two weeks and the third, three weeks. Amazingly, they were won by a Senior Aircraftman, a Corporal and a Sergeant, in that order! I wasn't allowed to raffle a fourth car, but Lord, it was fun, and we sent off a nice cheque for the British team.

My wife's father had been an athlete in his day and had thrown the javelin for England in the Empire Games before the war, so he was keen to go to the Olympics. Over time, I had been buying pairs of tickets for the Olympics in dribs and drabs for the morning and the afternoon sessions of the athletics. Some I got in Holland, some in Germany and some from the UK, but the problem was that you could not buy them unless you could prove that you had already booked accommodation. The cheapest way to do this was to buy a caravan slot near Munich, which seemed to satisfy the red tape.

In the early summer, we drove down to Venice to hire a caravan *in situ* on the Venice Lido, and, as we were approaching Munich, my wife suggested that I try to get a zimmer, if one was available. Incredibly, almost the first place I asked at in a tiny village only some five miles from Munich had the necessary B&B, so I booked it there and then. Amazingly, it was only some fifteen minutes from the stadium, so we were very lucky. We had a lovely holiday in Italy, while I continued to gather tickets for the Games. In the end, I had pieced together tickets for the first five days' athletics (both morning and afternoon sessions), plus some for the boxing, which would take place in the evenings.

Naturally, I could not leave my wife without a car while I swanned off to the Olympics, but sometimes you get lucky. I had ordered a Volvo Estate and delivery was promised for 3rd August. I wanted a sunshine roof and other extras, but Volvo said no. They did not hold up the production line for any special stuff; what you got was a straight Volvo which you could modify as you wished after you had got it. I had ordered the car some months earlier, but heard nothing in the meantime. With the Olympics due to start on the 11th, I was twitching like mad, so I rang Volvo to enquire about my car. "Yes, sir," they said. "Your car will be delivered on 3rd August. Was there some doubt?" That's the way to do it.

The other slight problem was a further ultimatum from my wife. "Don't think you can swan off to the Olympics leaving me and my mother here. We can't possibly watch the Games without a colour TV!" Nice one. So we bought a Sony Trinitron (which did us very well over the years), and I was allowed out to take her father to Munich. He was getting on in years and suffering a bit from glaucoma, and almost the first thing he did to my beautiful Volvo was to put his case on the roof and then slide it across to me, making a nice groove in the paintwork!

So, off we went to Munich in the most glorious weather and had five days of excellent athletics. We realised that sitting all morning and then standing all afternoon was quite enough for us, so we got rid of the boxing tickets and went to an excellent Italian restaurant which had a huge TV screen – so we watched the boxing anyway. All the great athletes of the day were competing, so it was a fabulous time, with all the girls looking wonderful and an excellent atmosphere throughout. I was much taken with Ulrike Meyfarth, winning the high jump aged only sixteen, and the bronzed Heidi Rosendahl in the pentathlon. However, I lost my heart and my voice to the wonderful Mary Peters, who won the gold for Great Britain, always smiling and always apparently enjoying herself. What a joy to watch her.

We drove back north on Day 6, and that was when the Black September Palestinian terrorists captured a number of the Israeli athletics team and held them hostage. Sadly, all eleven were murdered when German police attempted to rescue them. It was a dreadful time for all concerned, but the Games went on. They had to.

One day, as I was sitting at my desk, I saw the announcement of the Shackleton being run-on in the Service and being converted to the Airborne Early Warning role. I had already done two tours on Shacks, so I sent an immediate arrow prayer to the heavens saying,

'Dear God. Please don't put me on those.' But, as it says in the Bible, 'And some fell on stony ground'!

Lo and behold, despite the advice of my postings officer, after only a year and a half, I found myself being promoted to squadron leader and, you've guessed it, being posted to northern Scotland to become Flight Commander Operations on No 8 Squadron, on the Airborne Early Warning Shackleton. And, just to put the icing on the cake, I had to pay duty on the Volvo and the caravan on our way home. It is called planned careers.

My job had been incredibly busy and I had thoroughly enjoyed all the different facets. I was so lucky with having such an excellent boss and had been much helped by discovering the joys of a shorthand typist, which made my life so much easier. The chap who took over from me had a nervous breakdown, so I often wondered whether Rosa Klebb had anything to do with it.

Chapter 19

Airborne Early Warning

A little bit of history. In the late 1960s, the Wilson government decided that Britain would no longer have any interest 'East of Suez', so one wonders, incidentally, what we have been doing in Afghanistan and Iraq over the recent past. But, by declaring this policy, the government did away with our need for aircraft carriers. Thus, at a stroke, they effectively did away with the Fleet Air Arm and, significantly, the Airborne Early Warning (AEW) provided by Gannet aircraft which flew from our carriers. Apart from the shock to the RN, they rightly asked the question, "Who is going to provide us with AEW?" The RAF stepped into the breach and said that we would.

At that time, the Government was considering joining the NATO AEW project which would require the purchase of Boeing 707-based airframes, modified to the AEW role. We were also withdrawing our Nimrod anti-submarine Maritime Reconnaissance squadron from Malta, so we seemed to have eleven airframes surplus to our needs. British Aerospace and GEC thought that they could configure these Nimrods to make a Nimrod AEW which would meet the UK's needs. Thus, Britain pulled out of the NATO Boeing Airborne Warning and Control System (AWACS) project; it was proposed that the Nimrod AEWs would be our contribution in kind. These aircraft would take a bit of time to produce, so, as an interim measure, eleven of the youngest Shackleton airframes were modified to have the Gannet radar installed under the nose, and the Shackleton AEW Mark II came into being – I repeat, as an interim measure.

And, just to keep up with the story of the RN, instead of aircraft carriers, they invented the 'through-deck cruiser'. This was essentially a large ship with a flat deck (eventually with a ski-jump on the bows), but it wasn't called an aircraft carrier – so honour was satisfied. But, without that thinking, the story of the Falklands War would have been very different.

Chapter 20

RAF Lossiemouth, Scotland

And so it was that in 1973 we went up to Lossiemouth, on the Moray Firth, for me to learn the new role. We bought a cottage in the town, which gave us lovely walks on the fabulous beaches. We also had woods near the River Lossie, so we and our dogs had a lovely time in a beautiful part of the country. Meanwhile, I did a very short conversion to the aircraft because I had flown it before, albeit some eight years earlier. It was assumed that I would pick up the AEW role as I went along, so I was a bit behind the curve to start with. We had a mix of RAF and RN (ex-Gannet) aircrew on the squadron, so we were all learning as we went. When we detached anywhere, it was not unusual for comments to be made about our crews, but one was nice when someone thought we had cracked the Duty Free problem because it looked as though we carried our own Customs Officers with us! My Squadron Commander was a navigator, so I was effectively senior pilot; and, as we built up, I had over a hundred aircrew on my flight, which by far was the largest flight in the RAF. Fighter squadrons had about a quarter of that number on the *squadron*, so I was nothing if not busy monitoring and supervising all the pilots and the aircraft captains.

As a part of Harold Wilson's 'east of Suez' policy, we had closed our base in Aden and everything was withdrawn. No 8 Squadron, which flew Hunter aircraft, was disbanded, so we took over the number for our Shackletons. We took over the squadron standard, the squadron silver, the Line Books and everything else, and we painted the aircraft in the same colours as those worn by the Hunters. This included painting the squadron colours of yellow, blue and red either side of the roundels on the aircraft. Nobody said that we couldn't do this, and nobody said that they were actually fighter flashes, only worn by fighter aircraft. More to the point, nobody told us to take them off; so, overnight, we had invented the only four-engined fighter in the world! These colours are still being worn by the latest AEW aircraft flown by No 8 Squadron some fifty years later, so that is how traditions start.

The airframe of the AEW Shackleton was essentially the same as it always had been, although we now had former Gannet equipment in use in the aircraft. We also had a large radar scanner which was housed under the nose of the aircraft. Significantly, I had taken part in a trial in 1961 to see what modifications were needed to make the Shackleton cockpit safe to fly. We identified fourteen major items which needed to be fixed, but, over the intervening years, not one of them had been actioned.

I mean, the aircraft was due to be phased out in the late 1960s, so why bother? How little did they know? Amazingly, the aircraft staggered on into the 1990s, still with these problems in the cockpit, let alone other bits and pieces which needed urgent attention down the back. The aircraft were so old that a lot of things had worn out. For example, the rubber surrounding the escape hatches had largely perished, so, immediately after take-off, I used to ask for a loo roll to be passed to the cockpit so that I could fill all the cracks and reduce the awful hissing noise from the airflow. The engine and propeller noise was bad enough, so anything one could do to reduce the noise level was a bonus.

So, we pilots flew in an archaic cockpit, but conditions down the back of the aircraft can only be described as an ergonomic slum. The radar operators had to stare at tiny seven-inch cathode-ray tubes, trying to pick out aircraft contacts from all the other clutter created by radar returns from ships, oil rigs, seagulls and the bright reflection from the centre of the screen which was largely caused by reflections off the sea. Quite how the radar teams managed to find anything defeats me, but they did a brilliant job in really awful circumstances.

The aircraft was heated by ancient flaming petrol burners (seriously!) which had little thought for the comfort of all. Thus, if we pilots were comfortable at the front of the aircraft, the radar team boiled. If we got the heat right for the boys down the back, we froze in the cockpit. Character-building, I think you call it. So, there we were, in a 1940s-designed aircraft with a 1940s-designed radar, flying in the 1970s. It was the equivalent of the Sopwith Camel being our front-line fighter in the Korean War! Quite amazing, but somehow we got the job done while we awaited the much-vaunted Nimrod AEW Mk 3.

As the first and only AEW squadron, we were technically controlled by No 11 Group, which was essentially Fighter Command in a smaller guise. The headquarters was staffed by fighter pilots who knew little or nothing about large aircraft operations, so we spent much time trying to get them to understand how we should operate. It was rather like beating your head against a brick wall, and it took ages to get them to understand even the basics. For instance, ensconced in their Ivory Tower at Bentley Priory, just north of London, I was worried by their concern over statistics. "You are very short of night flying, old chap. See what you can do to catch up." They were greatly surprised when I pointed out that we didn't actually have much night in Northern Scotland during the summer. Why didn't they come and visit us occasionally to see how we worked?

Running the operational side of the squadron was quite a task, but it was also great fun. We had a lovely bunch of people, all of us striving to make the ancient aircraft and its ancient kit work as well as it could. We exercised with our fighter aircraft, which was excellent training both for them and for us; and, of course, we kept an eye on the Soviet (in those days) aircraft which approached the UK airspace. As part of NATO, we got messages from all the Norwegian radar stations as they noted the passage of intruder aircraft coming round the top of Norway. The large Soviet Bear and Bison aircraft were usually on their way to either Cuba or to Conakry (in Guinea on the west coast of Africa), but sometimes they came towards the UK to see if we were alert to their presence. We were often sent up to Icelandic airspace to monitor these aircraft and to let them know that we knew. Sometimes we had a couple of our fighters with us (and a supporting tanker) so that we could direct them on to the Soviet aircraft, just to keep them on their toes. It was all a part of the Cold War, keeping an eye on each other to make sure things did not get out of hand.

There are always pressures to reduce one's budget in the military, and we were often hounded to cut back on various aspects of our training. One of our problems was that we relied on our fighter aircraft to give us the necessary practice, but they, too, had their training requirements. We used occasionally to detach an aircraft to fly with the Americans at Keflavik in Iceland, which was always good fun and good training. However, because it was fun, there was an effort to get us to cut down on the 'jollies'. As a result of this pressure, I wrote a paper explaining what good training this was and how it all helped us to keep up our skill levels. This paper was passed through the station and then on down to our group headquarters, where it was given further perusal. When I left the squadron to become the AEW expert at HQ Strike

Command, my paper was passed to me for comment. Naturally, I said that it was a well-argued document and recommended that Iceland detachments should be continued for the foreseeable future! I am happy to say that my paper was approved and the boys were also happy. It is called timing.

On any squadron there are extrovert characters, and we had quite a few. One star who sticks in my mind was the sort of chap a station commander might write up as, "In the event of war and his being captured, this officer would make the prison commandant's life absolute hell. Unfortunately, he insists on practising on me!" Mick Geoghegan was one such man, who had a heart of gold. He volunteered for everything, and I had to make a special case for an extra pair of flying boots for him because he was always falling down cliffs to give the neighbouring Search and Rescue helicopter squadron practice in cliff rescues where they had to winch him to safety. Mick had a serious twinkle in his eye and, thankfully, he just about knew when to stop.

At some stage, we had a purge on the wearing of name-tags, and people were always being reminded to wear them. The cry went up, "Where's your name-tag?" Naturally, Mick had the answer. He had a name-tag made up with the word 'NAMETAG' on it, which did little to endear him to the hierarchy. And then we had the truly epic story of his suits. Unknown to us, Mick had been into Elgin and had two suits made which actually were very smart. He turned up one Saturday night in the

Officers' Mess wearing a very loud dayglo yellow suit which really startled everyone. He was immediately accosted by the station commander, who said, "Geoghegan, get out of here and don't ever wear that suit in my Mess again."

Deflated, Mick left the Mess; but, not to be put off at all, he turned up the next Saturday night wearing an incredibly bright dayglo *green* suit! Yet again he was thrown out by the station commander and told never to wear that suit in the Mess again. The next Saturday night, Mick was back in the Mess, this time wearing the dayglo yellow jacket and the dayglo green trousers! What a star! The station commander banned him from using the Mess Bar for a month, but that didn't worry Mick. We all went and joined Mick to have a drink in his room!

Before we went to Scotland, we decided we would like to adopt a West Indian child. We had been through the selection process and, almost as soon as we got to Lossiemouth, we were called from London to be told that they had just the chap for us in Lewisham – only some six hundred miles away! So we all drove south, leaving Sally and Daniel with my wife's parents near St Ives, and then went on to meet him. You may imagine the sort of anxieties we were going through, but there he was in what I can only describe as a well-meaning but not very good foster home – one lady looking after some twelve children, all of different ages. And there we met Michael, strapped in a highchair and talking to a television and a macaw. We were told he said no when he meant yes, yes when he meant no, and that he called himself Carcu – and he was almost three! We took him for a walk in Lewisham Park and he started staggering backwards. We worked out that he had never been outside for a walk and that going up a slope was something completely new to him. He did not know what trees were or where to look for grass. He must only have gone outside his home in a pushchair and thus had had very limited exposure to what would be a 'normal' life. We went back to see him again the next day and were startled to be told, "If you like him, we can rush the paperwork through and you can take him with you tomorrow!"

Incredible, but the thought of flogging up and down between Lewisham and Scotland any number of times was not appealing, so we said, "Yes!" Some time later, we were told that our case was being used to demonstrate how not to carry out an adoption process!

I have said many times that we did not really bring up Michael. Both Sally and Daniel were pretty sharp, so Michael had to run to keep up with them. There was much, however, that he didn't have a clue about, so we all had a steep learning curve. For instance, as soon as we got home, the first thing that Michael did was to fall down the stairs! He had evidently never been down any before, so he had to be shown a less painful method. Amazingly, Michael seemed to be the only black person for miles around, and many people came to Lossiemouth just to see him. An indication of the sort of times we lived in was when my station commander's wife asked a friend, "What will happen when David wants to take him into the Officers' Mess?"

I am delighted to say that my friend replied, "I imagine he'll just take him in there."

When we got Michael from Lewisham, we were handed off to the Social Services of Aberdeen, who were supposed to keep an eye on us. The fact that it was sixty miles each way to and from Aberdeen did not help, but they seemed incessantly to ask us when we were going to adopt him. Eventually, I had had enough and got quite cross with them. I told them that they really had no idea what they were talking about. They had only ever placed a brand-new baby for adoption, whereas we had a much older child who had to fit in with our quite bright children – apart from us. We were all finding out about each other and, until we were all happy, I would be grateful if they would leave us alone. We would adopt Michael when we were ready to do so.

Living on the Moray Firth was a great experience, although sometimes the weather could be quite exciting. Yes, it rained quite frequently, but it always swept through fairly rapidly, leaving the most fantastically clear visibility. When we returned south after this posting, it was very noticeable that the sky was much reduced in size, with invariably poorer visibility. The thing I really missed was the *size* of the sky in Scotland. Such was the visibility, you could see right down to the horizon. But, when we first went up there in 1973, the local area seemed to be steeped in the past. There were nice little shops in Elgin which hadn't had a face-lift or an upgrade in years. And, when one went shopping for groceries and asked for something mundane like cornflakes, you were often faced with the answer, "Noo. I'm afraid there is no call for that up here!" It was only in 1974, when the first supermarket appeared, that things improved. And, moreover, the price of petrol immediately dropped to that similar in England!

When we left Germany after only eighteen months there, my one aim in life was to return to the continent to see the rest of Europe. However, we found it all so beautiful and unspoilt up north that we never left Scotland! We had a large caravan and we sped off in the holidays to see the glorious countryside and wonderful scenery. There was very little traffic anywhere, so it was almost unrestricted. The breaks at Easter and in October (delightfully called Tatty-Picking, because that was when the potatoes were harvested) were lovely, sometimes in snow, but mostly in wonderfully clear weather. It was a lovely experience for us, but mostly for the children, and we had some fabulous moments.

Sally was quite precocious so, aged six, we took her to an American lady who had a notice in her window which said, 'I give guitar lessons.' Having searched the country, we managed to get her a half-sized guitar in Lossiemouth, so off she went. While we were camping in Glencoe in the spring, we went for a walk and came across a group of hippies sitting beside a stream, with one of them quietly strumming a guitar. Sally wandered up to them and said, "I can play the guitar."

This hairy monster looked at her and said, "Yeah? Well, like, play it then."

So she sat down with this full-sized guitar on her lap and plucked out *Cavatina* absolutely flawlessly. There was a moment of stunned silence and then the hippy said, "Well, that wasn't bad. But if you really practise, you might be quite good!" What a brilliant comment to a young child.

Another time, we were camping on the banks of Loch Tay with those wonderful golden autumnal colours. Each morning, we sent the children out of the caravan so that we could reorganise it for daytime use. This time there was a frantic banging on the door, with Daniel calling, "Daddy, Daddy." Thinking the worst, I was met by my small son saying, "Look. It was autumn last night!" And how do you explain autumn to children? It is when the leaves come down and, following quite a strong wind in the night, we now had a golden carpet of leaves with the branches now bare.

We had a lovely holiday on the Isle of Skye and with nothing to do, we decided to climb up to the Old Man of Storr, the pinnacle of rock which is a famous landmark. It was an incredibly steep climb up scree and rough rock, with all of us, including our German pointer and the children, all scrambling away, but we got there unscathed. We were greatly surprised to come across a group of climbers, swathed in ropes and other accoutrements, who looked at us in amazement. It hadn't occurred to us that we might have been hazarding life and limb – although the climb down was quite exciting.

Meanwhile, after only a year, Sally's guitar teacher said that she couldn't teach her any more because Sally was apparently better than she was. We asked what we could do and she suggested that we go to a lady called Kim Murray, who had been teaching music in Elgin for fifty years! Kim was delighted to meet us and went straight up into her attic and got Sally a half-sized violin. I then asked, "How young do you like them?"

"As young as I can get them!"

I then asked, "What about Daniel?"

Off she went and came back with a quarter-sized violin! "See you on Saturday for orchestra practice!"

Quite amazing. They had separate individual lessons every week and orchestras on the Saturdays.

When I was at Prep School, I had tried to learn to play the piano, but all I did for a whole term was to try to play interminable scales – so I gave up. I don't think Kim made them play any scales. Before we left Scotland, Daniel had been learning the violin for a year, and I went to his last lesson. Kim said, "All right, Daniel. I don't want to do anything new with you today. I just want you to play everything you have learnt with me."

I sat there and listened spell-bound as he played uninterrupted for her for an hour. She really deserved her MBE.

Chapter 21

Back Down South

We left Scotland in the summer of 1974 amid floods of tears from the children, who did not want to leave their friends. In an effort to change the subject, I explained that we were going to go over an amazing thing called Spaghetti Junction, but this turned out to be a bit of a mistake. The rest of the ten-hour journey was spent with cries, "Are we there yet?", which drove us crazy. But the real nonsense was, when we actually got there, the junction is almost invisible from a car as you speed on your way, so that was not a very clever ruse at all – but at least the children had stopped crying.

We were given an RAF married quarter at Booker, which was just to the south of High Wycombe, on the road to Marlow. The children went to the local schools there, while my wife juggled all the toing and froing with the different school times. She was unable to get a job as a physio, so she did various manual jobs just to keep her sanity and a few pennies coming in to keep our heads above water.

I became the AEW expert at HQ Strike Command at High Wycombe, which was some ten miles away from home. While it was a desk job, it was quite fun, as I seemed to be the only chap who knew anything about the role. Perhaps the highlight, from my perspective, was my being sent to the USA to join the aircraft carrier the USS *John F Kennedy* for a three-week exercise. Quite why I was chosen I really haven't a clue, because it seemed that my role would be to brief the Americans about the UK low-flying system, something about which I knew nothing! I therefore spent some time learning all about it, which was quite useful, because I was then probably the most up-to-date chap at the time.

I spent the whole flight across the Atlantic completely lost, listening to Jaqueline Du Pré playing her wonderful cello, and then flew down to Norfolk, Virginia, to join the ship. I had been on British carriers before, but nothing compares to the might of an American one. The *Kennedy* was absolutely huge: eighty-five thousand five hundred tons, four and a half acres of flight deck, a ship's company of five thousand and anything up to eighty aircraft on board. Wow!

I arrived late in the evening and was shown to my bunk. The bottom bunk appeared to have been taken, so I levered myself to the top bunk and went to sleep. I really had no idea where I was in the ship, but next morning I was surprised to see a figure emerge from beneath me. It turned out that he was the Executive Officer (XO) of one of the squadrons, so he took me along to meet his buddies. I was immediately made welcome and was delighted that they were all so friendly. All American aircrew have some sort of nickname, and it wasn't long before I was known as CB – short for Crazy Brit.

They would not let me fly in their E-2C Hawkeye AEW aircraft because the Department of Defence sent me a personal letter informing me that 'flying off aircraft carriers is inherently dangerous', so I was looked after by the various squadrons. They very kindly gave me a tour of the ship. Perhaps I should tell you that I hate the sea and I hate heights, so going on a vast ship like her was a real test for me. Because I was a pilot, the first man we went to see was the chap who stands at the stern of the ship and who goes by the name 'Paddles'. In the old days, before they had the mirror landing system which accurately guides aircraft down to the deck, they were flagged down by a man waving paddles. He's actually called the landing safety officer, the LSO, and, because all these modern things can go wrong, they still have a Paddles at the stern of the ship so that he can take over if there is a problem. So, this was the chap we were going to see. And how do you get there? Well, I had no idea, but this naval aviator just said "Follow me", and leapt off the side of the ship, eighty feet above the waves!

He actually jumped into a net which was about two feet off the side of the ship, so you could see the Atlantic thrashing past us down below. He then climbed up this net and disappeared above me. The honour of Britain was at stake. So, in a mad, reckless manoeuvre, I jumped off the ship into this net, and I was absolutely terrified. I then scrambled upwards and eventually found myself standing on the deck at the rear of the ship, beside the famous Paddles. Wow! It was, of course, fascinating to see the whole operation, but most of my attention was fixed on my having to do the return journey. Terrifying! But what I find amazing is that, after I'd done it about three times, it all felt so ordinary and I just leapt out and up without a care in the world. You just have to get used to these things when the honour of the country is at stake! But it was fascinating watching the aircraft coming in to land and effectively crashing on to the deck in an attempt to catch the arrester wires with their tail hooks. The noise was quite incredible.

On another occasion, one of my new friends said, "Come on, Dave. Let's go see the airplanes!" Naturally, I headed for the lifts to take us up to the flight deck, but he said no, it was quicker this way. He simply opened a door in the side of the ship and we stepped out onto a flimsy 'aloominum' platform – again, with the Atlantic below us and ready to carry me off, the while being buffeted by some forty knots of wind. He then led the way up another flimsy ladder which literally flapped in the wind, with only a piece of wire on the outside between me and certain death. How I made it I'll never know, but what a thing to have to go through. Thank goodness we returned to the crew room the sensible way.

Watching the US Navy at work on a large aircraft carrier was a real experience for me, and I only wish more people could see it at first hand. On the flight deck there is an incredible amount of noise with aircraft manoeuvring and taking off and landing. Aircraft are shunted around the deck at incredible speed as they reconfigure the deck from launching from the forward catapults to launching using the beam catapults beside the angled flight deck on the port side. They only land on the angled flight deck, so, when landings are in progress, all the non-flying aircraft are parked at the forward end of the flight deck or off to the side. Essentially, you cannot launch aircraft and land aircraft at the same time – which is why you have to keep moving the aircraft around. Fortunately, by design actually, the aircraft can fold their wings so that they take up much less space than they might otherwise, but it is still an incredibly tight squeeze – and a very slick operation.

Having seen them operate, I can quite believe the oft-quoted expression – if you stop aircraft carrier operations, it will take you at least five years to be able to work up a new ship to anything like the previous efficiency.

It is a staggeringly efficient operation and really quite wonderful to watch. While I was there, I watched them launch twenty-two aircraft. They then reset the deck and landed the previously launched wave of twenty-two aircraft. Incredibly, the whole exercise took less than half an hour. It really is very, very impressive.

It was during this cruise that the *Kennedy* had a collision with another American warship. I was lying in my bunk when I heard a thump and then a grating noise. This was followed by the sound of a lot of running feet, so I got up to see what was going on. We had been refueling at sea when the USS *Bordelon* made a bit of a nonsense and the two ships came together fairly firmly. I didn't know it at the time, but the *Bordelon* had been quite badly damaged and, as a result, was apparently immediately sent to the scrapyard. But what was interesting was the reaction of those on board.

The *Kennedy* had had a collision at sea less than a year earlier, which had been something of a disaster. So those who had been on board when that happened, ran like crazy to their muster stations. Those who were newly on board, like me, just wondered what was going on.

What had happened on 22nd November 1975 was this. They had been exercising at night and did a particularly complicated manoeuvre. Alas, the USS *Belknap* apparently turned the wrong way and cut into the *Kennedy*, just under the angle of the flight deck. She then slid down the port side of the ship. Significantly, under the angle on the port side is where aviation fuel is kept; so, as the *Belknap* went down the port side, jet fuel from the *Kennedy* just poured into her. The flames came up over the deck of the *Kennedy*, over a hundred feet above the ship. It would have been an appalling disaster except for one thing. The *Kennedy* was so large, with this enormous flight deck, that, on that cruise, they were doing a trial. They carried what I call a normal airfield fire truck to help cope with any crashes on deck. As soon as the collision occurred, the firetruck drove to the angle and into the flames and started pouring foam into the *Belknap*. It then drove down the side of the *Kennedy*, continuously pouring foam as it went. What a fantastic effort. The *Belknap* had been lit from stem to stern, but the foam kept it very much under control. Yes, it was a terrible accident and seven men were killed on the *Belknap* with one killed on the *Kennedy* through smoke inhalation, but had it not been for the fire tender, it would have been very much worse. Significantly, all American aircraft carriers now carry the large fire truck as a standard piece of safety equipment on the flight deck – and it is manned whenever there are flight operations in progress.

All this happened in the Mediterranean during an exercise off Sicily, as I said, on 22nd November 1975. Now here is the creepy bit. President Kennedy was assassinated on 22nd November. And if you transpose the time of the accident to the time in Dallas, it was the same time that he was killed. I find that staggering, and I still get that creepy feeling down the back of my neck whenever I talk about the incident.

The other near disaster we had when I was on board was when we lost an F-14 Tomcat fighter over the side. I tell this story, not against the US Navy, but to show how well they operate in sometimes very hazardous circumstances.

On this occasion, they were launching aircraft from the two catapults on the port side of the deck. They launch each one individually and separated from the other aircraft. For this to happen, all the non-flying aircraft are stacked forward on the bow. Those waiting to fly are parked to the rear of the launch catapults. Ah, ha, you might think. 'Won't those behind be blasted by the jet engines of the aircraft taking off?' Well, they would be, except that behind each catapult is a Jet Blast Deflector, the JBD, which deflects the jet efflux upwards – so this large flap of steel has to be in the up position for a take-off. Once an aircraft has taken off, the JBD is immediately lowered so that the next aircraft can manoeuvre forward to the catapult. And this is going on at each catapult.

The noise is staggering and the slickness of the operation of what are really two runways within feet of each other is wonderful to behold.

On this occasion, they had an F-14 Tomcat ready for take-off. The last thing they do before a launch is to arm any missiles on the aircraft; the signal to do this is when the pilot holds both hands up so that the crew chief can see that he is not anywhere near the throttles or the switches. A bombardier then goes under the wings and removes the safety pins. At this point in the proceedings, for no apparent reason, the Tomcat's port engine went to full power. The aircraft lurched forward to the right – the pilot still had his hands up; he hadn't even got them anywhere near the controls – and the bombardier was blown backwards into the JBD, which stopped him being blown over the stern or into the aircraft behind. The aircraft continued to the right and cannoned off a couple of parked aircraft before the pilot could turn it back towards the angle. It was still going at full power on the port engine, but naturally, without the boost from the catapult or the other engine, it was much too slow for any take-off. As the Tomcat started to tilt over the angle, both the aircrew ejected and the aircraft disappeared over the side. It actually floated down the port side of the ship before it eventually sank into the North Atlantic.

Meanwhile, we now had two aircrew in their parachutes, heading for the deck. The first down was the navigator, who was heading for the aircraft on the next catapult. It had its engine running and there was a real fear that he would be sucked into the intake. Most fortunately, his parachute collapsed over the top of the aircraft's wing, while he was whipped under it. Amazingly, his parachute cords got tangled in the bombs and rockets under the wing, so he was left suspended in this sort of spider's web. He never even touched the deck!

The pilot, meanwhile, was heading straight down the angled flight deck and landed as advertised in a crumpled heap. However, his parachute was still full and he was being dragged down the deck at about thirty-five miles an hour – heading for the stern and over the back. One of the deck team, seeing this awful scene, ran flat out for the pilot and dived into his parachute, collapsing it and keeping him on deck. It was an incredibly fast reaction and a really first-class effort. Yes, they'd lost an aircraft, but all the men were saved.

What also impressed me was that, very shortly after they had cleared the deck, the Captain came on the Tannoy and said, "I want you all to know that we lost an aircraft over the side not long ago. However, everyone is safely on board. The pilot sustained slight injuries, the navigator is unharmed and the bombardier, who was blown into the JBD, has suffered a broken leg. All men are in the sick bay and are fine." That was it, a short, crisp situation report which immediately stopped any rumour or conjecture.

I wish we could have done that in the RAF. A ship is an enclosed capsule, so it is easier to keep a check on loose talk, but an airfield is huge by comparison, with people scattered around it and outside it. It is very difficult to stop what we in the trade call 'rumour in confidence'. News of an accident spreads like wildfire, often with completely wrong statements and speculation, and this can be very upsetting for wives and families – let alone the chaps on the base.

Just to complete the Tomcat story, the position was well marked by the Americans because they wanted to recover the aircraft, and particularly the armed Phoenix missiles which would still have been attached, but we had to press on with the exercise and headed south towards Scotland. Significantly, throughout our time at sea, we had been shadowed by a Russian frigate, so they would have known about the loss of the Tomcat and would have been monitoring the radios anyway. There was thus obvious concern that they might have got to the Tomcat first.

A recovery vessel was dispatched with diving equipment on board. They got to the datum and searched and searched and searched. Eventually, to everyone's surprise, they found the Tomcat about three miles from where she had plonked into the water. She had gone in with her wings swept forward – to give the aircraft maximum lift for the take-off – and it is assumed that she virtually glided down at a very shallow angle – hence how far away she was from her expected position. I am happy to report that the aircraft and the missiles were recovered intact!

But, back to reality. At HQ Strike Command, I was the only AEW chap; so, when NATO wanted a briefing, I was much too junior to be considered as Strike Command's representative. With much reluctance, I was allowed to accompany a much more senior group captain who knew very little about the subject. And, while I was asked to give the presentation, I was under strict orders not to answer any questions. Apparently, that was what the group captain was for. We were welcomed at Ramstein in Germany and met the senior man, the distinguished Air Marshal Alan Davies, with whom I had served some years earlier and who was really delightful. We then had the ridiculous situation of my giving the talk, followed by many questions asked directly to me because I was the specialist. Alas, the group captain did not get a look in, so it was all a bit embarrassing for him.

When I was a young officer, you were expected to spend the afternoon of the first Tuesday in December in the Officers' Mess, watching the Varsity rugby match on television. But since those halcyon days, things had been tightened quite a bit, so we were expected to be slaving at our memoirs or whatever instead. However, still something of a rebel, I determined to watch the game and took my portable TV to work. My friends knew of my intention, so, at the appointed hour, we slipped away and found a deserted office, before settling down to watch the game. You may imagine my horror when the door opened to reveal the Group Captain Operations looking in on us. "Ah," he said. "Thank God there is still some spark of life in the Headquarters. Can I come and join you?"

Also, in the summer of 1976 (that fabulous summer), when I was working as a staff officer in the Headquarters of Royal Air Force Strike Command at High Wycombe, I was given a somewhat strange task which had nothing whatsoever to do with my job.

I was summoned to see a senior chap, who asked me to try to fill a day for a very important CENTO delegation which was visiting the country. I was told that they were very important, because anyone with initials like that just had to be important. However, you may imagine my concern when it was revealed that CENTO stood for the Central Treaty Organisation, a sort of

NATO for the Middle East. The members of CENTO were Iran, Iraq, Pakistan, Turkey and the United Kingdom, who formed an alliance ostensibly to show the Soviet Union that we were all together and thus dissuading them from expanding southwards. And, while this alliance was in being, we had the Arab-Israeli conflict going on to the west, while India and Pakistan decided to have wars of their own to the east. I need hardly add that during this time, Pakistan called on CENTO to help them, but this request was quite rightly turned down.

I asked David Maurice-Jones, a fellow officer in my department, to help with the task, but it was evident from the off that we might be hard-pressed to entertain, let alone look after this strange bunch of visitors who, apart from anything else, were not natural English speakers. So, what could we do with them? We didn't really wish to expose British secrets to these chaps or take them to see a Royal Air Force station, so we had to plan something different. I then had a brainwave and wondered if we could take these allies to Windsor Castle to give them a bit of culture.

Thus, I telephoned Windsor Castle to see if we could have an organised tour for this very select delegation and was told that for important visits, we should have a Military Knight to show us round. I would have to ask St James's Palace for one. This sounded just the job and, on enquiring what a Military Knight was, I was given a brief history of the Knights of the Garter. Apparently, when appointed Garter Knights, they make a promise that, amongst other things, one of them will pray in St George's Chapel every week. However, in the fourteenth century, there were so many away fixtures requiring the Garter Knights to go and whack infidels overseas, that they ran out of knights to do the praying. Thus, retired senior military officers were appointed Military Knights to help the Garter Knights and generally to help around Windsor Castle and in St George's Chapel. It was one of these that we sought, so I was given a London telephone number.

I put on my most pompous voice and rang St James's Palace.

"Good morning," I said. "My name is Squadron Leader David Greenway and I have a very important group of foreign officers whom I would like to take to see Windsor Castle. I understand that you can help me."

"Hello," said this lovely-sounding girl in London. "And where are you ringing from?"

"I'm calling from Headquarters, Royal Air Force Strike Command."

"Oh!" she said. "Daddy works at Strike Command."

"And what does Daddy do?" I asked.

"Oh, he's the C-in C!"

Collapse of stout party, as PG Wodehouse would have it. But the outcome was that we managed to obtain a Military Knight to show us round. He would meet us outside the entrance to Queen Mary's Dolls' House on the day in question.

And so it was that we set off by coach for the castle with this strange bunch of people. Somehow, they had been augmented by a few disinterested American officers who doubtless had similar difficulties with the English language. Happily, we were expected at the castle gates and made our way to the North Terrace to meet our guide. The place was completely deserted except for a somnolent figure lying on a bench – with a Solar Topi over his face. I respectfully approached, gave a polite cough, and enquired, "Brigadier Robinson?"

There followed an explosion of coughs and expressions such as, "What-what-what? Ah, ha... Whhoaaahhh!" I couldn't believe my ears or my eyes. It was Bloodnock! Truly wonderful, and it wasn't an act, because that was how he was all through our tour. What a star! He rose from the bench and then led us through the magnificent State Apartments. We saw some of the Leonardo cartoons, the awesome displays of exquisite china, and eventually we found ourselves in what I think was called the Trophy Room in those days. In there they have objects taken from various battles in which Britain has been involved. Items such as Napoleon's cloak and the bullet that killed Nelson are on display, and we looked in wonder. I say we, but I am not sure what the CENTO chaps got out of it.

We wandered around looking at the exhibits, when I saw what I can only describe as a pair of ugly pugs which were probably solid gold – so I asked Brigadier Robinson for the history of these items. I'm not actually sure about the metal of the dogs, but his description was pure gold!

"Ah... yes," he said. "Let me think. Right. Er... Seringapatam... Clive, y'know. Spot of bother... 43rd saw 'em orff!"

David Maurice-Jones and I realised exactly what must have happened, but we just stood there with tears pouring down our faces as our 'allies' just gazed on in amazement at this coded language of which they knew nothing. It was all too difficult.

We pressed on through the State Apartments, passing through the beautiful rooms and gazing at the most wonderful collection of paintings – Holbeins, Constables, Canalettos, Van Dycks, Rembrandts, Gainsboroughs and so on. You could even walk up to the paintings for a closer look. Eventually, we emerged back into the outside world, reeling at the magnificence of what we had seen.

At that point, an American officer turned to me and said, "Say, wasn't that outstanding. Where do they keep the originals?"

You can't make it up, can you? I'd like to think it was one of those ignorant Yanks who turned round and said, "I can't believe the Brits would be so stupid as to build Windsor Castle so close to Heathrow."

Our daughter Sally was getting quite good at music, so we tried to get her a decent violin. We had heard of a man in Southall who knew about these instruments, so we set off to find him. I had not been to Southall before and, as we approached, it was as if suddenly we were in a different country. It wasn't a gradual process. It was an immediate change to all things Indian. There were wonderful curry fumes in the air, beautiful saris being worn by the ladies, and Indian movie posters all over the place. It was quite a culture shock as we pressed on to find our violin man. I told him of our experience as we came through the town. "I know what you mean," he said. "They've driven the blacks right out!" I hadn't thought about it like that, but, at the time, driving through High Wycombe, one was very conscious of the different sections of the town being divided into the various racial groups. Indeed, the railway bridge to the north of the town was referred to as the Khyber Pass!

Also, in that amazing summer of 1976, we decided to take the children to Paris. We had a lovely sixteen-foot caravan, so we set off to cross the Channel on the overnight ferry from Portsmouth, arriving at Le Havre at a ridiculously early time, and set off down the autoroute. It all seemed to be so simple and, in no time at all, there was the Arc de Triomphe in front of us. Without thinking, I drove round the Arc with sixteen foot of caravan streaming behind me, accompanied by the most incredible cacophony of Parisian car horns giving me a typical French welcome. It was only later that I discovered that it was totally illegal to enter the centre of the city accompanied by a caravan. Fortunately, the Gendarmerie had a day off or something.

We camped in the Bois de Boulogne and had fun sending the children off to do some shopping in French, which was a great step forward for them. And then we went to the Eiffel Tower. I really don't like heights, but I couldn't be shown up in front of the children. We sped to the top, changing lifts on the way, where I had to hang on for dear life. On the way back to sanity, Madame and Sally decided to get off at the Premier Étage, while Daniel stayed with me. The lifts are very big and we must have been at least ten people deep as we readied for the descent. At the last moment, Daniel decided that he wanted to go with Mum, so he dived through this mêlée of legs and got to the outside door as it closed. The inside door then started to close with Daniel about to be trapped between the two doors, so that, if the lift went down, he would have hundreds of feet behind him if he fell to the ground. As you may imagine, I was shouting my head off, seeing this awful incident unfolding before my eyes. Thankfully, they managed to stop the doors and we escaped to live again. I wouldn't wish that experience on anyone.

We lived in an RAF married quarter at Booker, just south of High Wycombe and some ten miles from the headquarters, which had its pluses and minuses. There was a coach to take us to and from work, but I cannot stand any form of clock-watching. I decided to commute on a scooter, which at least gave me a bit of freedom and allowed me to finish what I was working on without racing for the coach.

The children were happily settled at local schools when, in 1977, I was suddenly short-toured to go to the RAF Staff College.

Chapter 22

Staff College

The Staff College course was usually a year, but our course was something of an experiment in that they did without the two leave periods and some of the more interesting visits. However, they kept the same lectures and exercises and so on and compressed us into only a five-month course. One of the great things about a year-long Staff College is that you all move to their married quarters, so all the course members get to know each other so much better. Because of schooling, a number of us chose to leave our families where they were and attended the shorter course unaccompanied. It wasn't the best solution and, after our trial short course, they sensibly returned to the year-long version.

The Staff College course was actually great fun and we learnt quite a bit along the way. For some exercises, we combined with the Army Staff Course from Camberley, so we cross-bred a bit. But the Army came into their own during one joint exercise when they all downed tools to watch the Queen's Jubilee Review of the British Army in Germany. The RAF were left to carry on with the exercise while the Army chaps spent the afternoon watching television, with tanks and other kit driving past Her Majesty in clouds of dust such that one could hardly see anything of the display. Never mind, it all gave rise to cries of, "Oh, I say. Damned fine show, what?" They were, however, somewhat miffed that we had completed the exercise without their input.

We had many interesting speakers (including the wonderful Leonard Cheshire VC), and students were asked to join the Commandant at lunch to help entertain them. I was at lunch during Wimbledon, and we were all a bit miffed that we could not take the afternoon off to see the Ladies' Final because we had to complete an exercise.

"Ah," said a visiting Air Marshal, "why don't you record the tennis so that you can see it afterwards?"

"No, sir," I said. "It would be much better to record the exercise and to let us watch the tennis live."

He turned to the Commandant and said, "Is this chap one of your brightest students?"

Alas, we had to complete the exercise.

There was quite a bit of pressure put on us during the course, with short deadlines much in evidence. But quite the hardest work I did was to produce the End of Course Review, which usually resulted in the students bad-mouthing the staff. I determined that we would be different and I set out to entertain them rather than have a go at them. I also wanted to leave the wives in tears at the end so that they would know that they had had a good time! A few of us got together to see what talent we had among the students, and amazingly we had piano players, violinists and other instrumentalists, so we had a band! My great friend Tony Wober and I sat giggling long into the night while we worked on writing sketches, often crying with laughter. Thankfully, lots of silly skits went down well, but the finale was something else.

I don't know if you have seen an orchestra play Haydn's Farewell Symphony? The last movement is often played by candlelight, and it has many solo parts in it. As each instrumentalist plays his part, he blows out his candle and leaves the stage so that the lighting gradually reduces, leaving only the last violins to complete the work before they, too, leave. It is a lovely idea, so I wanted to combine that with our singing 'Now is the Hour', mainly because we had Commonwealth officers on our course as well. Picture the scene: we had a horseshoe of us standing in the dark as the curtains came back. From the front you could see nothing except the candle I was holding in the middle. A lone violin played the first verse, as gradually those on either side of me slowly lit their candles from mine so we had an ever-increasing crescent of candles – just candles, because you could not see any of us holding them. We then sang the first verse, and you could hear a few sniffles from the audience. And now to the *pièce de résistance*. We hummed the last verse, but now we started to blow out candles in sequence so that, on the last note, I blew out the last one accompanied by weeping from the stalls. Success!

After much speculation, at the end of the course, we all got our postings. Staff College thought they knew better than the postings people, so they had to approve everything. It was all a bit precious, but finally the postings were put up on the college noticeboard – effectively set in tablets of stone. Much as expected, I was posted to a job in the Ministry of Defence, something to which I was not looking forward. Unbelievably, after a couple of weeks' leave, my postings man rang me at home and said, "I'm afraid there has been a bit of a cock-up, David. The job you are supposed to be going to is a navigator's job, and, of course, you are a pilot. Would you mind going to Cyprus?" What a question! Would I mind?

We had been moving towards adopting young Michael, but my overseas posting put an immediate hand-brake on this, while the Social Services had another think. Incredibly, they asked all sorts of naïve questions, such as, "Is it safe to take him to Cyprus?" and "Are there schools in Cyprus?"

I pointed out that he was about to be given the opportunity of a lifetime; so, as a compromise, we were allowed to take him, 'Fostered with a view to adoption'. What a performance.

Thus, we were transferred to the care of a lovely SSAFA sister who visited us periodically and drank a lot of our sherry and brandy, but who otherwise left us alone to get on with life. At one stage, we all went to Israel for an excellent holiday, so I sent the Social Services a postcard on which I said, 'I suppose we should have asked you, but we are having a lovely time in Israel!' Apparently, this put them all into a tremendous flap, until they were reassured by our SSAFA friend.

Chapter 23

Cyprus

We arrived in Cyprus in November 1977 to have the most wonderful tour. I was to be the Plans Officer in the Air Headquarters at Episcopi. There were two other squadron leaders on the Air Staff, so, if we had a problem and it wasn't Maritime or Air Transport, it had to be me – so I wound up looking after all sorts of different topics as well, which was fun. I was also the Group Flight Safety Officer, so I had an interesting mixed bag to keep me busy. There was also a much larger Army Headquarters in the same building, so we all effectively mixed in and all got on extremely well together. At that time, the RAF personnel on the island were outnumbered by about 3:1 by the Army, so we had our work cut out to keep our side up – successfully, I might add.

We lived in excellent married quarters some three miles across hills and valleys from the Headquarters, with the children going by bus to the military school. With the wonderful weather and temperatures in Cyprus, I bought a Honda motorbike, which was an excellent means of transport for me and which left my wife with the car. We all worked the brilliant seven a.m. to one p.m. every day, so the afternoons were free for sport, bathing or even skiing up on Mount Troodos at six thousand feet in the winter. The choice was endless. I sum up my life out there by my inability to speak Greek – so I had to get our maid to give our gardener a rocket! What a wonderful life!

We had one epic Keystone Cops moment when a swarm of bees came and settled in our garden, hanging off the branch of a tree. There were bee hives near the Fire Station, so I rang the firemen to see if they could take the swarm back to the hives. They seemed a bit reluctant, but agreed to come and have a look. Eventually, a large red fire engine appeared outside my house and we went to investigate the problem. I explained how easy the operation would be. It was simply a case of my getting a large cardboard packing case and dropping the bees into it. All was then required was to close the top and to have the firemen take the bees back to the hives. Schimple!

With some hesitancy, a fireman elected to put on his space suit while I remained in a T-shirt and shorts. In his full firefighting kit, including his helmet with leather flaps over his shoulders and an extra-thick glass faceplate through which he could hardly see, he began his task. He picked up the packing case and approached the swarm while I climbed a step ladder beside the bees, which seemed to be somnolent and nicely behaved. At the appointed moment, when our spaceman was ready, I whacked the branch and the bees all fell off into the packing case in the expected manner. I thought all was well, until the bottom of the cardboard case opened and the whole swarm fell out! I now saw the spaceman blundering around, trying to beat off many bees, still unable to see clearly, so I ran in to the kitchen and seized the fly spray in order to help him get rid of this menace. He covered himself in spray and it was only then that I discovered a slight problem. In my haste, I had seized a can of Pledge furniture polish instead of the expected Flit or whatever, so we ended up with highly polished bees and a desperate spaceman running blindly down the road pursued by a fire engine! I never did find out what happened to the bees, but we were glad to see them depart.

When we got to Cyprus, we used to go to the local Taverna for a wonderful meal with the best pork chops I have ever eaten – huge and succulent. My wife and I would share a bottle of the local wine, while the children had soft drinks, and the whole bill came to £5! OK, so they were Cypriot pounds, but it was fantastic value and a great night out. After some three years, the bill had gone up to £8, but it was still excellent.

During our time in Cyprus, they changed all the cookers in the married quarters to gas appliances, but my wife asked if we could keep the electric stove because she was used to it. Amazingly, the system agreed, so everyone was happy. In the autumn, as the season changed, we had tremendous thunderstorms which usually resulted in power cuts. With the houses plunged into darkness, initially we searched the house for the children. However, after a short time, as soon as the electricity went off, we didn't bother. We knew that they would be found in the car, waiting to go out to the local taverna to eat by candlelight!

The weather in Cyprus was just wonderful, with long hot summers, so we spent much of the time on the beaches. Sally and Daniel could swim like fishes and we had taught Michael to swim at High Wycombe before we left. However, when we got to Cyprus, he seemed to have forgotten how to swim, so we took him to the school swimming pool and tried again. He was hopeless and constantly made for the side, so I did the only practical thing I could and stood on his fingers. He soon got the message.

We had a lovely beach near us with a raft moored about fifty yards offshore, so we made it a rule that nobody could go to the raft on their own unless they could swim there and back. Happily, they all succeeded and, after his initial reluctance to get in the water, Michael improved dramatically. He is very black and, at the end, he spent most of his time, head down, looking for pebbles under the sea. Thus, he was almost invisible, and all you could see of him was his pink soles sticking above the surface!

It was really too hot to play any sensible golf in the summer, so our season was largely confined to the winterish months. We had a wonderful membership at the

Episcopi Golf Club and we had the greatest fun, putting on browns, which comprised an oil and sand surface, rather than greens. There was intense inter-Service rivalry with much banter and good humour, and we had wonderful competitions. I managed to get down to a 4 handicap and we beat the Army every year, which pleased us immensely. We even had three RAF chaps who played off an 8 handicap, but they were not good enough to get in the team.

My great friend Gerry Hinnigan and I devised the Cyprus Open Foursomes and we managed to get Rothmans to sponsor the event, which was very good of them. We played eighteen holes on the Friday, eighteen on the Saturday and then thirty-six holes on the Sunday, and it was a fantastic competition. Foursomes is a relatively quick way to play golf, with each couple playing alternate shots using the same ball, but it was a close-run thing to beat the rapidly approaching darkness in Cyprus, where there is very little twilight.

Because of the shortness of daylight, we reduced the field on the Saturday evening so that we could complete the event before dark. Those who had failed to make the half-way cut played a Stableford competition on the Sunday, fitting in between the two final rounds. People came from the UK, from Egypt and from further afield, and it was a tremendous success. I am delighted to report that Gerry and I won the Open in 1979, which made our day. And it was at Episcopi that I managed to play my only sub-par round of golf, which was exciting for me if nobody else. My score card hangs in my downstairs loo.

As I said, I was the Group Flight Safety Officer and, in this capacity, I attended the inquiries into two aircraft crashes. In the 1970s, the Americans were flying their U-2 reconnaissance aircraft from RAF Akrotiri. There was ridiculous secrecy surrounding these operations, and people were told not to talk about it. They were not to photograph anything and, if asked, to deny that anything was going on. All this was patently ludicrous because the U-2 made an horrendous amount of noise on take-off so that everyone within ten miles of the base must have heard it. It always took off at 0600 hrs, so there was no point in denying anything. In fact, the U-2s were monitoring the Israeli/Egyptian ceasefire lines on behalf of the UN, so what was the point of all this cloak and dagger stuff?

The first U-2 crash during my time was a pretty horrible one. The aircraft took off and immediately turned left towards the air traffic control tower. It caught its port wingtip on the ground and then rolled over the top of the Met Office and covered the Ops Room in highly volatile fuel. There was a tremendous fire and sadly a number of people were killed. It was really an American accident and nothing to do with us; but, as the Group Flight Safety Officer on the island, I was invited to go and sit in on the American Safety Inquiry. It was a fascinating experience because they do things very differently to the RAF. For starters, all the members had

183

nicknames. Thus, we had Frisbee, Snake, Leopard, Knife and others, so it was all very informal. The board was chaired by a colonel who seemed to be very grateful for my inputs. My views were frequently met with his observation, "Hey, Dave. That was a very, very germane comment!" We agreed on the findings, which were sent off to the States.

What had happened in the accident was pretty clear to me. On that day, the first three hundred yards of the runway were being worked on, so the aircraft was lined up for take-off some distance from the threshold. When the aircraft crashed, it had apparently made a heaving turn to the left and almost hit the air traffic control tower. On arriving at the crash scene, the American doctor said, "Well, they've done it this time." The implication was that they had obviously done that sort of manoeuvre before. Patently, the crash seemed to be the Americans' fault. I believe, to ease their boredom, the U-2 pilots had been in the habit of turning very close to the air traffic control tower to give them a thrill. On that day, I think the U-2 pilot forgot he was three hundred yards closer to the tower and thus miscalculated the aircraft's turn and just made an appalling error.

While the American inquiry continued, an RAF Board of Inquiry also sat to see if there was anything wrong with our RAF procedures. They asked the air traffic controllers if the U-2 had done this sort of manoeuvre before and were told that they had done it on numerous occasions in the past. They were then asked if they had reported this to anyone, which, of course, they had not. It seemed a rather pointless question since everybody on the station who lived in the married quarters could not have failed to hear the earth-shattering sound on take-off and must have seen the U-2s streaking over their houses and away to the south at low level. All the senior officers on the station must have known about this. I should point out that the U-2 was designed as a high-level reconnaissance aircraft which should have taken off straight ahead on the runway and then climbed to considerable height to carry out its role. It had no business fooling around at low level. However, having noted that the air traffic officers had not reported to anyone senior, the RAF Board concluded that the accident was the RAF's fault! I took their findings in to my AOC, who, at my suggestion, wrote 'BOLLOCKS' all over it.

The second U-2 crash involved the pilot dragging his aircraft in at low level from about twenty miles. He had suffered a partial hydraulic failure and managed to get only half his flaps down, so his approach would be something non-standard. There is precious little difference between the U-2's approach speed and its stalling speed, and, instead of flying the aircraft using the airspeed indicator to measure its speed, the aircraft is actually talked down by a U-2 pilot standing near the runway threshold. The latter judges the correct aircraft speed by looking at the nosewheel of the aircraft so that, if he sees too much of it, he tells the pilot to increase his speed by lowering the nose a bit – and vice versa. On this occasion, the aircraft came in and crashed just short of the runway. Again, I was on the American Safety Inquiry and listened to all the comments. They concluded that it was just bad luck because the wind had changed shortly before touchdown. At this point, I made another 'germane' interjection. I said I thought they were crazy to try to land the aircraft on the numbers, rather than some distance down the runway. I knew they trained in the USA, where there was practically no wind, so the aircraft tended to float for ages, waiting for the speed to reduce. Thus, over there, they seemed to want to land as early as possible on the runway. However, at Akrotiri, on the day, they had fifteen knots' headwind straight down the runway. Moreover, they had three thousand yards of concrete ahead of them, so why did they try to land it on the beginning of the runway? It all seemed unnecessary to me. "Very germane, Dave!"

During exercises in Cyprus, I was in charge of the Joint Services Reinforcement Cell, going through the motions of what we would do if we needed to seek help from outside the island. On this occasion, reinforcements were called for from the UK, and the exercise seemed to be going swimmingly. In order to reduce problems to the minimum, we all worked to the same time-frame. Cyprus is some three or four hours ahead of UK time, so we always use the one standard time. In this case, we used GMT, which is called Zulu in military speak; all times used in the exercise were in Zulu time. At one point during the exercise, an Army colonel wandered in and enquired at what time some reinforcements would be arriving. I did a quick calculation and told him, so he wandered off, back into Army territory. After a few moments, I realised that we had made a wrong calculation, so I went off to find the colonel to rectify the situation. I found him deep in Brown country. "I'm very sorry, colonel," I said. "I gave you some incorrect information just now. The reinforcements will not be here until 131400 Zulu."

"Ah," said the colonel. "Umm... er. I'm afraid that is not very clear. What day did you say?"

"The 13th, colonel," I replied.

"Ah," he said again. "And what time did you say?"

"1400 Zulu."

"No... I'm afraid that is still not very clear."

Before I could try again, a tired, laconic voice came from an old major in the corner, who said, "About teatime on Friday, colonel."

"Ah," he said. "Thank you so much."

All the RAF's worst fears came home to roost!

Throughout my tour, we had a wonderful time playing sport with all the Services. These included the Army, a lone naval officer, and many civilians, and we all got on extremely well together. In fact, I captained the Headquarters British Forces Cyprus cricket team and we had a wonderful time, playing on all the excellent sports facilities and really enjoying each other's company.

The top man in Cyprus rotated between an RAF appointment and an Army appointment, and shortly before I left, I was very disappointed to hear the incoming Army man say, "Right, I don't want to see any of my Army officers fraternising with the RAF."

Lord, what a waste of time. At a stroke, he had destroyed all the co-operation and *esprit de corps* that we had built up during my time; and, sadly, the island went downhill from that moment. I don't think it was ever the happy posting again, which was a terrible tragedy.

The tour in Cyprus was really the greatest fun. The climate was wonderful and we managed to go everywhere, sometimes camping on the beach to see the turtles lay their eggs (and later to watch the tiny babies making their way to the sea, being shepherded by a team of American students who were trying to protect them from scavenging birds or foxes). We had fantastic ruins to look around and we had the lovely Curium amphitheatre in which visiting entertainers played to us. It was amazing, just sitting in the lovely warm evenings, with the Mediterranean backdrop, listening to military bands playing. It seemed almost natural that they set fire to the dried grass and bushes with a very realistic 1812 Overture, firing their guns at the appropriate moment! It was just typical of the Army. We had Combined Services Entertainment shows which were always good fun, and we had Patrick Moore out to do a *Sky at Night* with the velvet, clear night sky overhead.

When Patrick visited us, I was detailed off to look after him. The first morning I picked him up, it was almost as if he had deliberately dressed as a scatty scientist. He had buttoned up his loud Hawaiian shirt one button out, and he had the remains of his breakfast down the front of his shirt – evidently boiled eggs! But he could not have been nicer and he was great fun. He was an ardent cricketer, despite his considerable age, so I asked him if he would like to play in my team. He acquitted himself admirably, despite being not very fit, and we all thoroughly enjoyed his company. I picked him up from St John's School one morning and, as we were driving away, he said that he had just had the best interview he'd ever had with a young boy. "He was wonderful," said Patrick. "He had all his questions down pat and he was so interested and intelligent."

I followed by saying how nice that must have been. "I wish more of the interviewers on the BBC were like him. For instance, I dislike Robin Day intensely, with his arrogant and aloof manner, always talking down to his subjects."

"Ah," said Patrick. "Robin is a great friend of mine!"

So much for that conversation.

The local produce in Cyprus was always excellent, and there was a never-ending supply of very good food in all the restaurants. The pork was truly outstanding, but we never saw the pigs – presumably kept out of the heat in caves? There were vast orange groves to drive through with the mesmerising smell of that never to be forgotten, lovely orange blossom. Vineyards seemed everywhere, and sadly, the local wine left quite a bit to be desired – but we drank it anyway. And, when the grapes were picked in the autumn, they were simply flung into open, high-sided lorries and taken to the factories. The great press of ripe grapes meant that the floor of the lorry was awash with grape juice which, when the lorry climbed hills, just spilled out of the back and all over the roads. Naturally, this made driving quite a challenge, particularly when the first rains came, with the surface not unlike an ice rink. Lord, it was fun!

All good things must come to an end, and, after three years in the sun, I was recalled to the UK to take up an appointment in the Ministry of Defence. The good news was that I was being promoted to wing commander.

Me flying a Piston Provost 1958

Awarded my pilot's wings 1958

Love from Diana

Being driven out of RAF Benson for the last time
On relinquishing command.

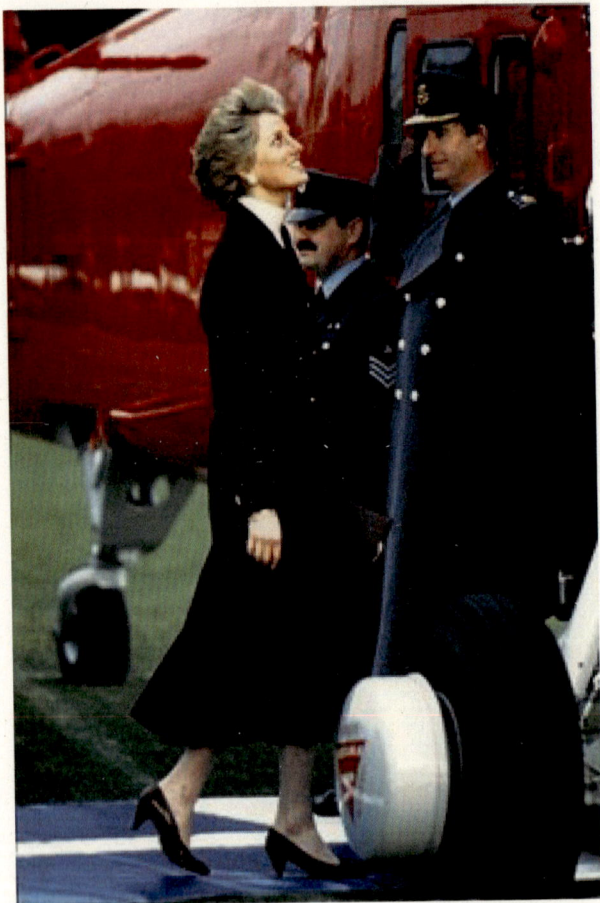

With Diana at Iffley Road, Oxford, 1990

HM The Queen and HRH Prince Philip
with The Queen's Flight 1990

Up country in Brazil, 1990.
We had just had a giggle about her appearance on *This is Your Life* because of the red folder she had in her hand.

Diana with the crew in Brazil 1991

Diana with the team in Chitral, way up in the North East
corner of Pakistan 1991

Chapter 24

Ministry of Defence (MOD)

On return to the UK in 1980, we asked to live at RAF Halton in Buckinghamshire, so that, while I commuted to London, the children could go to good schools. They still had grammar schools in Bucks, and that was the principal reason for our choice. We had a nice married quarter with lovely walks in the beautiful Wendover Woods behind us, so we were very lucky.

The children had continued their music lessons in Cyprus, so we enrolled them into the wonderful music-teaching set-up in Aylesbury. Sally went straight into one of the orchestras, while Daniel, now aged ten, was put with the younger ones. The conductor asked Daniel if he could play something for the twenty-plus children, but, puce with embarrassment, he refused. I managed to talk him into playing something from behind a screen, so he then proceeded to play the 'Skye Boat Song' flawlessly, which amazed me. The orchestra burst into applause, which completely flummoxed him; but, blushing profusely, he was accepted with increased standing.

My job in London was concerned with the introduction of the Nimrod AEW, which was being jointly produced by two firms. The airframe (which was essentially a modified Nimrod *maritime* airframe which itself was a modified Comet airframe) was manufactured by British Aerospace (BAe). The radar and all the avionics equipment was being produced by Marconi Avionics, who kept changing their name. They eventually became GEC Avionics, but the same team continued working on the systems.

My job in MOD was to oversee the introduction of the Nimrod AEW in the Operational Requirements office. I had two excellent people to help me, which was a real blessing, and I spent much of my time visiting BAe and Marconi to see how the project was progressing. The short answer was that it wasn't. BAe seemed to be ahead of the problem, but Marconi never seemed to make a great deal of progress. In the 1970s, you have to remember that computers were huge things like wardrobes which filled what was basically a Comet fuselage. That was part of the problem, but Marconi was trying to invent something which was really beyond them. Matters were not helped by the companies operating on a cost-plus system, so they just billed the MOD for any work they did and we paid. It was a very unsatisfactory way to do business, and, despite the 1977 company estimate of £200-300 million, the final bill was something like £1billion. I need hardly add that Marconi impressed those that should know better by demonstrating that the radar would work by showing their kit monitoring traffic on the M1 – not what we wanted it for at all! You don't get many cars over the North Sea or the Atlantic Ocean.

The Nimrod AEW should not be confused with the Nimrod Maritime Reconnaissance version of the aircraft, which was well-proven and an excellent vehicle for the role. In the AEW aircraft, we needed the radar to scan three hundred and sixty degrees around the aircraft, and the proposed solution was to have a radar scanner at the front of the aircraft and another at the rear. The two scanners had to work in synch to give the three hundred and sixty degrees cover. Of necessity, these scanners were housed in great lumps in the front and the rear of the airframe, so it really looked nothing like the beautiful Comet on which the airframe was based. I'm afraid it did not look at all nice.

So, there I was in the middle of this unsatisfactory project, representing the RAF as 'the customer'. Most of the supervision of industry was carried out by the Ministry of Defence Procurement Executive – a largely Civil Service-manned organisation. We had periodic meetings with them to try to get to the bottom of the problems, sadly with very little real progress. It seemed to me that Marconi were happy to drift along, but this may be an unfair view of their efforts. Some of their equipment was quite good; but, overall, it was difficult to see any real enthusiasm. For instance, I attended the Farnborough Air Show and went to the Marconi stand, which was displaying the Nimrod AEW's operator's console for interpreting the radar picture in the aircraft. A man wandered past and enquired what this display was about, to be told that it was the Mission Systems Avionics for the Nimrod AEW. "Oh," he said, and wandered off.

I chased after him to see if he understood what he had seen. I brought him back to the stand and explained about AEW and then how we expected the system to work, filtering out all the known air and sea traffic and stuff we didn't want to see, so that we could concentrate on anything threatening us. He was fascinated and thanked me profusely. Meanwhile, the Marconi 'salesman' said that he had never heard such a brilliant explanation. He was amazed at how I put the points across. How did I manage to do it? I said to him, "I'll tell you why and how. It is because we *care*!"

I was the first RAF chap to fly in a Nimrod AEW, which was interesting. It was just the airframe without any Marconi equipment, but at least it was a start. The original programme had envisaged the delivery of all AEW aircraft to service by 1982, but they were still scratching around trying to get one working while I had the job. There were some excellent bits which they produced, such as the operator consoles themselves and the automatic management of the radio and intercom system (AMRICS), but co-ordinating the whole seemed to be beyond them. In fact, at the Paris Air Show, I stopped the conversation at one stage and said to the

Marconi chaps, "I don't think you people know what we mean by Airborne Early Warning. In order to carry out the role, we need the radar to work, and we want the IFF to work, and we want the HF, the VHF and the UHF radios to work, and we want the navigation kit to work, and we want the Electronic Support Measures to work, and we want the AMRICS to work. But what you chaps seem not to understand is that we want all this kit to work together."

"Together?" they said. I don't think anyone had told them that before, and they were all a bit stunned.

The introduction of a 'new' aircraft often has silly things installed, and you only discover these when you get your hands on it. We found a few on the Nimrod AEW. For instance, they had installed a coffee cup holder on the edge of the operator's keyboard below the tactical display. In order to get out of your seat, you had to tilt the keyboard away from you, and it was only then that you realised that your coffee would spill on the keyboard! Nice try, but do it again. Also, when sitting at your tactical display, you had your hands full of the controls, so they fitted foot switches on the floor of each position, with one foot switch used for talking on the intercom and the other for transmitting on the radios. This was fine in principle, but you had to rotate your seat facing forwards for the take-off and the landing. When asked if everyone was strapped in for the landing, you could not reply. You had to undo your harness, rotate your seat and press the foot switch to answer, thus defeating the purpose of the exercise. These were not insuperable snags, but they did nothing to speed the smooth introduction of the aircraft.

During my brief time in the job, very little progress was made, and it was all a bit depressing. At one of my last big meetings in the Ministry, I asked a very senior Air Chief Marshal if he thought we would ever get the Nimrod AEW into service. I was given a rocket for being so disrespectful, but my former station commander, who was also at the meeting, said, "I don't think you can say that, sir. The Air Force Department has asked a very proper question and I believe he should be given a proper answer." It was very brave of him, but all I got in response was a bit of flannel. It was noticeable that the big man left the RAF shortly afterwards and became a director of BAe.

While living at Halton, I managed to join Ashridge Golf Club, which was lovely. There were many senior RAF officers also as members, and they were horrified that I had to be interviewed to see if I was suitable. When we later returned to Halton, there was almost a riot when I was again interviewed before I was allowed to rejoin! At one point at Ashridge, I was playing golf with Air Commodore Al Deere, the famous New Zealand Second World War fighter pilot, when he was struck by lightning. He just shrugged his shoulders and carried on. We reckoned that if the Germans couldn't get him, God was probably looking after him still! Al was a really lovely man.

After only eighteen months in the job, I was posted to RAF Lossiemouth to command No 8 AEW Squadron, so off we went again, back to Scotland. I did a multi-engined refresher flying course on the Jetstream aircraft at RAF Finningley in Yorkshire, before I went up north on my own to do a short Shackleton conversion, while the children continued in their schools down south.

Shortly after I took over the MOD job, my predecessor was killed in a car crash. And, shortly after I left the job, my successor also died. I was conscious of the Sword of Damocles coming ever nearer, but it never ceases to amaze me that I have been spared when others, who were more worthy than I, were taken far too young.

Chapter 25

Words of Wisdom

In the summer of 1981, we were living in Buckinghamshire and I was commuting each day to and from London. Our children were aged thirteen, eleven and nine. As the summer holidays approached, we had the usual problem of 'Find yourself something to do'.

It was my wife's idea – at least she claims it – and, for a quiet life, I guess I'd better go along with that. We got the children to write to famous and well-known people to ask for their advice. As you will know, giving advice is easy – so it was a relatively simple question to ask. However, after some thought, we expanded it to ask for the best piece of advice they had been given *and by whom* – which actually makes the question and the response more interesting.

The original idea was to get perhaps a few replies, possibly to photocopy them, and to then sell them at the local church fete or whatever. That was the hope. However, things got a bit out of hand.

The children started on the project and naturally they went straight for the people who made an impression on them – so they wrote to the *Blue Peter* presenters and people from the children's programmes.

I insisted that each person should get a handwritten personal letter from the children, rather than a photocopy, so that the people were more likely to consider their request. They started scribbling away – and very quickly ran out of people to write to! It is worthwhile, perhaps, looking at what they wrote. For example, Michael, aged nine, wrote to Arthur Marshall as follows:

'Dear Arthur Marshall,

I am writing to famous people like you to ask them what is the best piece of advice they have been given and by whom?

If my sister, brother and I get enough replies, we hope to publish a small book and give some money to charity. I am going to do it for the refugees.'

Nice touch actually, the phrase 'writing to famous people like you'! I therefore regret to inform you that, unless you got a letter from my children, I am afraid that they didn't think you famous at all!

So, by the end of a couple of weeks or so, the children had written perhaps some twenty letters each. Two things then happened. First, on 29th July, we all got up at some unearthly hour and were seated in the dust in the Mall by four thirty a.m. to watch the wedding procession of the Prince and Princess of Wales – and what a lovely day that was. We were all pressed together, about ten people deep, while they went on their way to and from St Paul's Cathedral. But, during the service, there seemed little point in our remaining standing, so I suggested we all move back and sit down in a civilised manner. We could then return to our spots for when the royal couple went back to Buckingham Palace. But what was nice was, at the end of the service – which was being broadcast to us in the Mall – when they played the National Anthem, we all got up and sang our hearts out. Beside me, an American couple also sang with us, which I thought was lovely.

A few days later, we set off for a wonderful two-week holiday, staying with lovely friends in Florida, where we spent much time in Walt Disney's Magic Kingdom. We also went to a number of nightspots, including a Mississippi paddle boat nightclub, where *we* finished the evening by singing the American National Anthem. I thought at the time that if we could sing each other's national anthem, there wasn't much wrong with the world.

There was quite a bit of excitement when we arrived home to find a small pile of replies to the children's letters! Not everyone had replied, but there were enough responses to spur the children on to write more. So, off they went again, now being steered by parental ideas, so the field opened up dramatically. Off went more letters and, if I may give you a tip, this exercise was a wonderful way to ensure that the children were up bright and early, eagerly awaiting the arrival of the post. That, of course, was in the days when we actually had a post!

People often spend much time knocking the skill and efforts of the British postal system, but our experience was very different. For example, we wrote to Muhammad Ali, Louisville, Kentucky, USA – and back it came stamped 'insufficient address'. And we wrote to Brendan Foster, Gateshead – and we had his reply in three days. Brilliant!

A few more letters were written each week, and gradually the responses came in. Part of the problem, of course, was where to write to. A number of letters were sent care of the BBC or ITV, but I managed to raid the next-door general's office when I was at work in the Ministry of Defence, because he had a copy of *Who's Who*. Several important people had given their address as care of their club, but you would be amazed how many of them had their home address listed – so that was a help.

Naturally, we didn't write all the letters in one sitting. I suppose it must have taken about four or five months to send about four hundred and fifty-odd letters. With a strike ratio of about a third of the letters getting a response, we then had sufficient to go and see someone about it. And then, of course – because we had now gone beyond the 'village fete and photocopying a few of the responses' stage, who do you go and see? And how do you go about the business of perhaps getting a book published?

Several years before, I had been to a party in Maidenhead. At some juncture in the evening, I went to the loo and found in there a series of little books written or compiled by a chap called J. L. Carr. I remember it vividly because the books were very, very funny, and quite ruined the party for my wife as a result. I just wanted to spend the rest of the evening in the loo! But J. L. Carr had written on the back of these books that he was a publisher, so I went to see him.

He was a lovely old man with a wonderful twinkle in his eye and, it transpired, he was often called in for erudite discussions on the BBC. You may have heard of him? However, he said that he really couldn't help me, because he only published his own books. But he was adamant that the only way to get a book published was to have an agent. Without an agent, you haven't a prayer, because they know who might take your book. J. L. Carr suggested that I go and see his agent.

So, armed with these massive photograph albums with the peel-back pages to protect the letters, I set off to find J. L. Carr's agent. Naturally, as with most things in life, I had found the most inconvenient time for the publishing industry. Unknown to me, it was the time of the annual book fair, so everyone was eyes down and concentrating only on this. Nevertheless, I beat a path to his door to be told that it was impossible to see him or anyone else for that matter. "It's the book fair, you see, and we are all so terribly busy."

This nice lady asked why I wanted to see the agent and I told her that I had been recommended to him by J. L. Carr. That meant nothing to her, so I explained what our project was. Again, I got a complete blank and was told to come back in about a month when things had settled down again.

Naturally, I couldn't stand for this sort of nonsense, so, in my ignorance, I said that I didn't think I really needed an agent! All I needed was a publisher and, if they weren't able to help me, then I would go and find one on my own. I even said to her that I thought that an agent would only hinder our project. Moreover, I even had the temerity to ask her to write down the proposed title of our book, because I was sure that they would like to know that they were missing out on getting fifteen percent or whatever for absolutely nothing! Lord, what cheek, but it had been that sort of a day.

So, how do you get a publisher? Well, I had a look through the sort of books that I liked and decided that Sidgwick and Jackson had done a good job with Edward Heath's books, so I ought to perhaps chance my arm with them. I had also heard of others like Hamish Hamilton and the Bodley Head, so, once again, I sneaked away from my Ministry of Defence desk and headed out on my venture.

I went to Sidgwick's first in Bloomsbury Way – see how easily I drop into the vernacular of the publishing trade! I really had no idea what to say or who to see, but, at Sidgwick's, I asked to see the top man and was ushered in to see a Mr Armstrong, who seemed to be in charge. He was quite delightful and keenly looked through the letters. He explained that everything was up in the air – "It's the book fair, you know!" – and anyway, if he was going to take our book, he would have to make a fast decision; he was going on leave on Friday, in four days' time. Could I possibly leave the letters with him? I said that I couldn't because I had to go and see other publishers, but I would try to send him some photocopies.

I next went to see the Bodley Head people and was ushered in to see a very stuffy lady who kept turning over the pages, saying, "No, I don't think anyone would be interested in this sort of thing."

"In that case," I replied, "why is it that you can't wait to see who has written the next letter?" There was no answer to that... so I went to Hamish Hamilton.

Again, I was fed the 'book fair' line, but I was ushered into the presence of the number two chap, who also asked me to leave him the letters. Once again I refused, but I said that he could have some photocopies. Alas, he explained, all the secretaries were too busy to do any photocopying, so that was no good. He was really quite startled when I said that I could operate one of their machines. He asked me if I could leave him some photocopies because he was so terribly busy with the book fair. So, down I went into the bowels of their building, and photocopied like crazy, making three copies of everything! One for Hamish Hamilton, one for me, and one for Sidgwick's! They obviously hadn't met an RAF officer before!

I then set off home to Wendover in Buckinghamshire to try to beat the rush-hour, and, by the time I got home, about an hour and a half later, Sidgwick's had been on the phone three times saying that they just had to do it! So that was it really. Maybe I was lucky, but we'd got a publisher.

I was actually handed off to a nice lady, I suppose the deputy head or something. We talked the project through and we discussed how the book should look. Their original thought was that they should produce a book of extracts from the letters, but I pressed them hard to try to get the letters actually reproduced, spelling mistakes, crossings out, warts and all – and eventually they agreed. They did say, however, that we ought to try to get a few more responses to get a better-sized book.

And so, with a publisher behind us, the children set to, bashing out the last few letters while we scoured the reference books for people who we thought would reply. In the end, the children actually wrote a total of six hundred letters and got some two hundred-plus replies, which is considered, by those who know, to be quite a good strike rate, apparently. Surprisingly, there were a number of quite unnecessarily offhand, rude and I thought unkind letters to young children. My original intention was to have all the good letters at the front of the book and to put all the nasties at the back – so that people could draw their own conclusions. In the end, however, we decided that, because it was a happy project, we would keep it like that and just ignore the rotten people and their letters. And, with hindsight, I think we were right.

Back to the vernacular now: and so the book went to bed – or tried to. Tragically, despite being urged to look after everything, Sidgwick's lost the letter we had received from the Archbishop of Canterbury. Nothing ventured, a letter went off to Terry Waite, explaining the problem, and, within a couple of days, we had a replacement signed by the Archbishop again. Now wasn't that nice?

Significantly, despite writing to Cardinal Hume three times, we never heard from him personally. We did, however, get stuffy notes from his secretary saying this wasn't the sort of thing he did, so the chief Roman never figured in the book. We got the Chief Anglican and the Chief Rabbi and the lovely Trevor Huddlestone, Archbishop of the Indian Ocean, but not the Roman. A number of people have questioned this omission, but that's the reason. I am sure that, if the request had ever got to Cardinal Hume, he would have responded – but he had an over-zealous outer office!

The final thing we had to do was to decide which charity or charities we were going to support. In the end, we each chose one. Sally chose the British Kidney Patient Association, Michael chose the Somali Refugees, Daniel chose the British Heart Foundation, my wife chose Dr Barnardo's and I chose the Leonard Cheshire Foundation.

I was then posted to RAF Lossiemouth on the Moray Firth, in Scotland, so the whole family moved up to join me in the spring of 1982. Meanwhile, we waited for the book to actually be published in time for the Christmas rush. However, before that happened, we had to organise the necessary publicity to coincide with this, and it was here that the publishers realised who they had taken on. They rang and said that they would like to have the children down in Birmingham for an appearance on *Pebble Mill at One* – the lunchtime BBC TV programme of the day. "Excellent," I said. "We'll all be down on the appointed day."

"We can't afford to fly you all down – just one parent and the children." I pointed out that, since it was a family project, the family should see it through together, but they were adamant. Eventually, I managed to persuade them to put us all up in nice hotels in both Birmingham and in Glasgow, while they could pay for my petrol if I drove the family down. So that was what we did.

It was actually quite an adventure, and a very good experience for the children. They interviewed well on *Pebble Mill* and were live on the *P.M. Programme* with Gordon Clough on Radio 4. The children sat with headphones on in Glasgow while the great man spoke to them from London. They also had an interview in Edinburgh with Margot Macdonald, some-time Scottish National Party MP, and another with Highland Radio – all excellent stuff. Meanwhile, I had arranged a full-page article in the *Daily Mail* to coincide with the publication – as well as a big spread in the *Aberdeen Press and Journal*. All of it wonderful publicity. Remember, the publicity was planned to coincide with the publication of the book.

After a week or so, I rang John Menzies in Aberdeen to see how the sales of the book were going. Incredibly, the manager said, "I don't know what is going on. The telephone has been going virtually non-stop with people asking after it, but there isn't one book in the shop. Where can I get some?"

It was, sadly, a walking disaster, and it rapidly became evident that, while Mr Armstrong was the head man at Sidgwick's, everything had been delegated to a number of 'daddy's little girls' who were patently not up to the job. Quite ridiculous and very sad, really; I am afraid that people don't keep going back to check if the book they wanted to buy someone for Christmas is available yet. They move on to something else. Eventually, the book came out, but sadly we had missed the boat.

I am not well up in these matters, but I think that publishers, when they think they have a good thing from a relatively unknown source on their hands, print about five thousand copies for the first run. They printed fifteen thousand copies of *Words of Wisdom* and, despite their horrendous cock-up, they still managed to sell about five thousand copies, which wasn't a bad effort in the end.

At my insistence, each of the contributors to the book was given a copy, which was a good ploy. I know the children's letters said that they hoped to publish a book, but, to placate anyone whose nose might have been put out, I thought it was a good tactical move!

And who replied to the children's letters? It is difficult to be precise, but I think a lot of people who needed the publicity responded. Actors and MPs figure largely, but there were also some extremely kind people. Strangely, although perhaps not surprisingly, I think the letters were a mirror image of what I thought the person's character was like – so the funny people were funny, the dry people were dry, the arrogant people were arrogant and the serious people serious.

Among many, two letters stand out. One was from a Captain of Industry, who wrote back to Sally in response to her question, using a huge typewriter with a bigger font than that used by Chief of Defence Staff, saying, 'I would rather make a donation to the charity of your choice.' When the book was published, I got Sally to write to him to tell him the good news. By return, she got a huge cheque with a note saying, 'Please don't tell them where it came from!' Wasn't that nice? And what a nice chap.

The other lovely letter we got was to Michael saying, 'Many thanks for your letter. I am not a famous person and I suspect that it was Ian Wallace the singer to whom you were addressing your letter. His address is...

'However, since you asked for my advice, here it is...'

What a nice man – and, of course, he was right! In my haste to find anyone with their home address, I found

Ian Wallace in *Who's Who* and indeed it was the wrong one! He actually worked in bogs and drains in the Midlands, which sounds a bit damning, but he was awarded a knighthood in the next New Year's Honours List. I wrote to him to say how delighted we were and suggested that he had probably got it for kindness to children!

Sending a copy of the book to each of the contributors was actually a very good tactic, because it generated a whole lot of new letters. Some said thank you, some said well done, some sent contributions to the charities and some were very funny. For instance, David Dimbleby thought that it was a wonderful project. It was fascinating to see all the responses we had had – and it was particularly pleasing to see that his brother couldn't spell 'advice'!

Sadly, of course, a number of people who we had hoped would reply never actually got around to it, but even then, there were some very nice touches. We wrote to Morecambe and Wise and, of the two, I would have said that Eric Morecambe was the more likely of the two to reply. We had a reply from Ernie Wise, but nothing from Eric Morecambe, which was sad. However, some months after the book went to bed, Michael had a letter from Eric Morecambe, in his own hand, which said:

'Dear Michael. I am very sorry I didn't get round to answering your nice letter which you sent me some time ago, but I was a bit tied up. But I do hope you managed to get lots of letters and have raised lots of money for charity. Yours sincerely, Eric Morecambe.' Of course, we weren't to know that he was having heart attacks at that time and that he had been very ill. But what a lovely man to take the time and trouble to write a nice letter to a young boy.

There were some really lovely letters which are worth repeating. For instance, Richard Todd, the actor, wrote to say that his mother advised him to, 'Do right and fear no man; don't write and fear no woman.' As he said, 'My mother was evidently not a woman's libber!' Alan Whicker wrote that he got his advice at his mother's knee – or some other joint! The letters make wonderful reading, even after forty years. Humphrey Lyttelton quoted Louis Armstrong and wrote in his superb handwriting, while the names of those who contributed are remembered with gratitude – Denis and Margaret Thatcher, The Duke of Edinburgh, David Niven, Brian Johnston, Alec Guinness, Matt Busby, Alec Bedser and many, many more.

We now come to the crunch point. Having given it a fair crack, the time came for the publishers to move on to other projects. They thus asked me if I would like to buy any of the remainder of the books at a reduced price. Well, what should we do? We had started out with the idea of selling the letters at church fêtes, etc., so it was a question of putting my money where my mouth was. But how many should I buy? How many could we sell? Would anyone want it? The questions were endless. In the end, I took a deep breath and decided to buy two thousand five hundred books. Absolutely crazy, wasn't it?

So I bugled off down to Chichester, where the books were in storage, towing my caravan in which to load the books. On arrival, I met their head man, who naturally suggested that I was mad! He said that the last chap who had tried that trick had managed to get about two hundred and fifty yards before his axle broke. He suggested that it would be more cost-effective if I paid to have them delivered to my house – so that was what we did.

Have you ever seen two thousand five hundred books? No, nor had I. We were fortunate to be living in a decent-sized married quarter at the time, but the stack of books took up very nearly half our dining room! It was a very daunting prospect.

I was also concerned that I might be done for income tax if the sales of the books for charity came through my account, so I popped in to see the local accountant to make sure that I was doing the right thing. "No, that's fine," he said – and then sent me a bill for £45 for services rendered! Bastard. So much for his contribution.

I gave a bunch of books to Barnardo's and to the Save the Children Fund to sell directly in their own shops, while we set to, to sit at stalls around the local area – and gradually the pile of books reduced to respectable proportions. We were lucky, of course, that I was posted every two years or so, so that I was able to start again in a new area which had not already been flooded with copies of the book. I was also lucky in that I was a relatively senior officer, so loyal young chaps came keenly forward to buy a copy. I'm not proud! I'll use any technique!

It was a great adventure for our children, and a wonderful experience for them – and for us. We were also able to help the charities we had nominated. It is difficult to be precise, but we reckon that we raised about £15,000 over the years, which is not too bad for amateurs. Just think what we might have raised if the publishers had had their fingers out.

Chapter 26

Officer Commanding No 8 (AEW) Squadron

Before I went up to Scotland to take over the squadron, I was interviewed by the AOC of No 11 Group. It wasn't a nice chat – I was just talked at by the man who later went on to be the Chief of Defence Staff (before he was given his cards for ungentlemanly behaviour). He just told me what he expected and then came out with that winning line, "I hope I shall not have to give you a formal warning as I have had to do to your predecessor!" Now *that's* interesting leadership! Suitably inspired by this great leader, I headed north, back to RAF Lossiemouth on the Moray Firth, back to Shackletons once again.

On my arrival in May 1982, I found a rather unhappy squadron which lacked leadership. Things were undoubtedly not helped by my predecessor spending a lot of time with his girlfriend in Aberdeen when he should have been looking after his squadron. I don't think his wife approved of the arrangement either. The boys were longing for someone to come in and lead them forward, and I was the lucky man who got the job. But what was amazing was that almost the whole of my executive team changed at the same time, which was very unusual. Each was posted by a different section of the Air Secretary's department, so it was my luck to have virtually a clean sheet to start with. I got all the boys together and told them how delighted I was to be their new boss, but I was anxious to stress that it wasn't *my* squadron. No, it was *our* squadron, so we must all pull together. Moreover, we were an Early Warning squadron, so I needed early warning of any problems which might be on the horizon so that I could head them off before anything got out of hand. That set the tone, and really all I had to do was enjoy myself while the team did wonders with the ancient Shackletons and their archaic kit. I had a brilliant Senior Engineering Officer, David Tombleson, who led his ground crew outstandingly well, and lovely Flight Commanders who knew their stuff and who set an excellent example. There was only one way we could go, and that was up.

My crews were frequently detached to other RAF stations to exercise with their fighters, so I was anxious that, while they should have a good time, they should always leave the stations knowing that they would be welcomed back. I introduced the squadron scarf in the squadron colours (which would be worn with flying suits), and that made a big difference. The boys looked smarter and they were proud to wear it – and morale improved in leaps and bounds. We also had detachments to Malta, Gibraltar and to Denmark, which enabled us to work with the latter's F-16 fighters. They were very hard to see with our elderly radar and thus gave us excellent training.

We also had an aircraft on permanent standby to intercept any Soviet aircraft which might encroach UK air space. Yes, we took some time to get up to the area of interest, but we were usually forewarned of the aircraft movements as we were a part of NATO's forces, shepherding the intruders on their way. It was very like three-dimensional chess. We knew what they were doing, they knew we knew, and so, in a strange way, we were keeping the peace so that there were no sudden and threatening interjections which might be misinterpreted and which could lead to unnecessary escalation.

We continued with detachments to Iceland, so that we could exercise with their F-4 Phantom aircraft, which was always good value. It was always interesting, but in the winter the weather made things a bit unpredictable. One time, I was flying from Keflavik with the American Phantoms when they suddenly disappeared and returned to base. We lurked around for a bit, before I called Keflavik to enquire what had happened. They kindly informed me that all Keflavik aircraft had been recalled to base because the airfield was about to go out in snow. Nice one. They hadn't thought to tell us, so I had a very dodgy return in appalling weather, landing in almost complete white-out conditions, with banked snow on either side of the runway. I had to get a 'Follow Me' wagon out to lead me back to the hangar. Conditions up there in winter can be vicious, with horrendous chill factors, so you gratefully taxi into a warm hangar before they close the doors behind you. It had been an interesting experience.

Very sadly, Ian Weir, an old friend whom I had known since the early 1960s, died of some dreadful liver problem. His wife was naturally distraught and at a loss what to do with his body. She asked for my help, so I suggested that he be cremated and that we scatter his ashes over the Moray Firth – over which Ian had spent much of his flying career. She was grateful for this offer, so we chose the following Friday for the flight. Naturally, the weather on the day was atrocious, with the wind howling very near to our maximum crosswind limit, but we set off anyway. The aircraft was bucking all over the place in severe turbulence, but we had a nice service in the air, taken by our lovely padre, as we scattered Ian's ashes.

It is, actually, very difficult to release ashes from an aircraft in flight. Previous attempts reportedly found that the inside of the aircraft was subsequently covered in grey ash. Thus, we decided that Ian's ashes had to go down the flare chute in a cardboard tube – so messages were sent to the Map Store to dispatch a cardboard tube over to us. We needed a means of getting Ian down the tube, so his ashes were shaken into my IN tray in my office, before we tried the tricky problem of getting him down the narrow tube. Alas, the offered map tube could not hold all his ashes, so we sent for a larger one, meanwhile putting his ashes in my OUT tray. Happily,

Ian managed to get into the larger tube, but all the time, while we were all emotionally still much saddened by Ian's death, we were so close to erupting into hysterical laughter, knowing that Ian was hugely enjoying his journey across my desk.

After our scattering of Ian's ashes, I then had the problem of getting the aircraft back on the ground in seriously nasty conditions. As we crabbed in to land, I was very conscious of Ian sitting on my shoulder, laughing at me struggling with the aircraft in the turbulence, and, strangely, applauding me when I pulled off a good landing after his final flight.

We held a lovely memorial service for Ian in our hangar, with a Shackleton in the background. Many people came from miles around – including from Germany and from the USA. Our lovely AOC, Air Vice-Marshal Ken Hayr, also came up for the service, and afterwards, after I had spoken about Ian and had read 'Desiderata', he said what a nice tribute it was. "You should come down to London," he said. "You are so much better than all the dreadful speeches we get down there!" What a lovely man.

Now that we had lost our senior pilot, I took over all Ian's responsibilities so that now I really was 'Lord High Everything'. So, from the flying side, I spent much of my time ensuring that all the pilots were up to scratch and not making silly mistakes on an aircraft which could really bite you. The great joy for me was the fact that I had to do everything better than my boys, flying with greater accuracy and passing on tips to help them.

During my time, I was also made President of the Mess Committee (PMC), which meant that I was responsible for the smooth running of the Officers' Mess. And it was during my tenure that the Buccaneer squadron at Lossiemouth invited the German Tornado squadron at Eggebeck in Jutland to come on an exchange visit. These visits were part of normal service life so that we could better co-operate with other NATO squadrons who had a similar role. During this exchange, we had a formal dinner night to welcome the Tornado squadron and, as PMC, I naturally sat at the head of the table with a German Captain on my left and a German Admiral on my right. I also had the great pleasure of having my squadron piper, carrying my squadron's colours, playing during the evening – which must have got up the Buccaneer squadron's nose! I spent much of the evening explaining to my German neighbours that these modern noisy machines were all very well, but what they really ought to fly was a MAN'S aeroplane with catering on board. We also had leather upholstery, amongst other amazing assets.

The evening passed off well, but you may be as surprised as I was to see a signal asking the Buccaneer Squadron to visit Eggebeck for a return exchange visit with the added comment, 'And, of course, the PMC must bring his Shackleton!'

I had not expected this, so I rang Ken Hayr down south to seek his guidance, and he said, "Go and have some fun!" Brilliant!

The visit was at the time of *Fawlty Towers* and John Cleese saying, "Don't mention the war." The boys spent much time telling me that when I spoke, I wasn't to mention the war. I pointed out that the visit was not about us and that I would not therefore be speaking, but they persisted. Anyway, we headed for the formal dinner to see what might develop. Of course, things got a bit out of hand and I was called upon to speak after everyone else. So, I rose to my feet and said I had been advised not to mention the war! There was a stunned silence from the assembled company which put the mockers on the evening straight away, so I went on by saying, "It is absolute nonsense that we shouldn't mention the war. We cannot escape the fact that your parents and my parents went to war against each other, so not to mention it is ridiculous. However, we are all part of NATO nowadays, and one thing that this must ensure is that we must never, ever let that happen again." A great roar from the diners was followed by a standing ovation, much to my relief. I then went on, "And another thing. It is a long time since an aircraft looking like a Lancaster has flown over Germany with an empty bomb bay. Fortunately for you, we didn't have an empty bomb bay; we came with a full bomb bay – but ours was full of whisky!" And then all my boys stood up, brandishing bottles of Glenlivet which we had secreted in our trouser legs on the way to the dinner – and the evening took off. I'm afraid the Buccaneer chaps were rather outshone, but we all had a good time.

Throughout my time on the squadron, we were regularly inspected to make sure that we were ready for our war role. There were two sorts of inspection: one a no-notice exercise about which we knew nothing in advance, and the other a planned visit to see how we operated. Some were nationally run and others run by a NATO team; the whole testing business was called TACEVAL (Tactical Evaluation). Thus, our call-out plan was checked to make sure we could respond in the right timescale, and all our operating procedures were gone through with a fine-tooth comb. Our ability in the air was also tested, so we were given a thorough check. Quite a bit of it was deadly boring, but parts of it were fun. We were very aware that we were still in the steam age in comparison to other squadrons with their shiny jets, but we could still hold our own and we made a great effort to show ourselves in the best light.

During one planned TACEVAL, we had a truly wonderful moment. We knew that the thing was going to start on the Monday morning – so we deliberately started twenty-four hours before the inspection proper, so that we could be ahead of the game and up to speed before we were tested. Our guards were all deployed and alert so we were ready for anything. The TACEVAL team arrived on the Sunday night and, with nothing to do, the leader of the team suggested that they wander over to see how my squadron was getting on. They had no idea of our actual readiness state and, as a result, they were being a bit casual. As they approached one of our hangars, they rounded the corner in pitch dark to be met with a bellow, "HALT! WHO GOES THERE?" The guard was only some five feet from the team and they were frightened out of their lives! A minute or so later, they arrived in my Ops Room, looking pale and very shaken, and, indeed, very impressed. This set the tone for their entire visit and, as a result, we got rave reviews in their report.

On the other hand, whilst we might have thought we were pretty good, we were tested by the SAS. We had been warned that they would visit us at some time, but we had no idea when. They were apparently dropped at the far end of Loch Ness and then had to yomp their way to Lossiemouth, which was seventy-seven miles by car – but, of course, they had to do it unseen. We had all our guard posts manned and I had forewarned my team, but you may imagine my surprise to be presented with a photograph, taken by the SAS, of our Bulk Fuel Installation (BFI). The photo had been taken at night and, not only could you see my guards, but the top of the BFI had been beautifully covered in explosive wires, etc.! Not only had they done that, but they then dismantled all their stuff and disappeared into the night. One could only admire their work. I am just very glad that they are on our side.

We were, of course, flying the AEW Shackleton while we waited in vain for the Nimrod AEW to appear.

Meanwhile, the NATO AEW Force had formed with their Airborne Warning and Control System (AWACS). The aircraft was based on the Boeing 707 airframe, with a big rotating dome on the top of the fuselage. The force comprised individuals from all the participating NATO nations, and it was evident that certain nations did not get on very well with others. There was, therefore, a degree of uncertainty and possible friction within the unit. But now that they had formed, we were invited to go and visit them at Geilenkirchen in Western Germany.

Naturally, we arrived in time for Happy Hour, so we were given a lovely welcome, during which I was strung up and left hanging in a parachute harness while the party went on around me. Honour was satisfied when, at last, I was given a couple of beers while I rotated helplessly so that I could spray the jeering mass. They were extremely welcoming and we had a wonderful weekend with them.

The base commander was a delightful German, Major General Klaus Rimmek, and he was very interested in how we operated. The next day, we were invited to dinner in their brand new Officers' Mess, which had, if you can imagine it, white carpets in the public rooms. It looked fantastic, but it wasn't to remain pristine for long. Since we were getting on so well, my boys thought it would be a good idea to show the general a Shackleton starting drill. This entails chaps lying on the floor, representing the outline of a Shackleton, with four of them playing the part of the engines. With our contra-rotating propellers, when an engine was started, the relevant chap had to lie on his back and wave his arms and legs about as if he was a Shackleton engine. It actually looked quite realistic, before mayhem followed. Someone produced the checklist for the starting sequence and we got the necessary people in position. We even got the General lying on his back on the floor on the left of the fuselage, in the No 2 engine position, with the comment, "Don't worry, General. Just watch the others and you will soon pick it up."

And so the starting drill began as the No 3 and the No 4 engines on the starboard were started, with the 'engines' duly waggling their arms and legs. We then started the No 2 engine, with the General trying to turn his blades. As you may have expected, as I feared for my career, there was the dreaded call, "FIRE IN NUMBER TWO ENGINE!" To put the fire out, every beer in the bar was thrown over the helpless General! I have a wonderful photo of him, lying on the floor in his best uniform, with pints of beer airborne and coming at him from every angle. He was absolutely soaked and thankfully howling with laughter. There was also, of course, a dreadful stain on the bar carpet.

After the fun and games, the General took me aside and said that it was fantastic to see such high morale among my troops. He longed to get that feeling going with his mixed-nations force.

I had previously briefed my chaps that it was vital not to put up any blacks and to ensure that we would be welcomed back. To that end, there must be no stealing of trophies or similar items – and they all nodded wisely. There was a beautiful new, huge NATO AEW Force shield, about five feet by three feet, hanging above the fireplace in the Mess, and, despite my protestations, it disappeared shortly before we departed. I carried out a full search of the aircraft, but I could find neither hide nor hair of any illegal trophies. However, on arrival back at Lossiemouth, I was told to look away while the shield was brought out of the aircraft. Naturally, on their return visit, not only did the NATO boys claim their shield back, but, unnoticed by us, they lifted the lovely wind-tunnel model of the AEW Shackleton which we had in our coffee bar. Perhaps they were getting the message and the General was getting his troops in line.

And, it was during my time that we found a totally new way to treat a Shackleton. Ever since the aircraft was introduced into the Royal Air Force in the early 1950s, we had towed it with a fairly standard tractor. These were the usual beasts of burden which could not move an aircraft which had its brakes on. The poor tractor simply stalled. Thus, whenever an aircraft was being towed, there was always an airman in the cockpit to work the brakes. The problem was that the tractor was, in the case of the Mark II Shackleton, attached to the tailwheel of the aircraft. Thus, there was quite a distance between the chap on the brakes and the tractor driver. There was also, invariably, quite a bit of noise in the vicinity, so there was, of necessity, a lot of shouting involved, with the chap theoretically in charge organising the operation doing most of it. With much shouting of "Brakes on" and "Brakes off" a number of times, the necessary towing was achieved. Amazingly, after some forty years, during this manoeuvre, we managed to pull the tail off an aircraft!

We had used the same procedures as normal, but only in hindsight did we discover the difference. The dear old Fordson or Massey Ferguson tractors had been retired, so we had used what we in the Service called a Queen Mary tug. The latter was vastly superior, much larger, and it could pull anything. In this instance, the aircraft brakes held, but the Queen Mary just pulled away until there was a fearful clunk from the back of the aircraft and the fuselage – minus the tail – just fell onto the hangar floor. It sounds awful, but the airframe boys did a fantastic job and the aircraft was flying again in no time at all. The boys were amazing.

One of my last flights overseas was to Gibraltar. It is a fair old stretch from the North of Scotland to Gib, so we had to set off at some ungodly hour in the middle of the night. It was chucking it down with rain before we left, so I was grateful that my co-pilot offered to do the external walk-round checks on the aircraft, while I did the internal checks in the dry. We were glad to escape the awful weather and settled down for the long transit to Gib. As the sun came up, you may imagine my surprise to see that the propeller spinners at the front of the engines had, for this occasion, been painted in the squadron colours of red, yellow and blue. What a nice tribute from the boys.

The aircraft looked very smart actually, but on return to Lossiemouth, the spinners were sadly repainted the customary battleship grey.

On my last flight in a Shackleton, I went off with my great friend Stephen Roncoroni, just to have fun. It is a sad feeling when you come to the end of a wonderful tour, but I still put the aircraft down for a final perfect landing. As we taxied in, Stephen asked me to give him my watch, which I thought a bit strange. As I left the aircraft, the fire brigade soaked me with their powerful hoses – with everyone else cowering in the aircraft. I was then piped in to the squadron with the fantastic and emotional 'Flowers of the Forest', played by the squadron piper. What a fabulous way to go.

All good things come to an end and, after two years in command, we headed south again for a married quarter at Halton, in Buckinghamshire, so that I could once again enjoy the commute to the Ministry of Defence.

But, before I leave Shackletons, it is worth remembering that we really were flying an anachronism. The Shackleton made its first flight in 1949 and, with a few modifications, which became various marks of the aircraft, the Shackleton AEW flew on until 1991. Incredibly, the Shack actually flew in five decades. Most of its flying was away from land, so we were largely out of sight and very much unknown. Other chaps had sleek fast jet aircraft, so we were rather conscious of being looked down upon – and almost an embarrassment. But the aircraft was, by and large, a faithful beast (although the engines sometimes gave us problems). We were thus out of the public eye, although at one Farnborough Air Show there was an attempt to show the aircraft off. A Mark III Shackleton took off at the end of one flying day and, to impress the crowds, it reappeared at the start of the next day's show, having flown for twenty-one hours. I don't know if this feat impressed the crowds, but the aircrew were somewhat unimpressed, just loitering around. They could just as well have landed back at RAF St Mawgan and then taken off to fly to Farnborough the next day, for all the good it did. I don't think that the public would have been any the wiser. But I will just finish this chapter with this nice description of the aircraft:

The Shackleton was a wonderful aircraft for getting you out of nasty scrapes and dangerous situations – which you wouldn't have got into if you hadn't been flying the bloody thing in the first place.

Chapter 27

Back to the MOD

We managed to get a married quarter at RAF Halton again, so I knew the routine of the daily commute up to London. This enabled us to put Sally and Daniel back in to Aylesbury Girls' School and Aylesbury Grammar School respectively, so that was a real plus. And, it was while we were there that they were both selected for the National Scout and Guide Symphony Orchestra, which was very pleasing. They went on various tours with the orchestra to America and to the continent, which was excellent experience for them. But one of my most satisfying moments was when they lifted the roof of the Royal Albert Hall playing Elgar's 'Pomp and Circumstance'. Now *that* was a proud Dad.

In 1984, back in the Ministry of Defence, I was looking after the operational side of the RAF's AEW force, while the much-vaunted Nimrod AEW was still no nearer any sort of effective capability. BAe and GEC Avionics were trying their best, but the aircraft capability fell very short of our requirements. In an effort to speed the beast into service, a few of the aircraft were moved to

RAF Waddington so that the RAF and Industry could put their heads together to try to solve the insoluble in an organisation called the Joint Trials Unit.

Over the years, as a result of the predicted shortfalls, we had tried a number of times to kick the Nimrod AEW into touch, but the Government simply told us to get on with it, which was all a bit disheartening. So, we had to grind on, while one of my first tasks was to write a paper suggesting that the AEW Shackletons should be run on in service, into the 1990s if necessary, for lack of a replacement and in order to retain a bit of skill and experience in the role.

My office overlooked the Thames, which was nice, so at least I had a decent view. As there was no AEW branch in the Ministry at that time, I was ensconced with the ground radar chaps, so we had a nice bit of banter. Looking back from this distance, it is amazing to remember that everything in 1985 was done almost with a quill pen. We had typing pools on every floor and much of our written stuff was sent to Glasgow to be turned into pretty typed papers. The whole system was very cumbersome, and it sometimes took days to get your draft back from the system. We had no computers, but we had a cunning officer who knew about things, who organised a 'trial'. Somehow, he got hold of three computers, and I was lucky enough to get my hands on one. I have no idea what model they were, but we used them as word processors, which was a huge step forward. It will come as no surprise to you to hear that the Air

Commodore wandered into my office at one stage and asked what I thought I was doing. I explained that I was writing a paper, and he immediately said, "Stop that. I don't ever want to see any of my officers typing anything!"

As soon as he left my office, I continued to process words and eventually took my document to him for approval. In his inimitable fashion, he drew lines all over my masterpiece, changed various sections and gave it back to me with the instruction to send it to the typing pool. I made a copy, did as I was told and returned to my office to re-jig the paper. After lunch, I took the altered version back to him and, yet again, he changed things around. I followed the same procedure and, by five p.m., we had the approved document. I then explained to him what I had done; I said that his amendments were probably still on their way to Glasgow. They would not return for a couple of days, probably covered in Snopake or Whiteout, so it wasn't a very efficient way to do business. Meanwhile, I had simply re-processed the words in my office and had a complete record of the required alterations – if they were needed. He was greatly surprised and, thankfully, we were allowed to keep the machines. Meanwhile, his shorthand typist PA was seen to be putting on her coat, having been shown the future.

And, on the theme of computers, in my next job at a NATO Headquarters, the new American Chief of Staff came blustering in and asked what we were still doing with pencil and paper. "Where is my computer?" he demanded. After a short study, it was agreed that computers should be purchased for the headquarters. But, true to fashion, all the generals said that they wanted them first, with the senior staff second. The drones, meanwhile, had to wait for the third tranche, all the while continuing to turn out the necessary paperwork in the usually slow manner. Thus, for two years, the generals and the hierarchy looked at blank screens with no electric input from the drones! You can't make it up, can you?

I was at home between Christmas and the New Year and we had quite a noisy party going on when the phone rang and a Scottish voice said, "It's the Director." I had no idea who or what this was and asked him to repeat what he had said a number of times. Eventually, he said, "It's the Air Commodore!" Of course, I wasn't expecting anything, so thought that there must be some sort of crisis in the offing. Why ring me when we were all on our Christmas break? He then said, "You've been awarded an OBE in the New Year's Honours List!" Wow! I'm not sure who was most surprised – but it was a close call between our reactions. So that was a nice start to 1985 and the New Year. Incidentally, when you are given an award such as a medal, you can look up the citation. But when you are given an honour, you are not allowed to even know what was said about you. Funny old life. I assume that I got it for running 8 Squadron, but it was significant that my station commander had no idea that I had been awarded it. The lovely Ken Hayr must have put me up for it, and I shall for ever be in his debt.

I was lucky to have the award given to me by Her Majesty the Queen, which was the icing on the cake. The numbers attending were restricted, so I had to ask my sister to keep an eye on young Michael in the Army and Navy Club, where my father was taking us to lunch. In one of the sitting rooms, Susan and Michael were playing Snap on the floor while we were at the Palace. There was a shuffling of feet behind them, and one of the club's retainers came up behind her and said, "Excuse me, Madam. No games of chance are allowed in the club!" I imagine the 'Black Lives Matter' people might have had a thing to say about that!

I then heard that I was to be promoted to the rank of group captain and that my relief was to be a chap called Rod Thompson, who was coming down from Waddington, having been running the Nimrod AEW Joint Trials Unit. Timing is all, but, as I left the office, it was then that George Younger, the Secretary of State for Defence, asked to speak to someone who knew about the Nimrod AEW. All the hierarchy immediately faded into the wallpaper and Rod was sent to talk to the great man.

At that time, Jim Prior had left the Government and was now working for GEC. Moreover, he could 'do Government speak', so he was making the right noises in an effort to ensure that GEC continued with the Nimrod AEW project. On meeting the Secretary of State (SofS), Rod was surprised that only George Younger and he were present. The SofS started by saying that Jim Prior was full of praise for the Nimrod AEW. It was a fantastic aeroplane and it could see targets at hundreds of miles! Why doesn't the RAF like it? Rod said that that was indeed true, but we didn't want the aircraft to see high-flying aircraft. That was what the radars at Fylingdales were for. No, we needed to be able to see low-flying aircraft at closer range, and sadly, the equipment wasn't up to it. Rod had flown on most of the Joint Trials trips and offered to show the SofS the videos of the sorties which he happened to have on him. They drew the curtains and Rod then showed how the radar could not cope with looking down; it gave up completely when it saw land. Sadly, the computers were completely overloaded by surface contacts and, indeed, by the surface of the sea, which reflected the radar transmissions and completely confused the system, making it useless. Suffice it to say, shortly thereafter, the project was cancelled and plans were made for the introduction of the AWACS into RAF service.

A short while later, Margaret Thatcher was visiting Headquarters Strike Command and, during the conversation, Air Chief Marshal Sir Peter Harding said to her, "Well, we don't want another fiasco like the Nimrod AEW!"

"Let's be absolutely clear, Air Marshal," said the PM – thereby demoting him – "The Royal Air Force made a complete nonsense of the Nimrod AEW!" She turned on her heel and left – a public hand-bagging if ever there was one. But it just goes to show that the Government is never wrong – no matter that the aircraft was selected by the Labour Government.

And, just to complete the Nimrod AEW saga, in my next job I was to work for Air Marshal Sir Benny Jackson, who told me this fascinating tale. A friend of his was the Labour MP Fred Mulley, who, you may recall, was at one time the Secretary of State for Defence. In fact, he held the post at the time of the Queen's Silver Jubilee Review of the RAF in 1977. The review was held at RAF Finningley, in Yorkshire, and was attended by the great and the good. It was a glorious day for the occasion, and Fred Mulley distinguished himself by falling asleep while sitting next to Her Majesty. The photograph of him slumped in his chair followed him for the rest of his life.

Benny Jackson had Fred Mulley to stay some ten years later and, during a quiet evening, Benny said, "Come on then, Fred. You were Secretary of State for Defence when the decision was made to opt for the Nimrod AEW when, to a man, the RAF said that we should go with the already proven American AWACS. Why did you make that decision?"

"Well," said Fred, "Roy Jenkins said that it was about jobs."

So that, in a nutshell, is how the system works. We in the Services spend our lives looking at the threat and then we tell our masters what we need to meet that threat. Eventually, the government decides what we can have and then, if it doesn't work or isn't good enough, they turn round and blame you!

Chapter 28

Belgium

I had already been asked if my family would accompany me to any posting, but I had to tell the system that I couldn't move the children for six months; they were locked into A and O levels until the end of the school year. I am pretty certain that, with my background, I was being considered for command of RAF Waddington. In the event, however, I was posted to SHAPE in Belgium, to the Supreme Headquarters Allied Powers Europe. The offices were near Mons and I was to take over from Don Drysdale (who had been my squadron commander during my first AEW tour). I was to be Chief Resources Policy, which covered a multitude of sins, but the bottom line was that I was effectively to be the bank manager in all things Infrastructure for the Supreme Allied Commander Europe (SACEUR). And, what did I know about any of this? Absolutely nothing!

I had a somewhat inauspicious start to the job when I was returning from a New Year weekend at home. The weather in England had been quite balmy but, on crossing to France, the temperature dropped and the place was almost a white-out, with everything frozen solid. I pressed on towards Mons, but, not far south of Dunkirk, while creeping along with all the other traffic, my car just went sideways and down a very steep embankment. It was just sheet ice, and lorries were passing me also going sideways. I clambered back to the top and asked a passing lorry driver if he could please call the police. Thus, I sat in my car in driving snow, awaiting rescue for about half an hour, before I climbed back up to ask a passing lorry if they had seen the police. "Oh, yes," said the driver. "They are about four hundred metres behind you, also blown off the autobahn!"

I arrived at SHAPE in the winter of 1986 and started the commute to Belgium, living in what are termed Bachelor Officers' Quarters (BOQs), which I found pretty dire. I was very lucky that a fellow group captain had arrived at the same time as me, so, with nothing better to do, Phil Wilkinson and I practised leading each other astray when we needed moments of light relief. He, too, was unaccompanied for the first six months and, as he lived in Maidstone, we combined our visits to the UK to see our families as I sped on to Buckinghamshire.

I spent the first month in the job burning the midnight oil, and was often in my office until eleven p.m. I had an incredibly steep learning curve from what was essentially a standing start. I had a team of some eight NATO officers working for me, and I was saved by a quite exceptional US naval officer, Commander Jim Dickey. Life without him would indeed have been grim.

Whilst we were in the Policy Division at SHAPE, it rapidly became clear that I was effectively reporting directly to the Supreme Allied Commander, the American General Bernard W. Rogers. He had already served for five years as SACEUR, and I thought he was a god. Everyone walked in fear and trembling of him, but I thought he was outstanding. The first time I went to see him, he asked me what I was doing. I explained that I was the new Chief of Resources Policy, and he looked me over. He then said, "I have a couple of things I need to say to you. First, don't ever try and feed me horseshit! Secondly, you need to understand that I am the best and the most experienced infrastructure officer in NATO – and don't you forget that!"

I smiled at him and said, "Yes, sir."

"Right," he said. "What are you doing here?"

I explained that we needed to get his approval of the Infrastructure Proposals which sought the necessary funding from the NATO nations. These were put forward to the nations every two years, so I was in at the deep end at the beginning of my tour.

"Right," said SACEUR. "Let's go!" He took off his jacket and we sat around his table discussing our suggestions. It was absolutely riveting, being probed by the Great Man, and really a fascinating meeting, listening to his discussions and requirements.

At this point, it might be helpful if I described how the Infrastructure programme worked. We provided buildings and facilities such as harbours, river-crossings and so on to support NATO forces in war. We did not provide manpower or war-fighting equipment. Each of the NATO nations paid into the infrastructure fund on pre-agreed shares, and the funds were used where the SACEUR saw the need – on the basis of from each according to his ability, to each according to the need. The interesting thing was that there was no real money involved because, very sensibly, we used Infrastructure Accounting Units – a sort of general false currency without the complication of an exchange-rate squabble.

SACEUR was a wise old bird and, to get his annual infrastructure programme (called a Slice) forwarded to NATO Headquarters for approval, he got his regional commanders to put forward their needs in priority order. Once these had been screened by the various staffs, it was up to my office to put the recommended Slice together for the SACEUR's approval. Just two of us went down to see the SACEUR in his den, and we had really enthralling discussions as to how he could influence various parts of NATO. The strange thing was, however, that SACEUR could ask the nations for more troops or more aircraft, etc., and they could just shrug their shoulders. With the Infrastructure Programme, they had actually given him real money to spend, so he could have substantial power in how and where he could bolster the alliance. He cared enormously about the programme and, as he had said, he was the best and most experienced infrastructure officer in NATO.

Working for General Rogers was an absolute dream, and, once you had earned his trust, you felt as if you were a glove puppet on the end of his hand. One of my early forays with him was during the Commanders-in-Chief conference, when I was called in to discuss the infrastructure programme with the European C-in-Cs. I was faced with a total of some dozen senior officers sitting round his table with thirty-six stars between them. I had not been briefed on what SACEUR wanted me to bring up, so it was quite a surprise when he turned to me and said, "Well, David. What shall we tell the C-in-Cs?" We! So I launched into the discussions with the great men all taking notes furiously, while Bernie just grinned at me as I pointed out how the NATO regions could do better. He was thrilled, so I was pleased with my thirty minutes of fame.

As we worked through the Infrastructure Cycle, we had to produce the annual Slice for NATO approval and we had to prepare the biennial Infrastructure Proposals. These were major efforts in my office, and it occurred to me that it would be nice if my team could meet the great man. Accordingly, I asked SACEUR if he would like to come and have a drink with my boys, and, of course, he agreed. I don't think anyone had ever asked him for a drink before, so there was quite a bit of sucking of teeth as he was accompanied by his heavy brigade of security. People were amazed that he actually came to my office and had a nice chat with my team. What a lovely man. Naturally, my boys were delighted to chat with the top man, so it was a win-win situation, but everyone not involved was wondering how I managed to get SACEUR up to my office. I *asked him* – that's how! Thereafter, he came up every time we had a major achievement.

General Rogers left SHAPE after a seven-year stint as SACEUR, and left a huge hole in his wake. It is not too strong a statement to say that I loved Bernie Rogers. To me, he was simply outstanding. After his long tenure, I understand that Margaret Thatcher approached Ronald Reagan to say that she had it in mind to offer Bernie an Honorary Knighthood. I understand that Reagan had replied, "Over my dead body!" They had, apparently, fallen out over the Strategic Arms Limitation Talks, when Bernie took a very different stance to that taken by the White House.

The following SACEUR was a very different man, and it was extremely difficult to get him to understand what was going on. He took over the job when the next set of Infrastructure Proposals had to be presented to the nations at the Defence Planning Committee (DPC). He had been briefed by his staff and the words to be used had been approved right up the command chain. However, we were not ready for what followed. The Proposals should have been presented by my immediate boss, a German Major General. However, he ducked the issue and said that I would do a better job, so I was suddenly in the hot seat. We had done all the work with the slides all ready for the presentation, when I got a message from Lord Carrington's office (he was then

Secretary General of NATO) to say that the meeting would now not be held in the Military Committee room, but in the much larger Council Chamber. I wondered why he had bothered to tell me – and then the penny dropped. There were no visual aids in the Council Chamber, so suddenly, at the last minute, we had to get the slides turned into glossy hand-outs. What a performance, but the reproduction boys did a fantastic job, working through the night so that, when I went up to Brussels the next morning, I was armed with the glossy brochures.

Before the meeting, we met with SACEUR in a side room, with all his senior team around him plus me, when he suddenly went apoplectic and started lashing out. I have never heard language like it, and I was greatly surprised that most of it was aimed at me, while the three-star generals made like wallpaper. Essentially, his comments were; who had agreed my words, who had seen them, who had approved them, how could he possibly know what I was going to say, etc., etc.? I pointed out that my speech had been approved by all levels of the hierarchy. Moreover, since SACEUR did not have a seat at the DPC, and would thus not be required to speak, he need not worry – but this set him off again. What a start to the day.

As I was only a group captain, I was not allowed in the DPC, but I managed to sneak in when one of the guards was distracted, and found a seat next to my general. We sat there steaming throughout the morning session, wondering what had got into SACEUR. He demanded another meeting immediately after lunch and once more he laid into me, which just left me completely incensed. How on earth was I supposed to represent SHAPE's views when the boss didn't know what was going on? Back in the DPC, I sat back with my general and was horrified to hear Lord Carrington say, "Well, it is obvious to me that the most important item on the agenda is the Infrastructure Programme, so I suggest that we take that now!" Infrastructure wasn't on the agenda until the next day, so I was thrust straight in.

The DPC comprises all the NATO Secretaries of Defence, so there I was, surrounded by these great men, about to deliver something about which my boss knew nothing. About fifteen feet in front of me sat Lord Carrington, the Secretary General of NATO, and to my right, about twenty feet away, sat Frank Carlucci, the US Secretary of State for Defence. While I was getting ready, he didn't look at his hand-out. He just said, "Go on, boy. Convince me!"

So, off I went, with Carrington grinning at me and encouraging me. I spoke for about thirty minutes, and afterwards Lord Carrington came and shook me warmly by the hand and Carlucci came and said, "Good pitch, boy."

So at least they were impressed, which was more than could be said for the SACEUR. Contrary to the rules, he blundered to the front and demanded to speak, which did nothing for my pitch or for his standing. We then went back into his room for me to receive yet another haranguing, which achieved precisely nothing. It was a truly horrendous situation and I was absolutely livid. However, despite SACEUR's appalling behaviour, my German general reported to the chief of the Policy Division that I had done a fantastic job and had delivered an excellent speech. And a fat lot of good it did me!

The next morning, I went to see the Chief of Staff to tender my resignation because I was so angry. I had been humiliated, but before I could say anything, he told me that SACEUR had been on the phone to him to say that of all the people at the DPC, he was the one who didn't know what was going on. I never received an apology or anything like it. It was just an appalling situation which the senior men should have resolved. I have never experienced anything like it.

Apart from the more normal work in the office, I was also required to go down to the NATO School at Oberammergau, in the Bavarian foothills, to give talks to the officers newly-arrived in NATO jobs. It was quite a trip down there, about five hundred miles, so it was worth taking the family down there for a bit of a break and to see the glorious scenery of southern Germany. I had, by this time, acquired a Renault Espace, which was ideal for us since it also had room for our three children and our dog as well as our luggage. It was all right in the summer, but in the winter I went by rail.

Throughout my time at SHAPE, we were encouraged to mix with all the NATO nations; but after a while we thought we should be allowed some British-only dinners.

Accordingly, we started the SHAPE Officers' Dining Society (SODS), which proved the greatest fun. You could only join by invitation, and we wrote the rules to say that any officer of any nationality could be asked to join. Our only failing was that we never actually asked anyone else, but we were at least covered. The aim was to dine together once a month, with each of us in turn choosing a restaurant and organising the dinner – with the proviso that you were not allowed to repeat a restaurant. Thus, we had some amazing meals in both Belgium and in France and some absolutely awful ones, but it was always fun. It was a wonderful way to keep in touch.

Phil Wilkinson (whose office was only about twenty feet from mine) and I also spent some time visiting the various NATO nations and, on our return, we tried to bring the most unpalatable drink you could find. This was referred to as 'The Challenge', and again it tested our friendships to the limit. Quite the worst brew we found was Garlic Wine, which was, as you may imagine, really awful. However, it wasn't accepted for The Challenge because someone had found only half a bottle. But, Lord, it was fun trying all the brews out and amazing that we seemed never to be ill as a result.

I had an interesting visit to both Turkey and Greece and flew out to Ankara. When we arrived, there was no sign of my luggage, so I went to accost the local manager, who turned out to be German. We had the usual pointless discussion as to where my cases might be, but, in the end, he had the temerity to say to me in his best film-star German accent, "If you had taken ze trouble to fly Lufthansa, zis vould not have happened!" I reached for my ticket and showed him that I had indeed flown Lufthansa, so he stepped up to see what he could do. Hmm.

I was in a suit which became progressively more crumpled during my visit, so I don't suppose the Turkish Chief of Defence Staff was too impressed, but at least he was very pleasant. My cases eventually caught up with me in Athens, so it was all a bit tedious. However, on my return to Brussels, there was absolute chaos in the arrivals terminal. Apparently, the Customs and arrival staff had gone on strike, as was their right, so we were asked to mill around. Eventually, this got to a ridiculous stage, so I seized my cases and, calling out, "The passengers are exercising their rights!", I just forged through the empty halls, followed by a mass of grateful passengers. What a leader!

As my time at SHAPE came to an end, I met the lovely Ken Hayr, who was on a visit to the Headquarters. "How do you like your new posting?" he enquired. I said I hadn't a clue what he was talking about. He then blew my mind to say that I was going to command RAF Benson, in Oxfordshire. Wow! Now that was something I hadn't been expecting, so there was much to look forward to. The job also included the appointment of Deputy Captain of The Queen's Flight, so all the RAF hierarchy had to approve my posting before my name was submitted to Buckingham Palace. Only when Her

Majesty had put a tick in the box was the appointment
ratified.

Chapter 29

Station Commander, RAF Benson

My first reaction to being appointed Station Commander was to ask myself, why me? Benson had been a transport station for as long as I had known it, so what was a Shackleton chap doing there? Well, there was no point in worrying about that. The main point was that someone seemed to think that I was the man, so I had to get stuck in. The station had a number of different units on it, including The Queen's Flight, which did not come under my command, although I was also to be Deputy Captain of The Queen's Flight (TQF). I therefore had quite differing priorities which would complicate my life. The saving grace was that I had a quite outstanding Deputy in Wing Commander Dave Shannon, who was well able to run the station on my behalf in my absence. Apart from TQF, the main unit under my command was No 115 Squadron, which was the RAF's Flight Checking squadron. Their job was to verify that all the approach and landing aids of the RAF stations were working as advertised, and, to do this, they flew Andover aircraft. On a normal flying station, I would have been expected to be current on the main aircraft type, but, because of my involvement with TQF, I had no hope of this. I did, however, fly the Andover when I could, which was great fun – although not as the aircraft captain.

With the almost constant pressure on military budgets, much of my time was spent in knocking down rumours about various moves of the assets on the station. This did nothing for smooth planning for my teams, who were obviously concerned about where they might move to in the near future. Fortunately, most of the rumours were unfounded, but it was nevertheless unsettling.

The Annual Formal Inspection was carried out by my AOC, one Sandy Wilson, with whom I had served before, and I had a bit of fun with him. The visit started by his calling at my house to change into his finery. The next thing on the agenda was his taking the salute to coincide with an Andover flypast – all of it done to pre-arranged timing. But while at my house, there was much twitching and looking at watches, all the while demanding why we hadn't left for the parade. I told him that my corporal would tell us when it was time to go, and this really got him going. I pointed out that the corporal had got a watch and that he was perfectly capable of organising us, but this seemed to concern him. Of course, it all worked out well, but Sandy liked to be in charge!

There were other interesting things in which I got involved. For instance, there was great concern about airmen and airwomen fraternising, and this came up at the AOCs' conference. Contrary to the perceived wisdom of the day, I said that I allowed the girls to visit boys in their rooms, which caused a bit of a stir. I said that, with the best will in the world, young people were going to bonk, whether you made it difficult for them or not. I said that, to me, it seemed that the current regulations were more concerned about avoiding a *News of the World* 'Shock-Horror story' rather than treating the troops sensibly. Moreover, if you treated them as adults, they would behave as adults. The rules were very sensibly relaxed as a result of my interjection, which was gratifying.

Apart from the usual activities at RAF Benson, we had one epic experience which could have gone horribly wrong. An officer had been restoring a German ME109 fighter which had been recovered from the desert in North Africa. He had been working on it for a number of years and, before I took command, much thought had been given to flying the thing. Historically, ME109s were notoriously difficult to handle on take-off and, since they had always been flown off grass strips, it was thought that a grass strip should be prepared from which the aircraft could be flown. We had two proper runways at Benson, but a grass strip was mown across the airfield in readiness for the great day.

There was, of course, much interest in its first flight, so we decreed that there would not be a 'first flight' as such, because there would be extra pressure to push for a particular day when all the VIPs, etc., would have the date in their diary. To keep it sensible, we had a 'roll-out ceremony', which actually worked very well. Lots of senior people came, together with the Press, and we had a few visitors from overseas – including some German officers. We were particularly delighted that the son of the last German to fly the beast came and presented an unused gunsight. What a fabulous gesture, since it was one of the critical items that we still needed.

After this jamboree, when the great and the good came to be seen, we had a quiet day for the first flight. Since we had nobody who had flown a 109, Ray Hannah (late of Red Arrows fame) came down to fly the thing. I was away flying with the Princess of Wales on the great day, but I saw the video. As you may know, it is almost impossible to get a grass strip smooth; there are always humps and bumps which add to the interest. The grass strip also disappeared over the brow in the middle of the airfield, so the far end of it was out of sight.

Ray Hannah set off and, before too long, the aircraft started bucking and jumping as he accelerated for take-off. On video, it was really quite alarming to watch, and, at the *moment critique*, having been thrust into the air a tad early, the last thing you could see was the aircraft heading nose-down over the hump – and disappearing from view! If you had not known that it had taken off OK, you would have thought that it was a certain crash coming up. However, following much roaring engine noises, the aircraft was to be seen clambering away.

Ray sensibly left the undercarriage down on the first flight and did a couple of passes over the airfield before he returned to land. The overall impression was that all was well, but people remarked on the rather unexpected whine coming from the engine. I should co-co! During the after-flight inspection, it was noted that all the prop tips had been bent backwards by contact with the earth when Ray porpoised over the horizon! The funny engine noise was caused by the bent prop tips. They were, of necessity, returned to Dowty to see if they could help. Rectification naturally took some time, during which Ray Hannah retired from the RAF, so who was going to fly the beast next time?

John Alison (then an AVM, and later an Air Chief Marshal, who had been on my staff college course) actually owned his own aircraft, an Auster. Thus, he was eminently well qualified to fly the 109 because they both have propellers, haven't they? Anyway, John came down to Benson and we sat around in my office discussing the pros and cons. I told him I thought it was madness to consider using the grass strip since we had masses of concrete which would be much smoother. I also said, with regard to the horrendous torque on take-off, that this was probably because the chaps usually had a pretty short field from which to operate, so they felt the need for a whole lot of power straight away – hence the big swing problems. I said that I didn't think rapid power application was needed because, with six thousand feet of concrete in front of you, you could start by taxi-ing and then gradually apply the power as needed to accelerate into the sky. So that was what we agreed should happen, but we didn't tell any of the powers-that-be.

On the day of John's first flight, I was again away flying with Diana, but, once more, some kind soul videoed the whole thing. It went as follows. John took off as we agreed and, as he was passing about three hundred feet, the engine started to fail. In true Flying Instructor fashion, he first selected a suitable field and then had a look round the cockpit to see if he could rectify the situation. He checked that the magneto switches were on, that the fuel was switched on – oh hell, the fuel cock was back in the 'off' position. He thus selected fuel 'on' and the engine leapt back into life, allowing him to climb away from about a hundred feet! Nice one.

As with most piston-engined aircraft, you blip the throttle to maintain taxi speed, particularly at a place like Benson, which has a few hills and slopes on the taxiway. The throttle friction was a tad tight, so John had relaxed it so that the throttle was easier to operate as he taxied towards take-off. The throttle friction lever is supposed to hold the throttle in the selected position. Hindsight is wonderful, of course, but only afterwards did he realise that movement of the throttle and the fuel cock were both restricted by the throttle friction. He had taken off and the usual vibration had allowed the fuel cock to quietly close through lack of friction! As a result of John's experience, after almost fifty years of operation, a modification was made to the ME109. A bungee cord was fixed to the instrument panel to hold the fuel cock in the ON position, which allowed a sensible amount of freedom for throttle use. Isn't that amazing!

The aircraft was transferred to Duxford, but, sadly, after a few displays, it was damaged when it went into the hedge at the side of the airfield.

PART 2

Chapter 30

Deputy Captain of The Queen's Flight

So, as I came towards the end of my thirty-seven years in the RAF, I had the great good fortune to spend some two years flying with the Royal Family. Actually, if the truth be known, they had the great good fortune to fly with me, but we won't waste time on semantics!

I flew with all the members of the Royal Family and often accompanied them on their visits on the ground as well. I was, therefore, able to see them operate at first hand and to gain just a small insight into how they worked. But I have no intention of turning this into, as the tabloids would have it, 'A kiss and tell exposé'. Far from it. I have great admiration for all members of the Royal Family – and I mean all of them. And, incidentally, I have no idea how they have managed to put up with all the constant flak and rubbish from the press in general. But I did have some wonderful experiences and lovely stories which I am very happy to share with you. My dual jobs of Station Commander and Deputy Captain of The Queen's Flight really did not mix, so I was torn both ways. However, TQF had a great pull on my time, so that was the reason I had a formal deputy to look after RAF Benson while I was away. I also had very strong support from my wife, who helped enormously with the family and welfare side, which is such a very important part of running a station. So, with these two behind me, I was allowed out to play!

People often ask how I got the job. Well, the short answer is that I don't know. Your name is noted and, eventually, after all the senior RAF chaps have made their views known, it goes forward to be approved by the Queen. Only when she has put a tick in the box is your job confirmed. But I think the real answer is that your face has to fit.

It is difficult to summarise all my Royal flying; but, for what it is worth, I flew some four hundred Royal Flights in the two years. I did well over a hundred with the Princess of Wales and over fifty each with the Duchesses of Kent and York. I also did over thirty each with the Prince of Wales, Princess Margaret, the Princess Royal and the Duchess of Gloucester. And, of course, lots more with Princess Alexandra, Princess Alice and, as it used to say in the Prayer Book, all the Royal Family.

I had originally been interviewed and approved by Sir John Severne; but, by the time I took over the job, we had a new Captain. It had been customary for all my predecessors to have been appointed CVO for their services. However, almost the first thing I was told at my first interview with the new man was that I would not be getting one. The reason was "because the Royal Household objected to the fact that we only served two years when they had to serve longer to qualify!" I was, quite frankly, gobsmacked; but, as the new boy on day one, I wasn't in a position to argue. I was encouraged to tell all my friends that I would not be getting a CVO so there would be no doubt from the start. Welcome to TQF! I remain the only Deputy Captain who was not awarded anything from The Royal Victorian Order.

I was then given a briefing on all the members of the Royal Family, their likes and dislikes and how they liked you to behave, etc., and was then asked if I had any questions. "Yes," I said. "You haven't mentioned the Princess of Wales."

"Oh," was the response. "She's just a silly little girl."

It seems that that was the view of the Royal Household, which appeared to me to have a ridiculous amount of power behind the throne. Remember, this was 1989 and the troubled Wales marriage was not then public knowledge, but I was amazed by this statement.

I flew with The Queen's Flight from 1989 to 1991 and had a truly fascinating time. I still find it hard to believe, but I actually got to Timbuktu and to the Khyber Pass in the same year – so that wasn't bad, was it?

My job as Deputy Captain (DC) was to escort members of the Royal Family in the air and sometimes on the ground as well. There were two of us doing this

Deputy Captain job: a full-time Deputy, who was called DC1 on the Flight, and me, a part-time Deputy, called DC2. At that time there were many members of the Royal Family, so the Captain flew the Queen and the Queen Mother, while DC1 flew with the Waleses and the Princess Royal, mainly on the grounds of continuity, while I did what I could with the rest. There was no brief to follow. You just had to keep your eyes and ears open and make sure all was well. My own view was that we ought to strive to make sure that the principal passenger had a better day, as simple as that.

I was also appointed ADC to HM The Queen, which meant that I had the EIIR insignia on my shoulders and I wore the gold dangly things called aiguilettes on my right shoulder. That, actually, is worth stressing. Lots of lovely chaps wear aiguilettes, but only those who work for the Royal Family wear them on the right shoulder. If you are ADC to a mere mortal, you wear them on your left shoulder. But, don't ask me what they are for. Their origin is lost in the mists of time, but my theory is that they are worn to make you very pretty. They are also quite useful as swizzle sticks at cocktail parties.

When he heard that I had got the job, one of my predecessors, Marcus Wills, very kindly asked us to dinner. At one point, he launched into a story about when he accompanied Princess Alexandra to Hong Kong. On arrival, he was horrified to discover that, whilst he had his khaki uniform with him (as is worn in hot climates), he had forgotten to pack a khaki shirt. "Oh, Lord," I said.

"What did you do? Did you ask someone to nip out and buy you one?"

"No," said Marcus. "I wore a white one. I thought it looked very smart, actually!"

"Good grief," I said. "What did anyone say?"

And Marcus came out with the winning line, "David, in this job, no one is looking at you!"

And, there I was thinking that my immaculate uniform and my gleaming shoes were vital to the role!

The Queen's Flight had a unique set-up. We had hand-picked aircrew to fly the aircraft and we had hand-picked ground crew to service them – about one hundred and eighty men and women all told. To manage the flight, as I said, we had the Captain of The Queen's Flight, who had two deputies – one a full-time appointment and the other sort of part-time, which was me; part-time because, as I said, I also had to run the station. Our role, as executives, was to supervise the Royal flying programme and then to monitor the flights. Bearing in mind that the men of the Royal Family were pilots in their own right, we assumed that they would understand any problems as they occurred. We escorted overseas trips which merited it and we also accompanied solo ladies on most of their trips, in the UK as well as overseas. It was rather like a travel organisation. You planned what was needed and then, when required, you escorted the more difficult trips. You sat between the aircrew and the Royal party, the theory being that, if something went wrong, the aircrew would resolve the aircraft problem, while you resolved the Royal Family's problem. And it worked very well.

In the air, however, you can have only one captain, and that is the captain of the aircraft. We were, therefore, referred to as Commodore in the air, which was a very sensible system. There were obviously long periods when not a lot was required, but you couldn't really relax. There was always something lurking around the corner which probably needed your attention.

At that time, we had five aircraft on The Queen's Flight, two helicopters and three fixed-wing. The helicopters were the twin-engined scarlet Wessexes, and they were, even then, about twenty-five years old. Incredible really. How many people do you know who drive round in a twenty-five-year-old car? Not many. The Wessex helicopters were actually twenty-nine years old when they were pensioned off in 1998, which I think is amazing. And, incidentally, I think it was jolly nice of the Queen to grant Prince Edward and Sophie a title named after a helicopter.

Surprising as it may sound, with those five aircraft we managed something in excess of a thousand Royal flights a year, which is a tremendous workload by any stretch of the imagination. It also, incidentally, shows how much work the Royal Family does, which is not necessarily reported.

When I joined The Queen's Flight in 1989, the last of the Andover aircraft, which had been with the flight since 1962, was about to be pensioned off. They were replaced by three British Aerospace 146 aircraft, which really were a great leap into the modern era. But as with most things, they were rarely exactly suited to the task. I mean, only two people going off in an aircraft which could hold about twenty on a good day is ridiculous. Equally, when we had a full load of passengers, there wasn't sufficient space to put all their luggage. And sometimes, there wasn't sufficient range for the big trips. Now, obviously we made no pretence to be an Air Force One *á la* USA with their huge Boeing 747, but it was a super aircraft and so much better than the Andovers.

A lot of people are surprised about that comment that there was insufficient room in the aircraft. The BAe 146 was designed as an inter-city hopper; it was expected to be used by commuters on the London-Birmingham-Manchester run, and all they had were laptops or briefcases and coats. There was no great hold for luggage and only minimal cupboard space. This was fine for day-to-day operations, but not for major tours by the Royal Family. They have to take many changes of clothes; so, occasionally, I had to leave my golf clubs behind!

With the aircraft really designed for short hops, we sometimes had to stop to refuel. For instance, when I accompanied the Princess Royal to The Gambia, we stopped for fuel at Casablanca, which is some distance south of Gibraltar, so that was pretty good range for anyone.

Naturally, the aircraft fit was very different to the civilian versions. Basically, we divided the aircraft into three separate but connected compartments, with the Royal compartment at the rear, normally with six seats in it. In the mid-section, we had the supporting cast like me and the personal protection officers and secretaries and so on. Then, at the front, we had the ground crew who serviced the aircraft – normally a team of four. We could change seating configurations quite quickly and we could put in a bed if one was required.

Only the Royal Family used the rear door of the aircraft, while everyone else used the front steps. I would meet them at the rear steps, salute and, when they had all embarked, I followed them up the steps and we closed the door. In that rear compartment was the royal loo and a dressing table where they could smarten themselves up before they went off to meet the dignitaries on the airfield apron. Interestingly, on long trips, the Princess of Wales used to get into a tracksuit so that her dress wasn't creased for the arrival. Very nice and sensible planning.

Coming forward, the Royal compartment had six seats, two on the left and four on the right, with antimacassars on the backs of the seats. When did you last hear that phrase? The young don't even know what macassar was! Between the seats we had very nice beech unfolding tables so they could eat and/or work. Government Red Boxes came on most flights, so they worked a lot of the time in the aircraft. In the Royal compartment, there were photographs taken by Prince Andrew and a St Christopher medal for Prince Philip.

As I said, I sat in the mid-section, pretty much over the wings, with the supporting cast, and I always sat in the aisle seat so that I could see into the Royal compartment to ascertain that all was well with the principal passenger. During long flights, the steward was popping in and out of the Royal compartment with tea or other meals, so it was always useful if you were tipped off about a possible disaster. Comments such as, "Terribly sorry, sir. I've just tipped a cup of coffee over Princess Margaret!" would give you a useful heads-up of an impending problem, so you could nip it in the bud before it got out of control. Thankfully, it never did on my watch, but you had to be alert – just in case.

Further forward, we had the compartment on the left for our ground crew, with four comfortable seats in it. On the opposite side was the crew loo. Then, just aft of the cockpit, we had the forward entry and exit doors (with built-in air stairs). We also had what I call a standard airline catering set-up, with roll-on food containers, etc. On long trips, at the end of the day, I did quite a bit of washing-up, and often Princess Diana came and did the drying-up, just chatting away. It was a lovely way to wind down after a tiring day. Then, in the cockpit, we had the aircraft captain and the co-pilot, plus a navigator. Sadly, as a result of one of the Defence Reviews, the services of the navigator were dispensed with. But I should say that the polished performance of both the aircrew and the hard-working ground crew was second to none. They all did a fantastically good job and the whole operation was a wonderful team effort. There was enormous pride in everything we did, and it was reflected in the great efforts we made to meet the programme timings exactly, with the aircraft doors opening precisely on time as requested.

So, my job in the air was to liaise with the principal passenger and to make sure that all was well. The role of The Queen's Fight was, quite simply, to ensure the safe and timely arrival of the Royal Family – strictly in that order, with safety absolutely paramount. No one else was allowed to touch the aircraft, and we spent much time ensuring that it was always in pristine condition. This included polishing it as soon as we landed so that we were ready to go at short notice. This may seem like over-kill, but remember, as soon as the principals stepped off the aircraft, there was an instant barrage of cameras popping off. It was the same on departure, so the last thing we wanted was a dirty aircraft in the background.

Whenever we went overseas, we always asked the Ambassador or the British High Commissioner if we could bring them anything, and the answer was always salmon. I'm sure the Royal Family think that salmon is the local fish all over the world, because they all served it!

It is impossible to cover all my flying on The Queen's Flight, so I will concentrate on the personalities with whom I flew and the fun I had with them. Let's start with the Queen.

Chapter 31

HM The Queen

I had one fascinating flight with Her Majesty. The Queen normally never flew by helicopter; but, in January 1991, when John Major wanted to tell her about the imminent war with Iraq, he needed a rapid audience. Two fixed-wing aircraft were out of the country with the Captain and the other Deputy Captain, so I was left holding the baby. One possibility was for the Andover (which we still had at that time) to leave the Prince of Wales in Aberdeen and to come on down for her to use, but Her Majesty said no; she said she'd be perfectly happy to fly by helicopter. This caused a bit of consternation on the flight, as no one knew what her preferred seating plan was, since there wasn't one. I believe the observed reluctance of the Queen to fly by helicopter stemmed from the fact that she usually had a large entourage with her – which precluded the use of helicopters. However, a helicopter was all we had, so we set off for RAF Marham (near Sandringham) in Norfolk. We had the aircraft in a standard two seats at the front and two seats at the rear configuration, and the weather was awful, with the aircraft lurching around; it really was very rough.

Her Majesty arrived in a downpour, wearing a scarf, and said, "I do hope it's all right. I suppose I should have asked, but I've brought my hairdresser as well!" *Fait accompli*, and not what we were expecting, but the fuel/weight equation was extremely tight. We did some instant maths and in we got, with the Personal Protection Officer and the hairdresser taking the two front seats. Her Majesty took back left, which left me sitting beside her on the starboard side – not what I had anticipated at all. We got away with what might be termed an overweight take-off because we were on an airfield. Thus, we used the runway to accelerate the helicopter in order to get sufficient lift. It is a perfectly safe thing to do, but we could not, for instance, have done a vertical lift at that point.

It was very turbulent and I had visions of Her Majesty being sick, followed by me – and I'm not joking, so I tried to divert her attention away from this swinging, lurching, smelly black box in which we were travelling. So I waved to my mother-in-law. Her Majesty immediately asked what I was doing. I explained, and straight away she joined in with glee. I then got the road map out and made her keep a check on the navigator's position – because we didn't really trust him, did we? We waved to John Major's house and we waved to Jeffrey Archer's house at Grantchester on the way past, and generally passed the time with pleasant and very funny chats – all the while keeping our minds off the turbulence. But I had to keep pinching myself; just me and the Queen. Ridiculous! As we were getting on so well, my mind wandered, and suddenly Her Majesty let out a piercing shriek. "BARNET!" she cried. "BARNET!" I enquired what was happening, but she allayed my fears for her sanity by saying, "Oh, it's all right. My hairdresser lives in Barnet and I just wanted to let him know." The really impressive thing, though, was that she was absolutely spot on. It is very difficult to navigate when you cannot see forwards, but she was an expert. All great fun, and we landed in the back garden at Buckingham Palace in the best of spirits.

For the return to Marham, Princess Margaret wanted a lift, so I had to get clearance for her from BP. All was well, but by now the Andover had come back from Aberdeen, so we were able to give Her Majesty a more dignified ride home. Princess Margaret came fifteen minutes early, so we stood chatting in the doorway until HM arrived. All very civilised, and both were extremely grateful for all the help we had given them. It was a fascinating day.

There is one apocryphal story about Her Majesty which I do hope is true. Apparently, the Lord Chancellor (or someone similar) was seen to be investigating the State Dining Room at Windsor Castle. He was suddenly aware that there was a figure behind him, so he turned to see the Queen looking at him. "What are you doing?" she said.

"Your Majesty, I'm trying to work out how to get hot food to your guests."

"Ah," was the response. "You don't seem to understand. They don't come here to eat hot food. They come to eat off gold plates!"

My final trip on The Queen's Flight was with the Queen and the Duke of Edinburgh. Her Majesty very kindly presented me with a lovely signed photograph of them, which I treasure.

Chapter 32

HRH Princess Alice

Princess Alice was a gracious lady who lived at Barnwell near Peterborough. I did most of my flying with her from her back garden in Wessex helicopters. She was the same age as the Queen Mother and a little frail, but she was as sharp as a tack and just as delightful. She was a really lovely lady. She also had extremely nice ladies who travelled with her who were also a joy to work with.

Perhaps one of my more memorable trips with Princess Alice was to Buxton, where the visit was a great success. However, to my consternation, the flight home coincided with a critical rugger international, and I was desperate to watch the game. Fortunately, Princess Alice sat in the centre left seat, so I was able to sit in the back left corner behind her and watch the rugger on my mini television. Most happily, both the flight and the rugger proved successful, so it was a happy day.

Amongst other visits, I also accompanied Princess Alice to Tidworth Garrison, where she was to see one of her regiments. We flew in by helicopter, landing on the cricket field, before taking to open carriages for the long drive to the parade ground. I had never seen a parade of tanks before, so I found it all very interesting, particularly when they drove past and then dipped their gun barrels in salute. All very much of an eye-opener for a pilot in the Royal Air Force! It later transpired that my son-in-law, Roland Dangerfield, who married our daughter Sally, was a participant in the parade. It's a small world.

I often had to help Princess Alice up and down the difficult aircraft steps in the Wessex, holding her arm and carrying her bits and pieces, and she was always grateful for my help. On one occasion, when we had some time to spare, she showed us round her garden at Barnwell and then insisted on giving us some plants. The honeysuckle she gave me has now moved four times and happily grows in our garden. She was a lovely lady.

Chapter 33

HM Queen Elizabeth the Queen Mother

To avoid any misunderstandings, with two Queens who flew with us (more if you include the flunkeys!), the Queen was always referred to as Her Majesty, whilst the Queen Mother was always called Queen Elizabeth. On The Queen's Flight we had to have a sort of shorthand or the flying programmes would have been huge! The Queen was always HM and the Queen Mum TQM, while princes and princesses were P or Ps. Thus, Diana was PsOW. All my trips with Queen Elizabeth were a real joy. She was quite delightful, very friendly and gracious, and she had a very clear memory. She always had time to talk to people and she made you feel very much at your ease, which, of course, makes it more pleasant for everyone.

One of my first trips with her was to France to collect her and her party. They had been staying in a chateau and we were going to bring them home. Various messages were passed to us, mostly concerning Ruth, Lady Fermoy, who was Lady-in-Waiting at the time.

Lady Fermoy had been unwell the previous day, so she missed the remainder of the programme; it was very hot, so she was sent to us at the aircraft so that we could look after her. On arrival, she was very pale and frail, so we cooled the aircraft as much as we could and fed her cold drinks. Eventually, the Queen Mother and the remainder of her party appeared some considerable time later than their planned departure. "I'm so sorry," she said, "but we were having such a lovely time and I do so enjoy talking to everyone! By the way, how is Ruth?" I told her all was well, although Lady Fermoy appeared to be a little frail. "Yes," said TQM. "At dinner last night she went all pale and just went 'Eugh,' and just slipped under the table. I feared that we had lorst her!"

On another occasion, I went down to Deal to collect her, following a visit in her capacity as Lord Warden of the Cinque Ports. All her supporting cast had filled the seats at the rear of the helicopter, so there was only the seat next to her vacant; so I sat down and strapped in – horrified to see that she didn't do so as well. She started chatting straight away and asked if we could make a detour to see Walmer Castle (where she had spent the previous night) because she had never seen it from the air. Obviously we could, so away we went. She was as pleased as punch and even more so because, when the inhabitants heard the helicopter, they all came out on to the ramparts and waved. I offered to take some photographs while she waved to her hosts of the previous night. The Queen Mum did not do her seatbelt up and was leaning perilously towards the sliding door which you also kick out to evacuate the aircraft in an emergency, so I was on tenterhooks! I mean, when do you grab? I am eternally grateful that she didn't fall out, but it was a glorious day and, I'm glad to say, she had a good view of the castle before we set off for London.

We then flew up the Thames and I got a map out so that we could follow our progress. She was absolutely entranced as I pointed out various highlights such as the Isle of Sheppey, Canvey Island and the Thames Barrier. As we came in over the East End, she told me all about her trips to see the people during the Blitz. Wow! I wish I had a recording of that conversation. It was so lovely and friendly and ordinary, and yet fascinating at the same time. It was one of those perfect days with unlimited visibility, and one could not have wished for a better day to fly up the Thames. Queen Elizabeth was extremely grateful and said that it was the best flight that she'd ever had – but I guess she said that to all the boys! It wasn't bad for me either, but her Private Secretary, Sir Martin Gilliat, was kind enough to repeat Her Majesty's words to me later. He, too, was a lovely man, having been a prisoner of war for a number of years during the Second World War. He had escaped three times before finding his way to Colditz Castle, along with all the other bad boys.

Meanwhile, back at the aircraft, when the Queen Mum had gone off, the crew called to me and said, "Did you see it?" Did I see what? "We were trying to attract your attention, but you were locked away in conversation with the Queen Mum so we couldn't interrupt you, but, on the approach to Kensington Palace, there was this gorgeous girl, sunbathing naked on the roof!" Well, no I hadn't, but I still reckon I had the better deal.

I had two marvellous episodes with Queen Elizabeth during the summer of 1991. On the first occasion, we were to fly her from Aberdeen to the Castle of Mey by helicopter; but, as it was a lovely clear day, I asked her if she'd like a tour of the coast rather than a less inspiring straight transit. She was full of enthusiasm, so we hugged the coast at low level all the way round via John O' Groats and had the most marvellous views of all the inlets and fascinating cliffs. On arrival, she immediately asked us all in for afternoon tea, so the four of us accompanied her and her Lady-in-Waiting across the lawn and into the castle. It was the most lovely, relaxing tea I have ever had, with Her Majesty sitting at the head of the table, surrounded by teapots and kettles and just chatting away. But don't talk to me about Health and Safety! The kettles were on her right, with their leads trailing under her arm – but they were so repaired with bits of black tape such that I feared that sparks would fly out and electrocute her. I sat beside her and it was just like an ordinary tea party almost in a farmhouse – except that one was constantly aware that one was dreaming. What a lovely lady!

The Queen Mother has a habit of asking people in. Once, when, alas, I wasn't on board, the boys took her back to Sandringham and landed on the lawn in front of the house. "Oh, you must come in for some tea!" she said. So, into the drawing room they trooped, with TQM leading. As the crew filed in, she suddenly turned round and said, "Oh, by the way, have you met my daughter?" And there, of course, was the Queen. Great fun!

Also in the summer of 1991, Queen Elizabeth opened the new bridge at Dornoch, on the north-east coast of Scotland, and I was lucky enough to escort her throughout. Unbelievably, I had turned down Sir Martin Gilliat's invitation to spend the night at the Castle of Mey beforehand – and I still can't believe it! The weather forecast had been suspect, so I decided to stay with the helicopter in case of problems. Alas, I wasn't invited a second time! Anyway, I was bidden to the castle for lunch the next day, and duly arrived at the appointed time to find her Equerry setting up drinks outside. We stood around chatting, when there was a sudden scurry of corgis hurtling around the corner, followed by a little old lady wearing a headscarf which was being blown all over the place. When out of the wind, she took it off to reveal that it was indeed the Queen Mother, beaming with pleasure. "I've just been down on the beach with the dogs," she said, "and there isn't a soul around. It was just lovely!" She hadn't even had a policeman with her – and that is one reason why she loved it up there. The local people were delighted to have her and, joy of joys, they left her alone to enjoy herself.

We went in to lunch, just the four of us, with me sitting down at one end of the table with Her Majesty. Again, another ordinary meal, just chatting away. And it was then that I had this wonderful conversation with her. "Where are you living at the moment?" she asked. I explained that we were buying a house at Cardington, where the R-101 airship was built in the late 1920s. It crashed in France in 1930, on its way to India. "Ah, yes," she said. "What a terrible disaster that was. I remember it all so clearly."

I followed up with, "Were you aware, Ma'am, that the R-100, the private-venture airship which, in fact, met all the parameters set by the Government, was designed by a chap called Barnes Wallis, the man who invented the bouncing bomb for the Dambusters?"

"Oh, yes," she said. "We went to the trials, you know! But, oh, that Guy Gibson; such a nice young man. I gave him his VC, you know. The King was out of the country!" Truly fabulous, with the conversation going past way over my head!

After one helicopter trip I did with her, she took me round her lovely garden at the Castle of Mey. Just the two of us wandered round as she used her stick to point out the various flowers which had been named after her. The gardens up there have very high stone walls to keep the strong wind at bay, so we were nicely protected, but what a wonderful experience. She was just a lovely, gracious lady.

She was also lovely and chatty when we went to her Christmas Drinks Party in St James's Palace. It was an enormous gathering, but, as I recognised her footman, Billy Tallon, we by-passed the system and I was asked to introduce my group. She had a lovely kind word for everyone and stayed with us for much longer than I would have expected.

It may have been the aforementioned footman who was involved in this great story about the Queen Mum. Apparently, she made her way down to the scullery, or wherever, one day and came upon a group of lackeys chatting. She is reputed to have said, "Excuse me. Would one of you old queens please get this old Queen a gin and tonic?" And I can believe it – except that she drank gin and Dubonnet! She was always bubbling with laughter.

Another marvellous trip I had with the Queen Mother was when I accompanied her down to see the Army at Shoreham, in Kent. She had a formal lunch in the Officers' Mess, which included me, and then she was going off to see the troops on the firing ranges. After lunch, a Range Rover was driven up to the steps outside the Mess and in we got, chatting away. After a five-minute drive, we drew up at the appointed spot, but Her Majesty just could not get out of the car. She had a tight skirt on and simply could not stretch to the ground. We had to stay in the car, both of us giggling almost out of control, while the Army went into recovery mode. With cries of, "Sar-Major. Slight problem here. Nip up to the Officers' Mess and get the stool from beside the fireplace in the ante room, so that Her Majesty can get out of the Range Rover!" We cried with laughter and oh it was fun. But perhaps the best part was that the Army had had this cock-up in front of the RAF!

There are many lovely stories about the Queen Mother, but perhaps my favourite involves Sir Thomas Beecham, who died in 1961. He was not only a famous conductor, but was also founder of the London Philharmonic Orchestra, and, indeed, the Royal Philharmonic Orchestra. You may remember that he had a small goatee beard and was a very distinguished-looking man. Rather strangely, he hated being recognised in public, so one wonders why he wore the beard. Anyway, many years ago, he was entering Fortnum and Mason's in Piccadilly when he was horrified to see a little lady waving to him across a pile of groceries. He made a run for the exit, only to see that she had got there first. "Good morning, Sir Thomas," she said. "And how are you today?"

"Oh, I'm fine, thank you, madam. And how are you?"

"I'm fine, too, thank you. And how is Lady Beecham?"

"Oh, she's fine, thank you so much. And how is your husband?"

"Oh, he's fine, too, thank you so much for asking."

At this point, the conversation dried up; so, in desperation, Sir Thomas said, "Do you know, I'm terribly sorry, madam? I cannot remember what your husband does."

And the little lady replied, "Oh. He's still King!"

There is one more story which I love. The Queen Mum liked visiting a house which had a wonderful garden. She called one day and, after lunch, she retired 'to use the facilities'. The son of the house, forgetting that this particular bathroom had been reserved for Her Majesty's use, was ensconced in there, resolving his particular problems. He completed his ablutions and, on leaving the bathroom, he met the Queen Mum awaiting her turn. Without much thought, he sped past her, saying, "I wouldn't be going in there for a bit if I were you!"

Chapter 34

HRH the Prince of Wales

The Prince of Wales normally flew unaccompanied within the UK, so nearly all my flying with him was on overseas trips. I found him extremely pleasant and hard-working and great fun to be with – particularly in difficult moments. I was, for instance, flying with him the day that the Conservative Party ousted Margaret Thatcher. I kept him up to date by keeping an eye on my mini television and, often thereafter, he asked after it and my other gadgets.

When I accompanied the Duke of Kent to Tunisia, the Prince of Wales asked if he could have a lift. Funny that he should have to ask, but we went via Sicily to drop him off for a private painting holiday. He and we had specifically asked for the arrival to be low profile with no protocol. Unbelievably, I counted fifty-seven people around the aircraft! Quite incredible! Heaven only knows how many would have turned out if we'd suggested some sort of formal arrival. It must be very difficult for him and for other members of the Royal Family to have any time to themselves. Practically everything they do is watched by hordes of photographers.

I also accompanied HRH out to the Gulf immediately before Christmas in 1990, so that he could go and see our troops before the start of the Gulf War. On the Friday before Christmas, we had an official visit to The Queen's Flight by Her Majesty the Queen and Prince Philip, at the end of which we had a formal photograph with them. Immediately afterwards, we leapt into a BAe 146 and sped off to Lyneham to collect the Prince of Wales. Prior to the trip, we had positioned a crew in Cairo; that would enable us to take him straight through to Saudi Arabia in the same aircraft, effectively in the one journey. For the trip we had modified the 'normal' Royal compartment by putting a divan bed in it, to enable HRH to get some rest en route. We left Lyneham in the evening and were able to speed him through the night, refuelling at Rome and at Cairo, where we slipped the flying crew. Thus, we were able to go on with a fresh team for the long two days to follow.

We went first to Jubail to drop HRH off so that he could visit Army units in the desert. We waited there for the remainder of the day in case there was a need to evacuate him. Thankfully, all was well and he then spent the night on board HMS *Brazen* in the Gulf, while we went to Bahrain to put the aircraft and ourselves to bed.

The next morning, we went to Dhahran and took HRH to Riyadh, where he met more troops. I then accompanied him to the Headquarters British Forces

Middle East, where I was glad to meet my PA, who had been snaffled by the British Force Commander for the duration! The Prince of Wales had numerous briefings and discussions, including one with our commander, General Sir Peter de la Billière, and the US commander, General Norman Schwarzkopf. During a lull, I told Sir Peter that his brother Fred was a friend of mine, to which he responded, "Bad luck!"

We then toured the Allied War Headquarters complex, which was fascinating, before setting off home again to be taken on northwards by the now refreshed crew from Cairo. It had been a very quick tour, but it was obvious that our troops much appreciated the Prince of Wales's efforts in going to see them. We dropped HRH at RAF Marham, so that he could drive to Sandringham for Christmas, while we headed back to Benson, getting in at 0745 on Christmas morning! I find it significant that there was absolutely no recognition in the Press of the efforts the Prince of Wales had made to meet our troops. There was no bad news to report, so they didn't bother. Alas, they seem to want to spread alarm and despondency, no matter who they hurt or who they drag down. They simply want to sell newspapers.

I accompanied the Prince of Wales on another short-notice trip when he attended the funeral of Rajiv Ghandi. This time, we went by RAF VC10. Also in the aircraft were Douglas Hurd, the Foreign Secretary, Neil Kinnock, Sir David Steele, Edward Heath and the lovely Commonwealth Secretary General, Chief Emeka

Anyaoku, who was quite delightful. It was an interesting trip, if somewhat boring because of the lack of a movie(!), but the aircraft was at times a hive of activity and, at other times, like a morgue. HRH had his private compartment forward and the rest of us mucked in together. Seeing the politicians close up was, if nothing else, an experience, and, as a result, I am convinced that *Spitting Image* is actually quite kind to them. I mean, seeing Douglas Hurd, who to me looks as though he's just woken up, actually waking up, is a sight to behold. I know that none of us is at his best having only slept fitfully in an aircraft, but the vision haunts me still!

When we refuelled at Bahrain late at night, on the way out I had a slight problem trying to persuade the politicians to go and buy their Duty Free then and there, rather than on the return journey. They only agreed after I pointed out that they were about to have a full hot day in Delhi before they started back. They would thus be in no fit state to do anything on the return trip. Most fortunately, sanity prevailed and I led them, sheep-like, to do their shopping. Incredibly, Edward Heath wanted to know why we were still flying old aircraft like the VC10 in this day and age. "Why don't you get something decent?" he asked. So I gave him a short talk on the Defence Budget, about which, to my great surprise, he seemed to know virtually nothing! Amazing. This was 1991; the RAF retired their VC10s in 2013, twenty-two years later!

Delhi was the expected hot and dusty shambles, so we were glad to see the VIPs depart so that we could put the aircraft to bed. I stayed with our Air Attaché and his wife for the day and they very kindly took me to see the house in which we had lived some forty-five years earlier when my father was in the Indian Army. We were unable to see any of the sights because virtually the whole of the city had closed down for the funeral, with the streets impassable. I slept for a couple of hours and then off we went for the return trip, which seemed incredibly long. I had to be on my feet at Bahrain again to see to any problems, but the rest of the passengers, as I had predicted, were out for the count. The Prince of Wales had had an extremely painful back throughout the trip to India, so I felt for him. He had the attentions of his physio to help, but he seemed to be very uncomfortable. Needless to say, we were all a bit shattered, having been virtually there and back with no time to recover.

During my stay with the Air Attaché in Delhi, he told me this wonderful story. As is common in India, all those with big houses and gainful employment have a number of servants, thus doing what they can to help the unemployment problem. Our Air Attaché was no exception and, amongst others, he had a *chokidar* – the night watchman who is responsible for guarding your place through the night. Unfortunately, on returning from a dinner party one evening, he found the man asleep, so he sacked him for dereliction of duty. It was then that he noticed that odd items were disappearing from his house, so he went to see the local headman to discuss the problem. He explained that a few items seemed to have been taken from his house and wondered if the headman could help.

"But, Sahib," he said, "you are having *chokidar*, are you not?"

"Well, yes," said our man. "But I came home one night and found him asleep, so I sacked him."

"Oh, Sahib. That was not a wise thing to do. I am recommending that you re-employ the *chokidar* immediately."

"But he was useless. Surely I should have one who can stay awake?"

"Sahib, I am recommending that you should re-employ the *chokidar* immediately."

So, much against his better judgement, our man re-employed the *chokidar*. And, lo and behold, all the items reappeared in his house! Only in India!

I had one helicopter trip with the Prince of Wales when we flew down to Highgrove to collect him. I wasn't supposed to be on the aircraft, so, when he came out of the house, the first thing he said to me was, "What are you doing here?"

No, "Good morning" or anything, just that rather brusque question. I explained that I hadn't been scheduled to fly with him, but, as I was flying with Princess Margaret on the next leg, it was easier for me to fly on this trip rather than try to chase the helicopter around the country by car. He agreed immediately and then blew my mind. "Do give Princess Margaret my love," he said. "I haven't seen her for ages."

Of course, I agreed to his request, but I started thinking, hang on, who lives in Kensington Palace? The Waleses, Princess Margaret, the Gloucesters, the Kents; they don't speak?

Shortly afterwards, I was flying with Princess Alexandra and she asked me to join her for a cup of tea in the aircraft. Apropos of nothing, at one stage I asked her if she was going to Sandringham for Christmas that year. "I don't know," she said. "We haven't been asked."

I was a bit stunned by this comment and I started thinking, what sort of dysfunctional family is this? On further thought, I came up with the question, when was the last time you had a cousin for Christmas? I certainly haven't, so why do we assume that the Royal Family should? We do have a strange view of the Royal Family when, with a bit of thought and better understanding, we might be less critical. They do a fantastic job and I cannot imagine how they must feel with cameras constantly pointed at them with their every move – or false move – instantly reported and picked on. What a life. We are so lucky to have them. Can you imagine the alternative?

Chapter 35

HRH the Duchess of Gloucester

I made a number of visits with the Duchess of Gloucester, and on each and every occasion she was a delight to fly with. I also visited a number of Service establishments with her and she was always interested and exceedingly pleasant to all with whom she came in to contact. She was served by two Personal Protection Officers, Tom Ruttledge and Jerry Gotleib – Tom and Jerry! – and they, too, were great fun, frequently testing one's sense of humour to the limit.

On one occasion, she was visiting a Royal Air Force unit and we were in the foyer of the Officers' Mess for the Duchess to meet the local hierarchy. There was a well-ordered horseshoe of a reception line, down which HRH moved; and, at the end, stood a young WRAF Flying Officer who was guarding the Visitors' Book. It was already prepared in beautiful Gothic script for HRH to sign. The girl was proud of her work and could hardly wait to be presented. As the Duchess got to the third from the end of the line, Tom started off. "I say," he said. "That book is beautifully prepared. Who did that lovely writing?" Naturally, the girl preened herself, took her eye off HRH for a moment, and said that she had. "Well done," said Tom. Then, as the Duchess was within an ace of speaking to the WRAF officer, he said, almost as an afterthought, "It's a funny way to spell Gloucester!" It was very unkind, but very funny; and, naturally, they did it everywhere they went! But happily, both the girl and the Duchess saw the joke. It had, of course, been spelt correctly.

There was, however, a precedent on a previous visit made to Germany by the Duke of Kent. He had had a super day with the Army, culminating in a formal lunch in the Officers' Mess. At the end of the meal, he was asked to sign the Visitors' Book, but he declined. The inscription had been made out... 'To commemorate the visit of His Royal Highness the Duke of Gloucester.' Yes, you do have to check!

Chapter 36

HRH the Duke of Kent

In the normal course of events, we did not commodore Royal Flights by male members of the Royal Family because, by and large, they were pilots in their own right and therefore they understood the problems of flying. However, it was usual to accompany them on potentially difficult visits within the UK (for example, to Northern Ireland) and those flown overseas. Thus, I had a number of interesting trips with the Duke of Kent, of whom I knew very little. He had, I had heard, a difficult reputation – but I only ever saw a charming, polite and quite delightful man who was always courteous to everyone.

My first epic with him was when he undertook a tour of the Commonwealth War Graves in Tunisia and Sicily in his capacity as President of the Commonwealth War Graves Commission. Prior to the trip, I visited the CWGC at their headquarters in Maidenhead, where they gave me and a number of senior people a briefing on their work. They gave us a tour of their facilities and showed us their nerve centre, where, without the use of computers, they boasted that they could trace any grave within two minutes. "Right," said Air Chief Marshal Sir John Barraclough. "A challenge! What about Guy Gibson?" Naturally, they traced him in very short order and even produced a photograph of his grave, which showed the simple inscription, 'Wing Commander G P Gibson VC DSO DFC RAF'. Whereupon, to everyone's amazement, Sir John said, "Do you know, I think you've got him wrong? Surely he had a bar to his DFC?"

Horror struck their faces and various tomes were consulted, but, lo and behold, not only was it proved that he had a Bar to his DFC, but he also had one to his DSO as well! I had visions of a man, many years after the event, hacking out a new headstone for Guy Gibson.

The tour of Tunisia was fascinating, and I spent much of it accompanying the Duke to the beautifully maintained Commonwealth cemeteries, many of which were far out into the country and a number of which followed the route of the 8th Army through North Africa. Our visit coincided, at one point, with that of some of the War Widows, who, under a recent Government scheme, were visiting their husbands' graves for the first time. Neither party knew that the other was going to be there, and there were some very touching scenes – particularly when HRH asked if they would like to have their photograph taken with him at the graveside. Many of the wives were overcome, despite in some cases remarriage and the passage of some forty years, and there were some very moving moments.

We also went to various sites in Sicily, and there was a priceless moment during what was termed a private part of the Duke's programme. In true Italian fashion, in order to allow the Duke some privacy at the Roman ruins at Syracuse, all the hoi polloi had been moved out. The carabinieri locked the entrance gate and held the people back, now keener than ever, craning and pressing to see who this very important person must be who had the clout to close national monuments. Some four of us then wandered around the ruins in peace until the crowd broke through the gate and this horde ran towards us. The Duke, who was wearing a very nice smart grey suit, faded into the background behind some ruins, whilst I, in my RAF blue uniform with all the gold scrambled egg and gold aiguillettes, seemed to catch all the attention. Much to the Duke's amusement, the crowd thronged around me and for some minutes I was pressed into numerous groups to be photographed. I hadn't the heart or, indeed, the language, to tell them the truth, but the Duke was extremely grateful for my service! "Thank you, David," he said. "Doing a grand job! Keep it up!"

I also did a number of trips to Germany with the Duke of Kent and, on one notable occasion, I had to ground him while we sorted out whether or not fog was going to clear. In true fashion, the Army was all for pressing on because it said so in the programme, but the meteorological services were totally unconvincing. What was really most reassuring was the fact that the Duke left the decision entirely to me and made no attempt whatsoever to influence me in what could have been a delicate moment. He was extremely pleasant throughout a very trying time, and thus made my life that much easier.

He was also excellent during a visit I did with him to Northern Ireland, seeing many troops and policemen and, as a consequence, he did wonders for their morale. Perhaps the down side of that was when we visited some soldiers undertaking some rest and recuperation from the rigours of patrolling the Belfast streets. Amongst other things, they were having a go at clay pigeon shooting – without, I may add, a great deal of success. It did nothing for their belief in their own abilities when the Duke, at their invitation, took up a shotgun and flattened all the ten clays to come out of the traps. It was wonderful to watch and, I am glad to say, the troops were most impressed as well. However, I have no idea whether the Duke's visit was good or bad for their morale!

The Duke of Kent was very nice at Garden Parties and always had time for a chat. And, incidentally, he was always very grateful for all that The Queen's Flight did for him. The Duchess also always went out of her way to thank everyone personally. They are a very nice couple.

Chapter 37

HRH the Duchess of Kent

I flew with the Duchess of Kent on many occasions and, in particular, accompanied her on several trips to Northern Ireland. On every visit she met the security forces and their families and, occasionally, visited Macmillan hospices, where she spent long periods with the patients. Perhaps the most moving visit was when she met some forty people of the RUC, each of whom had lost a husband, a wife or a father in the Troubles. I really do not have sufficient words of praise for the Duchess. She was, quite simply, fantastic, giving words of encouragement and hope to those who really needed succour. I do not know how she did it, because I was unable to speak myself, with tears running down my cheeks. I think she must be a saint.

On a slightly more mundane level, it was a great pleasure to be able to help the Duchess in what might be termed every-day problems. I usually carry an inordinate amount of junk in my briefcase, but you may imagine my delight at being able to kneel at her feet and remove chewing gum from her brand-new shoes. On the next leg, again on the new white shoes, she had ripped a heel in a grating, so I invisibly repaired a tear in the leather with superglue. I suppose you could say that I had found my niche in life! Sadly, there was no champagne to drink from her shoe!

I also flew with the Duchess to Leicester, where she had a number of engagements. Sadly, very shortly before we were due to fly her back to London, we discovered that we were unable to start the starboard engine on the Wessex helicopter. I had to do some rapid shuffling and liaison with the local police to line up a fast Jaguar to get her back for an evening engagement, and then I went to break the bad news. She was kindness itself, being more concerned about our welfare than hers. She was horrified to hear that I would have to make my own way back to Benson overland, while the crew limped the helicopter back to base on one engine. In fact, the Duchess got back to London only slightly later than originally planned, but again, as an illustration of her concern for others, she rang The Queen's Flight three times before we got back to ensure that all was well with us. What a nice lady.

Chapter 38

HRH the Princess Margaret

Perhaps of all the members of the Royal Family, Princess Margaret was the one of whom I had heard most before I joined The Queen's Flight. My understanding was that she was a difficult person with whom to get on and that the best thing to do was to be out of the way! I am delighted to say that, from my experience on the Flight, nothing could be further from the truth. She was always exceedingly nice to me, and I much enjoyed flying with her. Patently, as with all the members of the Royal Family, you have to remember that you are *not* one of them; you are very much a servant, and you step over the line at your peril. However, this is perhaps the most difficult thing to remember, because they are all so nice.

I had one potentially difficult flight with Princess Margaret during a particularly busy and complicated day. It was one of those relatively rare occasions when we were able to make maximum use of the aircraft by combining a number of tasks, so the dice were loaded towards the difficult end of the scale. The plan was to pick up Queen Elizabeth the Queen Mother at Wick and to fly her and her entourage to Aberdeen. We were then due to pick up Princess Margaret and Prince Edward from there and to drop the latter at Cambridge. Finally, we were to take Princess Margaret to Heathrow. All went well until the eleventh hour. As we were approaching London, the dreaded call came, "Commodore to the cockpit, please." We had been told that we were due to hold for an hour or more while Air Traffic Control sorted out some problem on the ground. Naturally, it fell to me to break the bad news. So, back I went, unsure as to how this particular piece of information would be received.

"Bad news, I'm afraid, Ma'am," I said. "We have to orbit for anything up to an hour while they sort out an Air Traffic problem. I am very sorry."

"Oh dear," she said. "What on earth are we going to do?"

"Well," I said, producing a bottle of whisky and four glasses from behind my back, "How about a drink for starters?"

"Oh, what a splendid suggestion," she said.

And so we had a lovely, impromptu drinks party, chatting and laughing all the while. Eventually, after about half an hour, we got clearance to proceed into London, but the cry went up, "Oh no. Tell him to go round again. We're having much too much fun!"

Chapter 39

HRH the Duchess of York

I flew many times with the Duchess of York, and I enjoyed each and every one of them. She was great fun and was always very grateful for all the help we gave her. She was, however, throughout my time on the Flight, frequently under the cosh from the tabloid press, and I am sure that this must have got to her after a while. However, from my perspective, she was very good value and, whilst she may have been nervous or apprehensive as to the sort of day she was in for, for my money she did a tremendous job.

One of the first flights I did with her was to Leeds, where, as Patron of Opera North, she was due to attend the opening night of *Porgy and Bess*. It was a Friday evening and the weather was set fair – clear and still and really a lovely day for flying. The Duchess came on time to Heathrow for a four p.m. take-off, some seven months pregnant and looking superb in a long black evening dress. We flew up to Leeds in good order and off she went to the opera. We, meanwhile, sorted out the

Andover for the return leg to RAF Marham in Norfolk later that night. We then went and had a meal.

With some two hours to go, we wandered in to the Met Office to see what, if anything, was happening to the weather. I say 'if anything', because the forecast had been set fair for the weekend. You may imagine our consternation, therefore, when Southend went out in fog. This had not been forecast, so I thought it prudent to call the Duchess's Personal Protection Officer (PPO) in the Royal Box to warn him of possible difficulties. I then rang Marham to see what they were forecasting, only to be told that they were expecting a lovely clear night with no hint of anything untoward. Very shortly afterwards, Norwich went out in fog as well. Patently, the fog was creeping westwards.

At this stage, the PPO used his head and asked me to alert the lady of the house with whom the Duchess had spent the previous night, not far from Leeds, as to the possibility of having to put the Duchess up again. I can just imagine the scene as the house party went into overdrive to put the place back together to receive HRH once more. A real French farce situation, which must have been wonderful to behold.

Meanwhile, in desperation, I called the station commander at Marham to try to ascertain exactly what was going on. He rang back shortly afterwards and said, "It is not foggy here, we are not expecting fog and, what is more, it is a lovely night. Come on in as planned."

So I rang the PPO and told him all was well; they could leave the theatre as arranged and we could depart on time. The drive from the theatre to Leeds airport took some twenty minutes, so we got ready for the departure.

Literally as we got the two-minute call from the police, I was told that there was a telephone call for me. It was the station commander Marham telling me that the airfield had just gone out in fog. Wonderful! I got back to the aircraft just as the Duchess's car drew up, so I knelt at her window and said that I was very sorry, but I had just scrubbed the sortie because of fog. "Never mind," she said. "I respect your decision as a pilot. Now, what time do you want me tomorrow?"

While I did the sums on the personal assumption that the fog might clear around midday, she dived into her handbag and rang Prince Andrew at Sandringham. Unknown to us, he had just returned from sea, so they were keen to meet up again. I told HRH that ten a.m. would be a good time to depart tomorrow, and, with that, she was taken back to the country house while we tried to find some accommodation.

That is exactly as it happened in the late autumn of 1989. The press was always hot on the heels of all the gossip and dirt that they could fling at the junior members of the Royal Family, so I guess this came as no surprise. It came to pass that, following that additional night at the country house in Yorkshire, after breakfast, a happy group photograph was taken of all the people staying at the house. And, lo and behold, the Duchess was still wearing her long black evening gown. Surely this was a sign of debauchery? There must have been a tremendous party, presumably still going on the next morning, and the Duchess must have been having a wild old time, probably more than most, since she was still in her long black evening dress. 'Fergie Still Whooping It Up After Breakfast!' was the spin the gutter press put on it, but, as you now know, it was very far from the truth. She got a very unfair press.

It seems rather mundane to report that the Duchess turned up on time the next day and that, possibly taking a chance on the clearance of the fog, we set off for Marham at ten a.m. on the dot. As luck would have it, when we got to Marham, the eastern end of the airfield was in thick fog and the western end was clear. We landed, taxied in and said our goodbyes in the murk. The Duchess then went off to Sandringham by car. She was still wearing that long black evening dress which she must have put on at Buckingham Palace at about three p.m. the previous day.

I flew with her again the following week and she was very kind. "Do you know, David," she said, "the fog at Marham cleared for only about fifteen minutes during the whole weekend. We were very lucky to get in at all." Yes, there is a God.

One other story about the Duchess of York was when I accompanied her to Northern Ireland on a visit to a number of venues. *Inter alia*, in Belfast she was due to name the new Royal Fleet Auxiliary ship *Fort Victoria*. I should point out that, for obvious reasons of security, apart from a very few people, there was a blanket of secrecy surrounding Royal visits to Northern Ireland. Thus, whilst the workers of Harland and Wolff knew that someone fairly high up in the pecking order was due to name their ship, they had no idea who it was and they certainly had no idea that it might be a member of the Royal Family. Anyway, we flew into the shipyard at Harland and Wolff and landed in a red Queen's Flight helicopter in the middle of this great press of men. As is customary, I stepped out of the helicopter first and stood to attention, ready to salute the principal passenger and to help her down the steps as necessary. As the Duchess of York came to the door and stepped down, there was a roar possibly louder than when David Beckham got England into the finals of the 2002 World Cup at Wembley. It was incredible and very moving. And it went on and on. They were absolutely delighted that she had come to Northern Ireland and were obviously very pleased to see her. That delight, incidentally, applies to all members of the Royal Family. But to see the Duchess of York talking and laughing with the workers was an absolute joy. She gave as good as she got and she was, quite simply, superb. Naturally, however, since there was no scandal or any bad news, the press chose to ignore the visit, but I was there and I saw and heard a very different story to that which you were asked to believe in the tabloids.

I flew with the Duchess of York on the day she got her new short haircut. We picked her up from the back garden at Buckingham Palace and, as was usual, as soon as the principal passenger appeared, I stood to attention by the door of the helicopter. I was, therefore, unable to see her as she approached from my right. She got in with a, "Hello, David." I followed her into the aircraft while the pilot started the engines. She then turned round and said, "What do you think of the new haircut?"

Almost without thinking, since I had just had a haircut myself, I said, "Whose? Yours or mine?"

"Mine, you fool," she said, pulling off her hat. She had had it cut short and looked very nice. That set the tone for the day. We flew to Winchester, where I wasn't required to accompany her, so I went to have lunch with my parents. I returned early as normal, but the Duchess returned earlier than expected, so I ran across the parade ground to the aircraft to welcome her. "Who were you talking to, David?" she asked. When I told her that they were my parents, she said, "Come on. Let's go and have a natter!" That was typical of her; she always was very kind and gracious.

When we flew on The Queen's Flight, the make-up of the Royal party was always known in advance. We were thus able to get the correct seating in the helicopter to suit the passengers. I was, on one occasion, a bit stymied when we went to pick up Fergie from Epsom to fly her to an appointment in Wales. To our great surprise, she was accompanied by her children and their nanny, whom we had not known about. The only way to cater for this number was for the oldest each to have a seat while I, in my smart blue uniform, had the little Eugenie on my lap, dribbling and snotting away with great aplomb – her, not me. I evidently did not make much of an impression on her; but, as she got older, she grew into a beautiful young lady.

There were many other trips, notably during the Gulf War, when she did wonders, boosting the morale of the wives and the people left at home, and I think she did a fantastic job. I doubt that any one of us could do so well if faced with that barrage of abuse, much of it ill informed, from all the gutter press. The point I keep trying to remember, and I repeat it for what it is worth, is that the press has only one aim in life – and that is to sell newspapers. Whether they tell the truth or whether they hurt people in the process seems not to matter one jot. I believe that they have an awful lot to answer for.

The Duchess was also excellent at the Paraplegic Games at Stoke Mandeville (which have now become the Paralympics), where she spent ages talking with all the competitors. For what it is worth, I thought she did a very good job in trying circumstances. Sadly, the Press were out to get her and, of course, they made her life a misery. What chance did she have? She was only with her husband for forty-two days in the first year of their marriage. Who would marry a sailor? I know I wouldn't.

Chapter 40

HRH the Duke of York

I only flew a couple of times with the Duke of York, but each one was a challenge! He was, of course, a pilot, so he understood the pitfalls of flying. It was, therefore, unusual to accompany him. In fact, both my flights with him were because we were doubling up the tasking and I was on the aircraft because I was escorting a solo lady on the subsequent flight. On the first occasion, at Leeds as it happened, I was having a cigarette away from the aircraft with apparently about twenty minutes to go before doors-closed time when, with absolutely no warning, there were the Duke and Duchess of York pulling up to the aircraft in their car! I put my cigarette out and then sprinted across the concrete while they said their goodbyes to their escorts. Thus, I was at the rear of the aircraft to welcome them on board. As he went up the aircraft steps, the Duke turned to me and said, "Funny place Leeds, isn't it? I could have sworn I saw a group captain running just now!"

When we were airborne, we discussed a recent trip I had made with the Duchess to Northern Ireland, which included flying in both a Queen's Flight BAe 146 and a red Wessex helicopter. He wanted to know why we were still flying the Wessex – then some twenty-six years old. We discussed the matter for some time and then he said, "But why do you insist on flying red Queen's Flight helicopters in Northern Ireland?"

I said that we always took the advice of the Northern Ireland Office. However, I thought that it was probably a desire of the Royal Family to show the world that they weren't about to have their proper way of life disturbed by terrorists; in short, raising two fingers to them. He thought for a bit, looked at me hard and then burst into laughter. He punched me on the shoulder and said, "Bloody good, isn't it?"

Whilst the Duke of York may have surprised me at Leeds, I caught him unawares a little later. I was in London and went to Buckingham Palace to speak to Prince Edward's office about a forthcoming visit. I hadn't spoken to his staff for some time and set off through the Palace to where I remembered we had last met. I walked along a long, wide corridor which was full of lovely paintings and furniture, in which members of the staff were polishing and dusting various items – just like *Upstairs Downstairs*! At the far end, I saw a figure in a hunched-over attitude and thought perhaps that someone had hurt his back. However, on closer inspection, it turned out to be the Duke of York – practising his putting! No wonder his handicap improved by leaps and bounds.

Chapter 41

HRH the Princess Royal

The Princess Royal prefers to fly unaccompanied in the UK, but she normally has a commodore when flying overseas. It was mostly in the latter capacity that I flew with her during my time on the Flight.

My first epic with her was on a tour of the Caribbean. We flew in a BAe 146 of The Queen's Flight and, because of the aircraft's limited range, we flew a route which went from Lyneham in Wiltshire, to Keflavik in Iceland, to Gander in Newfoundland and then to New York – round the edge of the Atlantic effectively. We then had a day's rest before heading off to Bermuda and then to Barbados, where, unbelievably, we had to spend four days. I was not involved with HRH at all, except as commodore when we were flying; so, by and large, it was a pretty demanding trip. The Princess Royal held a couple of functions on *Britannia* in Bridgetown, Barbados, before sailing off to Trinidad for more engagements. We then followed her and spent a night in Trinidad, before flying her on to Kingston, Jamaica, where we left her. She returned to the UK by civil air, so we then flogged our way to night stop in Bermuda and again in Iceland, before returning to the real world, having been away for ten days. Lord, it was hard work – but I don't expect anyone to believe me!

My other major tour with the Princess Royal was when she visited The Gambia, Senegal and Mali as President of the Save the Children Fund (SCF). It was absolutely fascinating and a real education to see her at close hand in some of the most amazing places. She is totally dedicated to her work and is marvellous at it, working non-stop throughout each and every day.

We flew in a BAe 146 of The Queen's Flight and stopped first in Casablanca, where we had planned simply to refuel. However, the King of Morocco had heard that a member of the Royal Family was passing through, so he had ordered the Royal Lounge to be made available, together with the Royal Honour Guard. I must say, they looked incredibly dashing and smart with their white flowing pantaloons, scarlet tops and flashing swords, but it was all to no avail. HRH had said that she was not intending to get off the aircraft and had no wish to put anyone out, so I was despatched to tell the waiting guard (in my fluent French!) that she was asleep. Perhaps it was just as well that the Princess Royal did not get off the aircraft. There was a very strong wind and it was actually quite funny to see their team of serfs attempting to control this amazing red carpet which seemed to have a mind of its own. Eventually, they gave up, hoping that it would stay where it was, and resorted to lying on it in various strange postures – thereby spoiling an otherwise impressive sight!

The Gambia is a tiny country, roughly on the centre of the bulge of the west of Africa. It is very hot and invariably sunny, although the country is largely green. The centrepiece of the visit was for the Princess Royal to attend the twenty-fifth anniversary of The Gambia's Independence. While HRH stayed with the British High Commissioner (BHC) in his Residence, we were forced to slum it in a superb hotel on the outskirts of Banjul, the capital. And there we stayed for three days, feeling sorry for the poor people in the UK in February!

On arrival in the country, with barely time to change, I was included in the party to witness the start of The Gambia's celebrations, which went on long into the evening. Amazing colourful processions passed, usually accompanied by the throbbing beat of drums, all being watched by the VIPs and us lesser mortals. Included in the latter, I am delighted to say, was the American astronaut John Young, the only man to have been to the moon twice and into space six times! He was quite delightful and totally unassuming. John Young was part of the American entourage which was supporting the top American official, President Bush's son, George W Bush Jnr. In true fashion, the latter was surrounded by deaf people with large lumps under their arms, a number of whom had been specially trained to walk backwards. It really was typical American overkill and very funny to watch – if only they didn't take themselves so seriously.

Eventually, with much over-running of the programme, the evening came to an end and we got to bed at about two fifteen a.m., after what felt like a very long day.

The next day was the Independence Ceremony, and I was lucky enough to attend as a spectator. It was held in an enormous hundred thousand-seat sports stadium which had been given to the nation by China. Apparently, the Chinese gave these sports stadia to a number of nations in Africa which had obtained their independence, presumably in an attempt to win friends and influence people. Again, there were many processions, this time under the burning equatorial sun, but what impressed me more than anything was the military parade, which was held on grass in the centre of the arena. It is incredibly difficult to march and carry out good drill on grass, but The Gambian Army was quite superb. If anything, they out-Sandhursted Sandhurst, and I was incredibly impressed.

Following the ceremonies, I was then invited to lunch at the BHC's residence; but, on arrival, it was immediately evident that there was an 'atmosphere'. I am pleased to say that it wasn't me who caused it, but the Deputy High Commissioner had been held up after the parade, I think at the President's Palace. But lunch kept on being delayed. The High Commissioner kept apologising and asked if it was all right if we delayed lunch a little longer, to which the reply was, "If we have to." This was a moment NOT TO BE IN THE FIRING

LINE. Anyway, after some time, we eventually sat down at a long narrow table where, much to my consternation, the BHC sat far away at one end and Mrs High Commissioner sat at the other. Various lesser people were placed around the table and then the Princess Royal was asked to sit in the middle on one side while I, for reasons I know not, was placed directly opposite and some three feet in front of her. Everyone looked at each other and then down at their plates, presumably waiting for someone to break the ice; so, typically, since no one else seemed to want to step into the breach, I launched into my Wimbledon story. It goes like this:

In the days before we had covered roofs at Wimbledon, whenever there was rain, they went into discussions with anyone who was around. On this occasion, to fill the time, Dan Maskell was talking to Arthur Ashe – the wonderful, quietly-spoken Wimbledon champion. The subject of seeding came up and they realised that, on grass, the seeds fell all over the place at Wimbledon. On the world circuit, on hard or clay courts, the No 1 and the No 2 seeds invariably got through to the final. Dan Maskell said, "You've played all over the world, Arthur. Is it any different on grass or Astroturf?"

Absolutely deadpan, Arthur Ashe said, "Well, Dan, I can't rightly say. You see, I've never smoked Astroturf!"

Maskell's face was an absolute picture!

Whilst the response was not unexpected in more normal circumstances, I was much relieved to see HRH going into peals of laughter. She then came straight back with, "That Dan Maskell is a terrible tennis coach, you know."

"Really?" I said. "I thought he was supposed to be good."

"No!" she said. "He's awful. He's been trying to teach me for years and I still can't play for toffee!"

So we took it from there and it turned out to be a nice occasion after all.

We had a lovely incident in Banjul, when we were delighted that the Princess Royal was able to accept the crew's invitation to dinner. She had an incredibly busy and draining schedule, but she made time to have a night out with the boys. We chose a quiet restaurant and it was just an ordinary fun and informal evening. During the course of conversation, we told her that one of the ground crew chaps called Reg, who was sitting beside her, tended to wear the most outlandish British Empire outfit when off duty. She was much amused and asked to see this the next time we flew. It so happened that on the flight out from The Gambia, we arranged for Reg to take in the royal cuppa, wearing his British Raj outfit. For what it is worth, he was wearing a khaki shirt, what can only be described as huge Empire Builder's shorts which came halfway down his calves, Union Jack socks with desert boots and, on his head, a solar topee in which was planted a Union Flag. It was very funny to see, particularly as the Princess Royal had forgotten that she had asked to see this apparition. She howled with laughter.

Following our meal with the Princess Royal, as soon as we got up from the table after she had left, mine host rushed forward and grabbed Princess Anne's chair and nailed it to the wall, some ten feet above our heads – next to another similarly positioned chair. "Nobody am sittin' on dis chair. It am sacred!" And why two chairs? Unknown to us, it transpired that George W Bush Junior, there to represent his daddy (who himself was then President of the United States) and accompanied by more heavies with deaf aids than I have ever seen, had had similar treatment! So that was his chair up there as well. I'd love to know if they are still there!

We then flew to Dakar, the capital of Senegal, where I was included in a formal lunch given by the President in honour of HRH. The next day, we flew a triangular trip round Senegal, visiting Bakel and St Louis. At the former, we visited very basic villages in the eastern desert, which were constantly under threat of drought and driving sand. The locals lived in tiny grass huts and they can only eke out their lives simply trying to survive.

St Louis is on the coast, north of Dakar, and is primarily a fishing port. In company with HRH, we were given a tour of the fish-drying area, which was probably the least attractive thing I have ever had to undergo. The fish arc gutted and left to dry under the sun on trestle tables, and the whole area must have stretched some three hundred yards by two hundred yards. As honoured guests, we were taken through the middle of this riot of colour and pressing humanity, but the incredible stench of it all was quite unbelievable. I found myself gagging on numerous occasions and, whilst it was interesting to have seen it all, it is not a visit I would wish to repeat. It obviously did not help that I had been unwell the previous evening and was still suffering to a degree, but it was a relief to return to the relatively pleasant atmosphere of an oppressively hot and dusty Dakar. The Princess Royal seemed to be completely unmoved during this walk through the fish market, and I thought she did a fantastic job. The next day we flew to Timbuktu.

Perhaps of all the places one has heard of in one's time, possibly the least likely place for me to visit, I would have said, was Timbuktu – but there I was. It is bang in the middle of nowhere and we had some slight problem finding it, with blowing sand reducing visibility and virtually no features in the desert to guide us. However, find it we did, and off we set in Save the Children Land Rovers for a look at the old walled city. The buildings and defences are made entirely out of dried mud bricks, and it must have been enormous in its heyday as the central point for all the camel trains. Sadly, all that is now left is a smallish town which huddles around very deep wells which have been dug like inverted volcanoes so that one can walk down to the water – if there is any. We then went into the desert, which really is brownish driving sand, to find a Tuareg camp. Again, the inhabitants have their work cut out just to survive, but the SCF has helped by providing a well for them, which found water at sixty-eight feet. It really was *Beau Geste* country, and I was not in the least surprised when a group of colourful Tuaregs appeared out of the blowing sand on their camels, looking absolutely fantastic and snooty from their high perch. And, quite naturally, they posed for photographs – for a consideration! Tourists had been there before!

Our next call was at Mopti, on the banks of the River Niger, where we spent two days. At that point, the Niger is a slow-moving broad river which is some hundred and fifty yards across, and, as one might expect, life revolves around it since it provides the only real irrigation available. It is used for everything – transport, bathing and washing, drinking and almost everything else one can imagine. We made two trips up the river, the first with the crew only and the second with HRH, and both were fascinating. Naturally, the odd sight caught the eye, like a dead, bloated cow floating past with vultures idly pecking on it; but most fascinating of all were the villages.

There were two distinct types. The first were the permanent ones, which were clusters of tightly packed mud huts, and the others were what I would call lightweight, with sticks and tents pushed into the ground to enable the nomads to move off to their next port of call with ease. On our first visit, there was a lovely, happy, bustling atmosphere, with children peering round their mothers' sarongs; but, when I visited with the Princess Royal, it was as if the Pied Piper had been – certainly to the first few villages. This may have been because we also had the local (much-feared) Governor with the party,

321

but it was a shame that HRH did not get to see the carefree happy places that we saw.

I also had the opportunity to discuss the work of the SCF with HRH. The aim is not to give the children a better life by providing food, etc., but to help the people to help themselves. Thus, teaching about irrigation and animal husbandry are high on the agenda, as are the provision of schools and help to train teachers. It was a fascinating experience.

We spent the last night of the tour at Bamako, the capital of Mali, before we headed back for home. We made great time across the Sahara, refuelling at Ghardaia in Algeria in glorious weather, and then sped across the Mediterranean to Lyon, where we were to refuel. Sadly, at that point the French chose to put the brakes on. So, despite having made up a lot of time to enable HRH to get home early, we then sat on the ground for an hour and a half for the doubtful pleasure of the striking French Air Traffic Controllers. It fell to me (it always does) to break the bad news, and suffice it to say that we were not amused.

Chapter 42

HRH Princess Alexandra

Princess Alexandra was a delight to fly with. She was always alert and jolly, and every time she went out of her way to make sure that everyone with her was also happy. My first flight with her was typical.

When the principal passengers have embarked up the rear steps of the aircraft, you and The Queen's Flight policeman enter the aircraft and wait at the rear while the steps are raised and the rear door is closed by the Flight Steward. The door between the rear entrance and the Royal compartment is closed during these manoeuvres, so there is a fairly tight scrum with three of you trying to keep out of each other's way – and even more so in the Andover, as we were on this occasion. The purpose of this is to allow the Royal party to settle in their seats without the threat of being knocked over by passing crewmen. Thus, you hover until you can see that they have taken their seats. So, there we were, hunched in the back, when there came a banging at the door and a cry from HRH saying, "It's no good hiding in there. We know you are there. Come on out!" And so the day started with all of us laughing, thus ensuring a happy day for everyone. She is a lovely lady.

I did a gorgeous trip with Princess Alexandra and Sir Angus Ogilvie to Guernsey, Alderney and Sark, and it was the greatest fun. They flew over by fixed-wing aircraft and then we used a Wessex helicopter for the remainder of the visit. For some reason, I was included in the dinner given for Princess Alexandra at Government House on the first night, and it was a really lovely evening. She was in cracking form and, after dinner, she went to the grand piano and sat down to play while we gathered round, expecting a sort of concert, I suppose. She played the first four bars of Tchaikovsky's 1st Piano Concerto, quite faultlessly, I would have said; she then stopped and threw the lid down. Amidst peals of laughter, she howled out, "That's all I know!" It was very funny and a lovely moment. We rounded off the evening by seeing an enormous fireworks display over the harbour, thus ending a memorable day for me.

We then visited Alderney, where HRH planted a tree at a school and opened an old people's home before we went on to Sark. We had a priceless moment on arrival when the helicopter downdraft blew the wig off one of the locals – much to his consternation. The impression we had was that no one else, apparently, knew that he wore one; so, if nothing else, HRH's visit made a number of the inhabitants' day. In fact, I am sure it is now known, not as the day that Princess Alexandra visited Sark, but the day old Charlie lost his rug!

Sark, of course, allows no motor transport; so, during that part of the visit, we were driven round in four open carriages with strong ladies, with leather aprons and bowler hats, heaving at the reins to try to control the horses. Apart from being fun and quaint, it proved to be very exciting indeed. As it was May, none of the horses had got used to pulling for the tourist influx for the season ahead, so they were, to put it delicately, lively, having taken their fill of the rich green grass. Thus, while the drivers tried their utmost to control matters, the horses had other ideas. Naturally, I was in the number four carriage, but, on a couple of occasions, we sped past the leading bunch in the best *Ben-Hur* manner, completely out of control, with great shrieks of delight from Princess Alexandra. It really was very funny, but it was also quite dangerous – particularly when the other horses thought that they should be leading. It developed into a real challenge for the Horsewomen of the Apocalypse, with the reins being tested to the full. Different, if nothing else!

Apart from trying to avoid the fallout from the horses, I spent much of my time carrying huge bunches of flowers which had been given to HRH; a photograph of me appeared on the front page of the Guernsey newspaper, which shows that it must have been a slow news day. It was a lovely visit and it was great fun being with Princess Alexandra on that and other trips.

When she heard that I was leaving The Queen's Flight, Princess Alexandra asked me to go up to see her to say goodbye, which I thought was lovely. I only flew nineteen times with her, but she was just smashing and such fun, and, undoubtedly, we had laughed a lot. But I was very touched that she gave me a signed photograph of her and her husband, which I treasure. I have often thought this procedure somewhat odd and have considered having some photographs of myself done to present to people – but, somehow, I doubt whether mine would have the same impact.

Chapter 43

HRH Prince Edward

I had one memorable trip with Prince Edward when I accompanied him on a visit to Northern Ireland. He was to open the Mary Peters athletics stadium in Belfast, and I thought it too good an opportunity to miss. When we arrived, I said to him, "I'm sorry, sir. You are going to have to forgive me for a moment. I just have to do this." I then rushed over to Mary Peters and gave her a huge hug and a kiss, which surprised her. She asked what that was for and I said, "I lost my voice and my heart to you when you got the Pentathlon Gold at the Munich Olympics in 1972!" I then turned to Prince Edward and said, "Thank you, sir. Please carry on." He was delighted and quite understood. He is an extremely nice man.

Chapter 44

HRH the Princess of Wales

In the normal course of events, I would not normally have expected to fly with the major households since, in The Queen's Flight pecking order of Commodores, I was number three – and then really only part-time because I was Station Commander of RAF Benson as well. However, as things turned out, I was asked to take over the Wales household, so I did the majority of my flying escorting the Princess of Wales – and great fun it was, too.

One of my very early flights with her was to Northern Ireland, and, unbelievably, it was the most awful day in January 1990. You may remember it when we had amazing thrashing wind; it was the day when bits were blown off buildings and Gorden Kaye, the star of *'Allo 'Allo*, was impaled through his forehead by a large piece of flying wood.

Talking of Gorden Kaye, people often asked why he spelt his name like that. He said that, when he started acting, he needed an Equity Card. On giving his name, an ignorant youth wrote it down as Gorden, so he decided to keep it like that to make himself a bit different. His explanation was that he got his name from a mis-spelt youth!

But, back to the Princess of Wales. Before we even set off to go flying, with the weather forecast so awful, I rang Kensington Palace to recommend that we scrub the sortie. However, the message came back, "I must be seen to try."

So, off we set in the Andover and arrived at Northolt in very blustery conditions. We pored over the weather charts and thought that it might be possible to have a go, but it would be a very rough ride.

The Princess of Wales came on time and, as usual, she looked a million dollars. I had managed to get her a disruptive pattern (DP) uniform (the sort of Action Man kit) with black flying boots so that she would be dressed similarly to the Royal Hampshire Regiment, whom she was visiting in Londonderry. However, the Palace tailor had obviously got at the normally shapeless sack and had turned it into a work of art. I have never seen anyone with slim legs look as though they have slim legs in DP, but she did. She was a knockout! So, off we went and battled our way into Aldergrove – as usual, amidst much secrecy and security. The Princess said that it was very important for her to go by helicopter to Londonderry, but I had to explain that any decision was out of my hands.

On arrival, the wind was only just within the Andover's limits, but we discovered that the station commander had already cancelled the intended helicopter flying – so we drove to Derry by car. The roads were not very good, with lots of snow and ice, but the police drivers did wonders and we hurtled up there in good order. There was, however, a very bad security gaffe. As we were still some distance from Derry, on the radio they announced that the Princess of Wales was visiting the city that day. Not very clever, so I can only assume that the press release had been tied to the original arrival time by helicopter – and no one had noted the change of plan. In addition, matters were not helped when we were informed that there were bomb incidents on two of the three roads into Londonderry. It did nothing for our peace of mind, which was already stretched, but we got there.

The Princess was absolutely fantastic during her visit to the Royal Hampshires, and the effect on their morale was wonderful to see. All the wives and children came out to see her, and she was superb, talking to everyone. You could see them all stand up straighter as a result of her visit. She was amazing.

Meanwhile, of course, I spent much time on the telephone with the Andover crew and with the Met men, trying to find out what the weather was doing. The answer was that it was not really getting any better at all, and possibly worse. We did, however, get a bit of a lull in the late afternoon, so the Northern Ireland helicopters came up to Derry and we were able to fly her back to Aldergrove. It was incredibly bumpy as we thrashed along at very low level to keep under the clouds. I sat beside the Princess of Wales, trying to reassure her, when she turned to me and said, "Hey, these are much faster than ours, aren't they?"

"No, Ma'am," I said. "It's the same model, but painted green. It is simply the fact that we have fifty knots up our chuff, so we are covering the ground that much quicker!"

When we got to Aldergrove, we discovered that all the airfields on the UK mainland had closed because of strong winds. Most unusually, even Heathrow had been closed because a building had been blown across the runway! It wasn't a very good situation because, naturally, there was considerable pressure to get her off the island. So, we put the Princess and her party in the VIP suite and fed them tea and coffee while I kept them up to date with information on the weather and our prospects for getting out of there. On the news, we heard that thirty-four people had died in the violent winds, so it was patently not a day to be fooling around flying. And so we devilled on, while the clock ticked on towards the time when we would have to night-stop for crew duty reasons if nothing else. They were, however, offering the possibility of a clearance in the evening, and so, after much thought, we decided to set off, once again being violently buffeted around.

I come now to a delicate matter. To match the Princess, throughout the day I had been in my Action Man kit as well; but, for the arrival at Heathrow, I thought I ought to be back in my poncy blue uniform. The problem, though, was, when do I change? There was

331

precious little room in the Andover anyway, so I would have to change in the aisle; thus, the only time available would be when the Royal Tea went back for the Princess. So, there I was, in my socks, shirt and shreddies, bent double over my suitcase, when from behind me came this shriek and a great peal of laughter, and there she was, laughing her head off. And she never forgot it, invariably bringing the topic up at the most inappropriate moments.

Fortunately, the weather then relented and we managed to get into Heathrow in fairly good order. She was, however, very uncomfortable and apprehensive as the aircraft bucketed about, so I knelt beside her on the approach and explained how an aircraft works. Happily, this seemed to calm her and helped her to relax. And, naturally, the next time I flew with her, she opened the conversation on arrival at the aircraft by saying, "Oh, I'm so sorry, David. I didn't recognise you with your trousers on!"

The Princess of Wales was Honorary Air Commodore of a few RAF stations, and, whenever there was a change of command, the station commander went to speak with the Princess. I had quite a few telephone calls from some startled station commanders, who said, "I went along to talk about my station and all we did was talk about your Y-fronts!" Fame at last!

My next epic with the Princess of Wales followed shortly afterwards. She and the Prince of Wales had been on a state visit to Nigeria and Cameroon. It had been, as you may imagine, very hot, with excessively high humidity, but matters were not helped by the air conditioning on *Britannia*, on which they were staying, breaking down. It had been a long and trying visit. At one point, in Nigeria, the Princess had been ordered not to walk on the red carpet, "Because only de Head of State am walkin' on de red carpet!"

She turned to her Personal Protection Officer and said, "What can I do?"

And Ken Wharfe said, "Bollocks, Ma'am, come with me." He took her by the elbow and together they walked up the red carpet. Quite right, too!

At the end of the visit, however, the Prince of Wales decided to stay an extra day to go and visit a rainforest. I was despatched, therefore, to go and collect the Princess, who was anxious to return to see her children. We sped down across the Sahara, refuelling at Palma and at Tamanrasset, and then we night-stopped in Douala, in the Cameroon, ready for the return the next day.

By then, of course, we had sussed out what had been going on, so we cranked up the air conditioning in the BAe 146 and got ready for the off. Meanwhile, a huge number of Press photographers got themselves organised to take pictures of the Princess's departure. There must have been some forty-plus cameras there, with many of the paparazzi on step ladders. While I was sauntering around waiting on the tarmac for the Princess to arrive, to my horror I suddenly found the entire battery of Press cameras turned on me, all whirring and clicking away. I was concerned that my fly was undone or there was some other glitch, but it seemed all was well. It took me some time afterwards to work out why I should be of such interest. It was my first public outing with Diana, and I suppose for that reason it might have been of interest. But I think the real reason was in case I foul up in later life. It really doesn't matter what I might or might not have done or do, but undoubtedly the headline would start, 'Diana aide in shock horror story'. The name Diana still sells newspapers. Anyway, I got away from the Press and eventually we set off, with the Princess looking drained. She promptly fell asleep, so we left her in peace.

I then had the problem of sorting out what she wanted to do at Tamanrasset while the aircraft was refuelled. I told her that we had lined up the VIP Lounge for her to use if she would like a cool drink or something, but she said she didn't want that. "Oh," she said, "I'm fed up with VIP things: can't we do something ordinary?"

I suggested a walk across the airfield to see a crashed Hercules C130, and she jumped at the idea. So, just the two of us had a lovely wander across the desert in the most beautiful clear dry weather, throwing a tennis ball back and forth and generally just being ordinary. We climbed all over the aircraft and it was a lovely relaxing time. On our return to the aircraft, she refused to sit in her seat and came to sit beside me. Then, for the next two hours, we told each other funnies until the tears rolled down our cheeks.

We refuelled at Palma, where, at her request, there was no protocol, so she and I went for another wander and a leg stretch on the airfield in the half-light (probably totally illegally), and then we set off on the last leg home.

It had been a really lovely trip. And what was particularly nice was the Buckingham Palace Press Officer coming back to tell me that he thought that the atmosphere in the aircraft had been absolutely smashing and just right. What a nice man.

Following those two trips, that amazing message came from on high, "I'd really rather prefer to fly with that nice young David Greenway." Wow, flattery indeed. So, I was switched to flying with the Wales household, which dramatically increased my workload. I loved flying regularly with the Princess of Wales, and each trip was a real pleasure. The vast majority were day visits within the UK, but I also went with her overseas as well.

I was very lucky to accompany the Prince and Princess of Wales to Tokyo for the crowning of Emperor Akihito of Japan. For this trip, Japan was simply too far for a BAe 146 with its limited range. The thought of going unserviceable in darkest Turkmenistan or somewhere similar was just not worth contemplating. You might expect that it would have been more appropriate to fly in an RAF VC10, but all our fleet had been excessively overflown during the Gulf War. They could not be taken out of service to be given the necessary additional servicing normally accorded to aircraft which are flown in by the heir to the throne. Additionally, with the VC10's shorter range, refuelling stops would have been required along the way, and this was not thought appropriate. We approached British Airways and asked if we could book the first class section of their Japan schedules for the trip. Their response was that this would completely foul up their regular schedules. Had we considered chartering one of their Boeing 747s which could make the trip in one jump and which would be much more cost-effective? So, we chartered a 747, with thirteen of us on board, outnumbered by the crew by about three to one! I need hardly tell you, however, that the Press, as expected, had a field day and made no effort to ascertain the truth. Again, they were simply concerned with selling newspapers, and it was another chance to have a go at the Royal Family with talk of royal junkets.

The long, boring flight was greatly helped by the provision of in-flight movies and, unusually with so much room, we were able to take some exercise. But it was still a grind. Nevertheless, we got to Tokyo as ordered, and really that was the end of my involvement in the visit. I did, however, attend the Remembrance Day service at the British War Cemetery, where the Prince of Wales laid a wreath. The engagement was covered by the British Press – but this time with a little more sympathy, although it was here that they saw the strained body language between the two principals. It seemed to confirm the awful conjecture about their marriage.

I spent some time in Tokyo trying to understand their underground system. Matters were not helped by the signs being written only in Bamboo, so it was something of a challenge! I also managed to turn the tables on the Japanese by going to Japan to play golf; normally, one hears of them coming to play in the UK because it is cheaper. And, with every other hole looking at Mount Fuji, it was worth every penny. I felt very superior.

Needless to say, the return trip to Heathrow was just as boring, but at least we had a different set of movies! But, if nothing else, it was interesting to see the manic reactions of the press to practically anything. It saddens me that they never, to my knowledge, write up what a marvellous job the Royal Family does. No one, for instance, pays the crowds to turn up to see them, or orders them to do so. And yet, the good that members of the Royal Family do as they go about their various duties, some of which must be unutterably boring, is really wonderful to see. People with smiles on their faces and walking taller as a result of having spoken with them. They also, incidentally, do an enormous lot for the Tourist Industry. One wonders, for instance, whether so many Americans would come over to visit the UK if we had no Royal Family. Would they come to see President Gordon Brown or President Cameron or, perish the thought, President Corbyn? The mind boggles at the thought of that!

I also accompanied the Prince and Princess of Wales on a State Visit to Prague. From my perspective, apart from being given the opportunity to see that lovely city and to wander in Wenceslas Square (which, incidentally, is a kilometre long!) the highlight for me was when the

Princess asked me where the crew were staying. "Well, Ma'am," I said, "it's a bit rough. We are forced to slum it in the best hotel in town. It only has a sauna, a swimming pool, a gymnasium, a squash court, a ten-pin bowling alley, two night clubs and a casino. It really is terrible."

"Bad luck," she said. "I'm staying in a castle. Neh neh neh neh neh!" Great fun.

Luck really seems to have been on my side, because I also accompanied the Prince and Princess of Wales on their State Visit to Brazil in 1991. Again, because of the great distances involved, we went basically there and back in a Tristar of British Airways. However, learning from the press reaction to the small numbers who went in the Boeing 747 to Tokyo, there were many more on the aircraft, including Lynda Chalker (Minister of State for Overseas Development) and Jonathan Porritt, the conservationist. The spare seats were offered to the Press, but, because they had to be there ahead of the Royal party to photograph the arrival, etc., they didn't fly with us! All rather self-defeating really, but at least we had called their bluff, and this time the press did not make a big fuss about it. I am pleased to say that there was no mention of a royal junket.

Again, we were saved from total boredom by the in-flight movies, and we passed the time on the first leg to Sal Island in the southern Atlantic by watching *Dances With Wolves* before it was released in the UK. As is usual on long over-water transits involving senior members of the Royal Family, we were given Search and Rescue support by RAF Nimrods. I was, however, somewhat taken aback to be asked on arrival by a senior member of the household, "Who owns these islands, David? And what sort of aircraft are those?" I explained that the Cape Verde Islands were Portuguese and that they were Nimrod aircraft; to which the response was, "Oh, I didn't know the Portuguese had Nimrods!" I didn't bother to enlighten him.

While the aircraft was being refuelled, we all got out for a leg stretch on the airfield and, in a moment of light relief, the Princess of Wales grabbed my RAF hat and put it on. "How do I look?" she asked. The answer, of course, was fantastic, and I only wish I had a photograph of her wearing it.

On we went to Brazil. Meanwhile, with its limited range, The Queen's Flight BAe 146 had gone out the only way it could have – via Iceland, Newfoundland, New York, Bermuda and Barbados, before getting to Brazil. On arrival, they then checked round the Royal party route to ensure that all the safety aspects were in place and that all the ground handling facilities were ready. That is normal procedure in out-of-the-ordinary places, and it has been found that that sort of attention to detail pays handsome dividends in ensuring a smooth and trouble-free trip. In fact, that procedure underlines the operations of The Queen's Flight, which probably looks from the outside totally effortless and rather easy. What really happened was that we tried to give the impression of a swan, quietly and smoothly going about its business

– but underneath, as you may imagine, like a swan's legs, everyone was working like crazy. There is intense satisfaction in ensuring a successful operation, and we took great pride in everything that we did.

We landed at Brasilia, the new capital, and I went to the hotel in preparation for the busy programme ahead – at 0500hrs body time! The next morning, we were up early to get the aircraft ready, so I caught a lift down to breakfast. Ken Wharfe, the Princess's Personal Protection Officer, was in there, making eyes at me, while in the far corner was a figure in a tracksuit with a cap pulled down over the eyes. It giggled, of course. Whereupon I said, "It's OK, Ma'am. I'm trying to ignore you."

"Oh dear," she said. "Please don't make me laugh again."

On the return from breakfast, this time I found one of the new heavies guarding the lift, saying, "This lift is reserved."

I offered to help, but was ignored. And then the same figure reappeared and, much to the heavy's concern, said, "Come on, David, I'll give you a lift!" She had been swimming while we had been stuffing ourselves.

The first day's trip was to Carajás, up in the Amazon forest. I was not directly involved in the visit, so we took the opportunity to follow the Royal route and visited the largest open-cast iron-ore mine in the world. It was staggering to behold, sitting amidst the lush vegetation, but what impressed me perhaps most of all were the truly enormous dumper trucks which they use to take the ore to the railhead. Standing beside one, the width of the *tyre* – not the wheel, the *tyre* – was twice my height! Wow!

The next day we went to São Paulo, where TRH made a short visit, and then we continued to Rio de Janeiro, where we landed in the dark in the early evening. Rio at any time is a picture and, at night with all the lights, it appears to be straight out of a Walt Disney creation. There seems almost an undercurrent of excitement running through everything, but we had work to do. We put the aircraft to bed and then, because we had a relatively late start in the morning, we visited some of the nightlife.

On the recce, before the Royal party had arrived, the crew had left their hotel on the Copacabana to find a restaurant. Literally, within two hundred yards, they had been bounced by a local gang and had been fleeced of all their money. Most fortunately, the co-pilot, who had the crew's detachment money on him, kept his hand deep in his pocket and thus managed to save the drinking vouchers; but it was a very nasty experience. They went straight back to the hotel to gather their wits and then discussed the incident. There they were, five supposedly intelligent men, and yet they were unable to give a clear description of any one of their assailants; they could not agree on colour of shirts, type of shoes, colour of hair or anything. Moreover, they could not even agree how many there had been. Amazing! It had obviously been a very professional operation. So, on my first night in Rio, we went out with money in our socks and without jewellery or watches – and that was my reason for coming back so late!

I had been to Rio in the early 1960s and, on returning to my hotel after a lovely evening out with a beautiful lady, I discovered that I had a cut in the back of my suit. How did it get there? Hindsight is wonderful, but I often wonder if I had been lucky to escape a knife attack with what appeared to be a stab in the back. I don't think it was my beautiful lady friend.

The next day, we took the Prince of Wales to Victoria, a smaller city on the coast to the north-east of Rio, where he had a number of engagements before returning once more to Rio. On the following day, he was due to fly in the Tristar up to Belém at the mouth of the Amazon, for a conference on the environment, while I was to accompany the Princess down to the Argentinian border. We were to visit a place called Iguaçu, where she was to see the incredible waterfalls (the Foz de Iguaçu) which featured in the film *The Mission*.

She arrived at the aircraft bearing a small canvas holdall and, when I asked her what she was carrying, she told me it contained her jewels! Naturally, I asked why, and she replied, "I can't just leave them in the hotel!"

The Prince had taken half the household to Belém with him, while we had the remainder with us; there were no royal staff left in the hotel. Stupidly, I offered to look after the little holdall for her and, without much thought, I pushed it under my seat and forgot about it – as you do.

The flight down to Iguaçu was about two hours, and, after about an hour, the Princess came back, knelt in the aisle beside me, and said, "Would you like to see my jewels?"

Wow! Would we? And so she opened this small grip and from within she produced the most wonderful selection of gems, the like of which I am unlikely to see again. It was all done so naturally and so nicely, with absolutely no side at all. Just a lovely, honest girl showing us some treasures in a simple way.

She started by producing the Spencer Tiara, which is literally wall-to-wall diamonds. It was the one she wore to get married in. And then out came that lovely teardrop pearl tiara. "This was Queen Victoria's and then Queen Mary's; it used to have a high front, but we've modified it to a lower profile and I think it's much nicer like this." And we passed them round! I asked her if it was uncomfortable. "Try it on!" she said.

Then, she went on, "This is a wedding present my husband gave me" – an exquisite emerald and diamond bracelet. "And this is a brooch the Queen Mother gave me" – an enormous oval sapphire about an inch across and two inches tall. "I don't like brooches," she said, "so I've had it made into this choker – what do you think?"

What did we think? The beautiful sapphire with seven rows of pearls. It looked fantastic. Next out was a set of exquisite aquamarine earrings, necklace and bracelet which had been given to her by the people of Brazil on her last visit; and so it went on. It really was an amazing experience and absolutely fascinating – with her quietly kneeling on the carpet in the aisle.

Naturally, with our handling all this wonderful jewellery, Ken Wharfe and I looked at each other a number of times. Eventually, this got too much for her and so she asked, "What are you doing, David?"

"Oh, it's nothing, Ma'am. It's just that Ken and I are considering doing a runner."

"You'll never get away with it," she said.

"Well," I said, "there's a chap down there called Ronnie Biggs who seems to know about this sort of thing! I'm sure he'd give us a hand! Anyway, it will simply be a question of opening the back door and jumping out."

"But you haven't got any parachutes!"

"Never mind, Ma'am. For this lot I'd be prepared to take the risk!" And then I said that surely these were far too valuable to be insured.

"Oh, no," she said. "They're insured."

"Ah," I said. "We can come to some sort of arrangement, then!" All great fun, but from then on, as you may imagine, I looked after that little bag as if my life depended on it – and it probably did!

The visit to the Iguaçu Falls was ostensibly private, but naturally the press saw a wonderful photo opportunity and were clamouring for the best shot. It was my first time in the firing line, as it were, in trail with the Princess, but I thought she handled them all quite superbly. She obviously had a very good rapport with them and, with a degree of bad grace, once they had their pictures, they let her get on with a private wander around the majestic scenery. We then had a stupendous private lunch before setting off back to Rio, where the weather forecast was supposed to be fine. However, as things turned out, this proved to be very far from the truth.

As we approached Rio overhead, completely un-forecast, the heavens suddenly darkened and, as if from nowhere, the most incredible storm erupted. We were literally thrown around the sky and, as luck would have it, such was the violence and ferocity of the ensuing downpour that both the city and the international airfields were closed for about an hour or more. Great sheets of lightning in the dark sky and hail battering at the airframe did nothing to persuade our passengers that all was well, so I set about preventing everyone being sick. I managed to give all the supporting cast some exercises to do which took their minds off the immediate problem; but, looking through to the Royal compartment, all I could see was the Press Secretary, sitting opposite the Princess of Wales, going greener and greener. Patently, it was time for action if we were to avoid a disaster.

It was too dangerous to walk, such was the violence of the turbulence, so I crawled up to the Princess to see if she was all right. She immediately turned to me and said, "It's all right, David. There's no need to kneel to me!'"

"No, Ma'am," I replied, "I am not kneeling to you. I was born in India and I'm facing East." Happily, that exchange broke the ice and the atmosphere improved from one of imminent disaster.

Eventually, we landed at the international airport, but, because we had been expected at the city airport, all the transport was at the wrong place. To compound matters, many of the streets were badly flooded and the usual rush-hour turmoil did nothing to help. So, there we sat, in the very warm and humid night, with great glops of rain quietly soaking my uniform while I tried to arrange a police guard. Then, there being nothing better to do, we had a much-needed drink.

I am pleased to say that the BAe 146 airframe survived the ordeal intact, but we had lost all the red paint from the leading edge of the tailplane. Naturally, the boys got to work on it to restore the aircraft to its pristine state, but it had been quite an eventful trip, one way and another.

The next day, we flew the Princess of Wales and her party north to Belém via Brasilia. For the first time on the tour we had no 'outsiders' on board, so we could just be ordinary, and it was a nice and relaxed trip before we met up with the Prince of Wales and his party and boarded the Tristar for the trip back to Heathrow. I was, as you may imagine, quite grateful to hand over the Princess's jewels to someone else for safe-keeping.

My last major tour with the Princess of Wales was also her first one on her own. It was to be five days in Pakistan, for which we once more needed the BAe 146 for in-country flying. We flew out to Muscat by civil air.

For this, we booked the Club Class section of the scheduled aircraft so that we could keep a secure eye on the party. The British Airways staff were excellent and it was a very easy, if long, transit.

We set off the next day in the 146 and landed at Islamabad, the new capital of Pakistan, where the Princess was met with garlands, red carpets and all the local hierarchy. After the Princess went off, the boys sorted out the luggage and put the aircraft to bed. I was then approached by a few Pakistani officers with the winning line, "I say, old boy, why don't we nip up to the Club and have a *chota peg* [a little drink]?" Truly wonderful! I was transported back to the days of the British Raj. Their officers were incredibly smart, with knife-edged creases in their immaculate khaki uniforms, standing around whacking their swagger sticks against their legs and saying, "Damned fine, what?" Most of them had bristling moustaches, straight out of our time in India. Sadly, I was unable to accept the invitation to the Club as we made preparations for the next day's flying, which involved only the crew on a recce sortie for later in the programme. We were to visit Chitral, right up in the Hindu Kush in the top right-hand corner of Pakistan and near to the Afghan border. Because the flight was very much out of the ordinary on the edge of the Himalaya range, it was necessary to prove that all would be well for the trip proper later in the programme.

We started the day at 0530 because we had been given the offer of nine holes of golf, and it was the only time we had available on the trip. It was beautifully hot, with a heavy dew, and just what we needed to set us up for the day. All those amazing cooking smells drifting over the course first thing in the morning. It was a real reminder of my time in India as a young boy. It was also a beautiful day for flying, and we were spellbound by the amazing views of the Himalaya mountains with their tops covered in snow. The descent into Chitral itself was really spectacular, with mountain walls either side of us as we dropped down into the valley.

On arrival, for our benefit as well as for the benefit of the Chitralis, the Princess's Private Secretary, Patrick Jephson, and I followed the Princess's programme so that they could practise what they wanted to get perfect for the visit proper. It was fascinating to see round the tiny hillside town and then to see the Chitrali Scouts dancing. Wonderful colourful uniforms flashing in the sunshine in the Governor's garden, with the amazing backdrop of the beautiful snow-capped mountain of Tirich Mir looking down the valley from twenty-five thousand feet. Really lovely.

On the following day, we took the Princess of Wales to Lahore, where she was met by a simply vast crowd, most of them armed with flower petals. There was also the most incredible noise, with the crowd being whipped into a frenzy with over-modulated shouts of "Pakistan-Britannia" from the loudspeaker system. In fact, the crowd was so large that we became alarmed for Diana's safety as the cars tried to get out in the press of humanity.

Ken Wharfe held on to one door of her car while I was inveigled into becoming a bodyguard, walking alongside the Princess's car and holding on to the other door handle for about half a mile until we were clear of the crowds. It wasn't threatening, but, with the enormous press of humanity, it was a sensible precaution. But it was a fantastic welcome and the note in my diary says, 'Shambles and glorious chaos!'

We then took the opportunity to see a part of Lahore, which was on the Princess's itinerary, though we took care to ensure that we were never anywhere near where she might be. We went round the vast mosque and then the castle, all the while battling with the wonderfully indifferent driving conditions. Rickshaws, trishaws, Lambretta-powered two-man Tuk-Tuk taxis, vast colourful lorries, police vehicles (invariably with their sirens going) and bullocks, all vie for road space – usually with at least a millimetre to spare on either side!

We then returned to get the aircraft ready for the off, while the enormous crowd reassembled amidst great excitement. Everything went well, though the Princess looked a little tired, having been out in that incredibly hot city all day. Once more, we were surrounded by vast crowds, still chanting "Pakistan-Britannia." Thankfully, all was well, and away we went. Then, much as happened during the tour in Brazil, the weather took a marked turn for the worse and great thunderclouds built up. There was a really serious deterioration, and then the heavens opened over Islamabad, where we were headed. In torrential rain, the visibility was reduced to ten metres and aircraft on the ground suffered structural damage. So, we headed straight back to Islamabad and put the aircraft safely on the ground. Meanwhile, outside on the dispersal, we had wonderful scenes of order and disorder while all the local dignitaries tried to get themselves back into a receiving line! Indeed, great efforts were made to recall the crowd! I had a long chat with the Princess of Wales and all she wanted to do was to stay put on the aircraft. So, I was dispatched to undo all that was being arranged on the ground.

Meanwhile, the Press gathered once more, sniffing a Royal disaster story. The Press Secretary tried to explain to them what was going on, but merely dug himself a deep hole, so I offered to help. I explained what had happened and all about the weather suddenly developing into unstable cloud and torrential downpour. I also pointed out that we had no business flying in those conditions when there was a more logical and safer place to be. Our business was to ensure the safe and timely arrival of members of the Royal Family, with the emphasis very much on safety. Thus, in an effort to avoid a repetition of what had happened in Brazil, here we were, safely on the ground, and here we would stay until it cleared up in Islamabad. No, the Princess was fine. In fact, she was now sleeping after a long, hot day and she would not be coming off the aircraft. I then left the Press and rushed back to the aircraft, where, quite clearly in the darkening evening, I could see through the window the

Princess playing cards with the boys! So, I had to ask her to draw the curtains!

As an afternote, it was interesting to see how the press reacted to that little incident – and it really was no more than that. 'Diana in Air Drama' ran the headlines. And this was followed by such phrases as, 'Group Captain David Greenway left the controls to reassure the Princess of Wales that all was well. A monsoon had erupted over Islamabad, so the Group Captain told the Princess that they were returning to Lahore. "The safety of the Royal Family is our business," he said.' There were other half-truths, but sadly there was no mention of dashing or gallant!

Meanwhile, in the aircraft, I was coming under severe pressure from the accompanying British High Commissioner, who had an important dinner party that night. Together with the Princess, he had the Prime Minister dining with him, as well as many other VIPs. He kept pressing and pressing in an effort to make me decide to leave; but, with the Princess's blessing, I stonewalled – thus keeping the pressure off the aircraft captain, whose ultimate decision as to when we might fly it would be. The High Commissioner demanded to know why, now that it had presumably stopped raining in Islamabad, we could not set off straight away. I pointed out that we had yet to confirm this, but I was more interested in what structural damage the airfield had sustained. For instance, had the airfield lights been damaged? Naturally, he was unable to tell us, so he went away to cancel the dinner party, much to the relief of the Princess, who had already had a long and tiring day.

The next day, we were due to set off for a visit to Peshawar, but the weather was initially quite nasty. Therefore, we delayed the flight and I asked the Princess to wait, not in the VIP Lounge as one might expect, but in the VVIP Lounge! Incidentally, I had great delight in watching the Pakistani authorities clearing the car park before the Princess's arrival. After much shouting and gesticulating, a forklift truck was brought in and the cars were simply hoicked out of the way! They don't muck about in Pakistan! Eventually, the conditions improved and we set off, having possibly jeopardised the programme for the day.

Amongst other engagements, the highlight of the first part was to be a visit to the Khyber Pass. The Princess's programme was rejigged to allow her to go, but we were told that it was out of the question for the crew to make a visit. Apparently, the necessary clearances had not been obtained, and that was the end of the matter. They had arranged, instead, for us to visit a local museum which was just as good. Not for us, it wasn't! I then had a little sulk and talked quite firmly to a number of high-ranking people and, lo and behold, all was sweetness and light. I almost had to stand on a brigadier's shoes as I explained that we were going to the Khyber Pass, before he relented. There was, naturally, no staff car to take us; so, as per normal procedures, a Volvo Estate was purloined from the car pound so that we could be properly carried! The police have considerable powers in Pakistan.

So we made this lightning dash to the pass, twenty-odd miles each way, stopping only to collect some guards who chose to travel behind us, using a confiscated pick-up truck! It was, of course, absolutely fascinating to see. Barren and rocky hills either side of the road, with many lookout posts to ensure that all remained clear. What appeared to be tribesmen were perched on every piece of high ground, passing on information long before we got anywhere near our destination. Carved into the hillside, alongside the Pass, are regimental badges from all the regiments who have served there in the past; the place reeks of history. We pressed on to the Afghan border and spent only five minutes looking down into Afghanistan (avoiding the Princess and her party), and then set off back to Peshawar. The guards who cover the Pass proper are incredibly impressive, with their coloured *pugree*s or turbans and smart sashes. The Pakistani officers are equally impressive. They are all immaculately turned out, with bristling moustaches and gleaming Sam Brownes. It hardly seems necessary to say that they all whack their legs with their swagger sticks. Ah, the legacy of the Indian Army! It was a fascinating experience, somewhat marred on our drive into the outskirts of Peshawar when, with the streets full of wandering Pakistanis, bullocks, goats and assorted traffic, most incongruously we saw the local branch of Marks and Spencer, green sign and all!

The next day, once more, the weather was suspect; so, to their chagrin, the accompanying Press entourage were unable to follow us and the Princess up to the top right-hand corner of Pakistan. However, we thought that, with our better navigation equipment, we might at least have an attempt at getting into Chitral for the Princess's visit. Again, having already seen the place, I briefed the Press on what they might have seen, showing them photographs of Tirich Mir just to depress them! Naturally, they were missing out on a wonderful photo opportunity, although, in an effort to appease them, we actually took a Press cameraman with us, so they all shared his photographs.

Most fortunately, as we approached Chitral, the weather relented and we were able to let down into the valley in complete safety. There were jagged and vicious-looking hills either side of us as we descended to the tiny airfield below. However, much to our sadness, cloud cover prevented the Princess from seeing the place in its full glory, although, as one might imagine, it was a lovely visit by any stretch of the imagination.

To our great pleasure, the Princess of Wales had agreed to have a photograph taken with the crew as a memento of the tour, and it was planned to take it at Chitral. We were, therefore, absolutely delighted when she returned from the town, not only wearing a beautiful white woollen coat which the Scouts had given her, but also a white woollen Chitrali Scout's head-dress. She looked fantastic; but, to cap it all, in the Land Rover with her, she had four small children in colourful local dress sitting on her knee. Naturally, they were invited to be in the group photo as well. As you may imagine, it made a lovely photograph which I treasure; a reminder of a very happy tour.

On the final day, The Queen's Flight crew flew the BAe 146 back to Benson with many stops in between, while the Princess's party travelled in the top bubble of the scheduled Boeing 747 – so we had some privacy away from the regular passengers. After such a busy programme, we spent the first few hours catching up on some much-needed sleep before we started to relax. Again, the in-flight movies helped to pass the time, but the highlight was undoubtedly to see Sam McKnight, the Princess of Wales's hairdresser, parading around in his newly-purchased bright yellow yashmak – but wearing his dark glasses on the outside!

And so ended a marvellous and very happy visit, during which the Princess of Wales worked extremely hard and did an outstanding job. It was a real pleasure to have been included in her party and to have seen the excellent work that she did.

Apart from these major overseas trips, I also accompanied the Princess of Wales on many of her visits in the UK. It was always fun and amazing to see the effect she had on the crowds who came to see her. She had a wonderful presence and such a lovely touch, particularly with the elderly and the young. Of course, all the men were in love with her as well, but unquestionably, she lifted the spirits of everyone who saw her. She really was a star and, to us outsiders, she was a real asset to the Royal Family. We, on the outside, were not aware of the awful breakdown of her marriage, but even with this going on in her background, she continued to shine.

A number of people have asked me if I knew of the dreadful time she must have been going through when I was with her, but the honest answer is that I did not. On a couple of helicopter visits I flew with her, I saw that she had been crying. All I wanted to do was to give her a big hug; but, of course, I couldn't. But, despite the downs, she still put in really excellent performances.

Quite a few of my trips with the Princess of Wales were noteworthy. I was with her when she took Prince Harry on his first official public outing when they visited RAF Wittering, near Peterborough. It was amazing, accompanying that tiny little boy, now well over six feet tall, beating lumps out of people on the polo field and now living in the USA. He was, of course, a helicopter pilot in the Army, and is now a father himself. He was very well behaved on this occasion, as, indeed, was Prince William when I took the Prince and Princess of Wales to Cardiff for William's first official engagement on St David's Day. There was a lovely moment afterwards when I said that I had seen them on my little television which I always carried. I said that I thought that Prince William had behaved beautifully. "That's nice," she said. "But please don't tell him. I don't want him to get big-headed!"

On a different visit, I was flying with Diana and the two boys. William was beautifully behaved, sitting there reading his book, while Harry was behaving like a proper little red-head, bouncing on all the seats, sticking his tongue out and generally being an awful nuisance.

Diana called to me and said, "Pssssttt!"

"Yes, Ma'am?" I said.

"I think I had them in the right order, didn't I?"

Lovely!

I used to pass her funnies for the boys and they, in turn, would pass some to me. Silly things like, 'What do you call a deer with no eyes?' *No idea.* 'What do you call a deer with no eyes and no legs?' *Still no idea.* 'Where do you find a dog with no legs?' *Exactly where you left him!* And one more I know she would have loved. 'What do you call a Camel with three humps?' *Pregnant.*

The Pakistan trip was my last major overseas visit, but there was one more treat in store. I left The Queen's Flight on 23 November 1991, and, shortly afterwards, I received an invitation to a farewell dinner which was to be given for me by the Princess of Wales – to thank me for all that I had done for her. If one has to leave a job like that, I cannot think of a better way. It really was a great honour for me, because she had gathered all her team around her to see me off. The dinner was held in San Lorenzo's in Beauchamp Place, and we had a private room for the occasion. It was, as you may imagine, a lovely evening, but the *pièce de resistance* was the pudding, brought in in the shape of a BAe 146 – with 'David' written on it. Words are not really sufficient to describe my gratitude, but all I can say is, what a super lady she was to work for. Now *that's* what I call caring management!

For two years I led what I suppose must have been an unreal existence. I had had an amazing task, and it was the greatest fun. I suppose it was also quite a responsibility. Sadly, shortly after I left the job, the whole edifice seemed to come apart at the seams – but I don't think it was my fault.

But perhaps the one saving grace, after all the sadness in the aftermath of the shambles of their marriage, is the fact that Diana will never grow old. She won't ever grow all wrinkly and grey-haired like the rest of us. She will always be that lovely girl that we all knew and loved. Oh dear. What a tragedy and what a waste.

I have, perhaps, not really said enough about the members of The Queen's Flight. To a man and woman, the ground crew were quite simply outstanding. They were all volunteers and they worked day and night, if it was needed, so that we could unfailingly carry members of the Royal Family when required. There was, naturally, great pride in the job, and I was conscious of being part of an élite organisation. They were always smart, unfailingly cheerful and a real credit to the Service. We always carried members of the ground crew with us, and they never failed to fix problems as they arose. It was also a joy to go overseas with them.

The aircrew, too, were excellent. All were highly experienced and were very professional in their jobs. Each crew was nominally allocated to a member of the Royal Family, mainly on the grounds of continuity, so that the passengers were comfortable, knowing their crew. Sometimes, with so many family members, it wasn't possible to keep to the usual crew for all their flying; but, by and large, it all worked out happily. There were eight aircraft captains on the Flight, all using the Kitty call sign. CO of The Queen's Flight (call sign Kitty 1) invariably flew with the Queen, while other crews were allocated (where possible) to a senior member of the Royal Family. When I was switched to fly with the Wales household, I flew the vast majority of my trips with Graham Laurie, who was Kitty 4 (also known as K4). Graham had an excellent young man, Buck Rogers, as his co-pilot, and, before one of the Defence Reviews, his navigator was Bob Shields. Sadly, navigators were withdrawn as an economy measure, but this made little difference. We all got on extremely well together and it really was a team effort across the board – including our ground crew. On top of that, because we always flew with the Princess of Wales, we had great rapport with Patrick Jephson, who was her Private Secretary, and with Ken Wharfe, who was her Personal Protection Officer. We were all working towards the one aim of looking after Diana, and I think we succeeded. Now that we have all retired, I am delighted to say that we meet up as regularly as we can and swap war stories, remembering that beautiful lady whom we all loved.

We are so lucky to have the Royal Family. The Queen did such a fantastic job for us all, and I, for one, am eternally grateful. In fact, all the Royal Family do a fantastic job, constantly hounded by the Press, so it must be so difficult for them just to be ordinary. Anything they do is immediately snapped up and invariably twisted to make a better story. How they have stood it, I know not, but it must be awful for them at times. Her Majesty worked tirelessly for us, as, indeed, did Prince Philip.

And, isn't it nice that we have William and Catherine coming along? They haven't put a foot wrong, and I am so glad that they seem to have the Press under control. Together with their lovely children, I believe the Royal Family is in good hands. Long may they all reign.

Chapter 45

Perks

One point worth bearing in mind is that, despite being a married man, as an ADC to the Queen I was always treated as a bachelor. The Ladies-in-Waiting were similarly treated as single people, because you simply cannot serve two masters at the same time. I had experience of this when I had been an ADC to a mere mortal in the 1960s, but this was a whole new ball game.

On the other hand, as members of The Queen's Flight, we were allowed a number of perks which, in the ordinary run of life, one might never have experienced. For instance, we were allowed to use the Royal Enclosure at Royal Ascot (which cost us quite a bit!). The Royal Family attended, and I have a lovely photograph (which appeared in *Hello!* magazine) of the Princess of Wales and the Duchess of York talking to me as they returned from the paddock.

Amongst other things, we were delighted to be invited to use the Queen's Box at the Royal Albert Hall (when it wasn't in use by the Royal Family) to attend a number of the BBC Promenade Concerts. They were lovely occasions, but it was also fun to see others craning to see if you were worth looking at!

We also attended a State Banquet in honour of President Mubarak of Egypt. To say we 'attended' is, in fact, a slight overstatement. We actually watched the proceedings from above the Ballroom – what is called 'Behind the Grille', because, quite literally, you look through a sort of wooden screen which is either side of the organ. All the members of the Royal Family attended, as well as members of the Cabinet and civic and military leaders. It was fascinating to see and really quite an experience – although it is actually rather boring just watching other people eat! But the choreography of how the meal was served and who sat where was interesting to see. There were some hundred and eighty people dining, so it was just a small gathering!

There is this lovely story which emerged during the Arab Spring, when the Egyptian President was overthrown. Apparently, David Cameron wrote to Mubarak and suggested he write a farewell letter to his people.

He replied, "Why? Where are they going?"

We were also very fortunate to be invited to attend a number of Royal Garden Parties at Buckingham Palace, which are lovely occasions where the great and the good get a chance to wander around the palace gardens and have afternoon tea. They also get a chance to see members of the Royal Family at close hand, and if they are lucky, they get to speak with them. I have been fortunate to meet several members of the family there, and was able to introduce them to my wife and children – or it may have been the other way round! Since leaving the RAF, we have been asked back a number of times, which is nice.

Also, when I was on The Queen's Flight, I received Christmas cards from the Wales family, which I treasure; lovely photographs of the Prince and Princess of Wales, with the boys growing up. Interestingly, when I sailed on Cunard's *Queen Elizabeth* in 2012, on board they were selling signed Royal Family Christmas cards for $3,000 a pop!

As I left The Queen's Flight, almost my last function was to attend the Buckingham Palace Christmas Dance, a lovely affair which took place in all the beautiful rooms of the palace. We had a marvellous meal and then lined the long corridor while all the members of the Royal Family came past and spoke to us. Again, it was nice to be able to introduce my wife and members of The Queen's Flight to them and to chat with them. We danced to the music played by the Joe Loss Big Band. It was quite a night.

Chapter 46

After the Lord Mayor's Show

For my last posting in the RAF, I was sent to RAF Brampton, in Huntingdonshire. This was a huge change from effectively constantly being in the spotlight, to my reverting to being a staff officer. I was to be in charge of Plans and Budgets in the Headquarters of the RAF's Training Group. And, yet again, what did I know about it all? Virtually nothing, so once more I had a steep learning curve. But, as with most jobs in the RAF, it was about people; so, while it was mainly about money and plans, we also had great fun, with wonderful people around me. In particular, I had two quite excellent wing commanders who looked after me so I didn't flounder around too much. Thankfully, they kept me on the straight and narrow.

The financial side of the job was an almost incessant battle with the Ministry of Defence Civil Service, who were trying to squeeze as much money as they could out of our budget. We were constantly being asked to offer up various aspects of our functions, while remaining a viable force. It was wearing in the extreme to battle away to justify our budget in order to meet the tasks placed upon us, and then, almost by return of post, to be asked to offer up something we needed in order to cut our costs yet again. Matters were not helped by 'our masters in the Ministry' invariably demanding answers at extremely short notice, and sometimes one wondered if they did this out of spite.

We were responsible for the costings of all RAF Training Command, which was bad enough, but somehow we were also responsible for the finances of the Red Arrows, so our budget was slightly tilted. The Red Arrows are not a function of RAF Training. They are simply a recruiting tool and a means of keeping the RAF in the public eye. However, whenever we were asked to offer cuts to our budget, we often suggested the Reds could be dispensed with – but this was always rejected!

All good things must come to an end, and so, after thirty-seven years of wonderful jobs and fun, I left the RAF in 1994. I was oh so lucky to serve when I did. The Services have been greatly reduced in number over the recent past, and I do not believe there is now much room for personal initiative. Everything seems to be computer-controlled, such that you can now be debriefed on anything which occurred in a sortie by someone who wasn't even there. We had so much freedom in my time (awful phrase), and, while we were occasionally brought to high states of readiness, we never actually went to war. In my case, we were constantly challenging the Soviet threat, facing down their aircraft, ships and submarines.

At times, it was almost like a game; but, in fact, it was deadly serious. It can be roughly summed up by knowing that we knew what they were up to and they knew that we knew what they were up to. It was a sort of Mexican stand-off, with both sides probing each other to ensure that nothing untoward happened.

Chapter 47

Wonderful People

After I retired from the RAF, I started speaking on cruise ships, which kept me on my toes and off the streets. I love the sound of laughter, so it has been great fun entertaining the passengers with my awful stories. Naturally, I have spoken about the fun I had with the Royal Family, but I have also spoken about recent British and European history, having compiled some twenty talks, which I have found fascinating – but I would say that, wouldn't I? But they seem to like what I say and, thus far, we have been on over fifty cruises, which is not a bad way to retire. We have, as a result, been all over the world, so we have been very lucky. More to the point, the vast majority of them have been free, which is a huge plus. I don't like having to pay for cruises. People sometimes ask me if I have to change my talks to suit a particular audience, but I usually say that it is easier for me to change my audience.

I have also helped people to record their memoirs on CD, which has been the greatest fun. As I tell them, you simply cannot record your own memoirs, just talking into a microphone. There is no feed-back, no laughter and no fun, and the whole thing seems to me to be boring – rather like talking to a dead blanket. It is so much better to have a conversation about your life, and I have found it a very enjoyable experience. We spend much of the time laughing and, as a result, my subjects come across as themselves, which is a lovely thing to pass on down your family. As a result of this, I have met so many fascinating people who told me some lovely stories. These are some of the gems I have gathered over the years.

I must start, however, with a tale my father told me from many years ago, when he talked about training the lovely Gurkhas. It was time to teach them how to jump out of an aircraft. There was great consternation that they were being asked to jump from two thousand feet. "Oh, Sahib, we cannot jump from two thousand feet. It is much too high. Can we please start at five hundred feet?"

The answer was, "Don't be silly. From five hundred feet, your parachute will not have time to open."

"Oh," was the response. "We are to have parachutes, are we?" Oh, the faith the Gurkhas put in their British officers.

I was talking to a ninety-year-old lady who was born in 1909. I said, "You must have been about five years old when the First World War broke out, so how did you get around? I mean, it was too early for cars, wasn't it?"

"Oh, no," she said. "We had no means of conveyance."

I found that amazing, because she had dropped right back into the vernacular of the day! When was the last time you heard anyone talking about 'means of conveyance'?

Another thing she told me about was her early working life. When she was nineteen or twenty, she went to work as secretary to a very high-powered chap in the South of England. He was apparently happily married, but, unfortunately, he took a shine to her – which was damned bad form, what? So, she was immediately withdrawn from his service – and quite right, too.

A bit later, she became 'engaged to be married', as they said in those days. And, the fact that she was now engaged to be married meant that it was now perfectly all right for her to go back and work for this bounder because, again as they used to say in those times, she was effectively 'orff limits'. Can you imagine that happening in the present day? Amazing! What a wonderful look into the more genteel ways of yesteryear.

We had a retired major called Esmond (better known as Es) in our village, who was a lovely countryman. He had had a pretty harrowing time at the beginning of the Second World War. He had been involved in the fighting around Ypres in 1940 and, during one particularly unpleasant barrage, a guardsman near him was felled by a German shell. Es could see that the man was very seriously wounded, but saw that he was trying to say something. He stooped and asked, "Can I help you?"

"Permission to speak, sir?" asked the guardsman.

"Of course, old boy. Go ahead."

"Excuse me, sir," said the guardsman. "Could I have a cigarette, please, sir?"

Before Es could get his cigarettes out, the guardsman died. Unbelievable discipline.

My Uncle Joe (who owned *the* jewellers in Aberdeen) came to stay with us, and Es was invited to join us. Having been introduced to each other, they realised that they had met before. It took them some time to work out where. They then realised that they had both been in the same POW camp during the war. Joe remembered that he thought it incongruous to be lectured on how to look after your partridges, while Es found it odd to be told how to look after his jewellery.

I used to play golf with a delightful judge who, at one point, had served in Ghana. He told me this wonderful story. As was usual in the far-flung corners of the Commonwealth, a number of important dinner parties were held by the Great and the Good. On this occasion, the British High Commissioner decided to have a dinner party and, naturally, he invited all the top brass, including the President. On the appointed evening, everyone turned up for the dinner party – except the President. The meal was therefore delayed, by first half an hour and then by an hour, while guests were given more drinks as they waited in vain. Eventually, when the dinner had almost turned to charcoal, they went ahead with the meal, but there was, naturally, something of a dampener on the proceedings. The next morning, the ADC was dispatched to find out what was going on. The obvious inference was that he, as the lowest on the totem pole, had made some sort of nonsense with the invitations, so he went to see his opposite number at the palace. He started rather nervously. "Can you please tell me if the President got an invitation to dine with His Excellency last night?"

He was somewhat taken aback by the response of, "Why don't you ask him yourself?" as he was pushed into the inner sanctum.

There, in front of him, behind a huge desk, was the leader of this nation. "I'm very sorry to trouble you, sir," he said. "But I wonder if I could ask you a rather difficult question? Did you by any chance get an invitation to dine with His Excellency last night?"

"Oh, yes," said the President.

Thankful that it hadn't been his mistake, the ADC then asked, "I'm afraid that this is rather embarrassing, sir, but did you by any chance *accept* the invitation to dinner?"

"Oh, yes, yes. I accepted."

Again, the ADC breathed a sigh of relief. And then, "I'm very sorry, sir, but you didn't come to the dinner."

"No, no. I didn't come."

"Sir, I'm very sorry to ask this question, but would you mind telling my why you didn't come?"

"Oh, yes," said the President. "I wasn't hungry!"

I had a lovely friend called Vic, who had a wonderful Hampshire burr, having lived in the county all his life. He had a somewhat hazardous war in North Africa and Italy, but naturally his early training days were somewhat different. After a fair amount of 'square bashing', they were sent on an initiative exercise. They were transported by three-ton truck to the darkest reaches of the countryside. They were then told to get off and to make their way as best they could to the rendezvous, which was some miles away. It was a freezing cold night and no one really knew what to do, so they decided to wait for the dawn in the hopes of thumbing a lift. Some recruits virtually gave up and sat on the roadside, getting colder and colder, but others knew better. As Vic said, "Them Lunnon boys was useless. They just sat there and shivered 'cause they didn't know what to do. It was wet on the ground as well, which didn't help. But us country bumpkins knew what it was all about. We just walked into the nearest field and kicked the cows until they stood up. Then we lay down on the lovely warm, dry ground." Initiative test? Brilliant!

In 1968, I was driving my father-in-law around East Anglia. He was looking at various villages and houses to see whether he wanted to move down from Manchester. We called in at a pub for some lunch and there, at the corner of the bar, was one of those wonderful old boys who just burble along, snapping out the repartee without a care in the world. For no apparent reason, he suddenly started telling us about his day. "Well," he said, "there I was in the cemetery this morning, scything away and thinking what a lovely day it was, when this big American car pulled up at the gate. Out got this huge man with a Stetson on his head. He leant on the wall for a bit and then he said, 'That's one big graveyard you have there. How many dead in there?' 'Well,' I said, 'I've been here all morning and I haven't seen anyone move, so I reckon they all are.'"

In 1989, when the situation in Northern Ireland was still tense, the Royal Air Force decided to change its smart white trim on its VIP communications aircraft for something which would be more difficult to hit with a missile. The selected colour was a sort of dull, non-reflective, battleship grey so that the aircraft would be more difficult to see. Margaret Thatcher, then Prime Minister, often used a BAe 125 of No 32 Squadron, at Royal Air Force Northolt, to get about the country. On this occasion, it was a miserable day, with rain cascading down; so, on arrival by car, she put up her umbrella, lowered her head and got into the aircraft as fast as possible. For the return to London, the weather had improved, so she was able to see the aircraft clearly for the first time. Horrified, she turned to the crew member who was waiting for her at the aircraft steps and said, "Is this something we have borrowed from industry for the day?"

"No, Prime Minister," said the unfortunate man in the headlights. "It's the new colour scheme for the VIP communications fleet for the Royal Air Force."

"Hrrmph," she said. "No, it isn't!"

Following his tour at SHAPE, Phil Wilkinson went on to Berlin to command RAF Gatow. He was there when the Berlin Wall came down in November 1989. Before that momentous event, Phil and his wife Angie used occasionally to go shopping in East Berlin. They bought crystal very cheaply from a little old lady in the East German Sector. After the wall fell, Angie went to see the lady and said, "Isn't it wonderful news?"

She got the response, "I don't believe it. I just don't believe it."

"But you are free now," said Angie. "What don't you believe?"

The lady replied, "I thought that you came to buy crystal from me because you couldn't get it in the West!" Amazing.

John was a lovely man, full of life and laughter, who I met many years ago. He was born with a silver spoon in his mouth, and this consequently made his observations on things around him all the more enjoyable. His opening phrase to me was, "Of course, my grandmother owned Hever Castle. She didn't much care for it and it wasn't any good for breeding cattle, so she sold it to the Astors and we moved north!" Wonderful! During the First

World War, the family lived in a big house with lots of servants. There was no class-consciousness and, in the holidays, John played happily with the servants' children; they all got on extremely well together. When the dinner bell rang, John went into the big house to dine with his parents, while the other children went to the scullery for their meals. John knew all the staff by their Christian names, and it was a happy childhood. When the cook retired, Rose took over the position, so John was a bit surprised when he greeted her the next morning with, "Hello, Rose. How are you today?"

She replied, "Master John. It's *Cook* to you now, if you please." The pecking order below stairs was just as important as that anywhere else!

Pam was a star. She was eighty-eight years old when I met her. She had had an incredible life and had travelled all over the world, often following her husband with her children on the hip. At one stage, determined to follow her husband, she made her way from Africa to the Northwest Frontier of India. She arrived in Quetta, when her husband was at the staff college, but he then went off to fight the Japanese in Malaya, so Pam stayed behind and ran the catering for the Staff College. She lived in a bungalow and naturally, in those days, the plumbing arrangements were somewhat primitive. One day, while seated on the thunderbox, she was horrified to hear the trap behind her being opened by the sweeper boy. "Very sorry, memsahib!" he cried.

"How did you know it was me?" she called.

"No balls, memsahib!" was the brilliant response.

On her own, Pam had travelled out to Africa and then all across it. She had travelled to India and then went on to Singapore and then back to Athens. She was a real tigress and an absolute star. Where would we be without ladies like her?

I was talking to the lovely Patience Tully, mother of Sir Mark Tully, the former BBC Delhi correspondent. We were going to talk about her life in India. "Have you got anything I can look at?" I asked.

"Oh, yes," she said. "This is an account my grandmother wrote of how she escaped the Indian Mutiny in 1857!" Wow! What a find! And then she went on, "And this is another write-up a friend of mine did about our journey home from India in 1945." Along the top of the document she had written, 'Lorna Boulton's description of our journey home.'

"Lorna Boulton?" I asked. "Wasn't she married to Walter Boulton?"

"Good heavens!" she said. "How on earth do you know that?"

"He was my godfather!" I said. Incredible, these coincidences.

Richard was another chap I met. Aged twenty, he went to the Royal Military Academy Sandhurst in 1950. In common with most people who had lived under rationing both during and after the war, he was very much on the thin side. He was also quite tall, so he looked a bit like a beanstalk. This seemed to upset the Sandhurst authorities, so they decided to try to put some meat on his bones. He was taken aside and told that, with immediate effect, he was on the Milk Parade. The Milk Parade was held every day at six a.m. ("0600 hours to you, sir!") outside the gymnasium at Sandhurst. A number of pale and slender youths were brought to attention in their gym kit and then were made to drink two pints of milk, under strict supervision to ensure that every drop was consumed. This was meant to fill them out and thus make them more presentable as officers. Richard manfully carried out this onerous task; but, try as he might, he signally failed to put on any weight whatsoever. Eventually, having tried his best for two months, he was taken aside by the RSM to be told, "Sir, you have failed the Milk Parade. You are dismissed!" Ignominy! What a wonderful thought! How can you fail a Milk Parade?

As the time to leave Sandhurst drew near, naturally there was much practising for the great Passing Out Parade. This is when the senior entry 'passes off' the parade ground for the last time and marches up the ancient steps of Old College in accordance with tradition. Sadly, as Richard was about to pass out, King George VI died, so all official parades and events were cancelled while the nation went into mourning. Consequently, Richard and his entry uniquely left Sandhurst with no pomp or ceremony to join their new regiments and corps. No drill, no fanfare, no bands playing, nothing. All rather sad, really. Happily, in 2002, they held a fiftieth anniversary reunion of Richard's entry at Sandhurst. Not surprisingly, having bored each other silly with their war stories, the subject of not having actually passed out came up. Thus, they sought the Commandant's permission to pass out, albeit fifty years late. And so it was that a group of seventy-year-old men, all smartly turned out with rolled umbrellas and bowler hats, marched up the steps of Old College – and into history. As they said, "Better late than never!"

I met a lovely lady called Judith, who lived in Cumbria. At the beginning of the war, she met Geoff, a pilot in the RAF who, in May 1940, was shot down and taken prisoner by the Germans. They kept in touch by infrequent, censored letters, so she knew that Geoff was safe. She joined the Auxiliary Territorial Service (ATS) for the duration of hostilities. Geoff escaped from Stalag Luft III three times, but, following the Great Escape and the subsequent murder of fifty escapers in March 1944, a message from London reached them to say that there must be no more attempts to escape from the camp. Thus, they continued in captivity until, in 1945, the Germans realised that the game was up and marched the prisoners out of the camp. Geoff and Rupert Davies, the actor who later became famous as *Maigret* on television, teamed up and made themselves a trolley on which to take essential items – and then they were marched across Germany for three months, sleeping where they could, mostly outside in the continental winter. Eventually, they got to Lüneburg Heath, while the guards tried to ingratiate themselves against the day when the Allies would be in control. The bombing of Germany was fearsome, and it was thought that the last POWs might turn out to be hostages. However, one night the guards just melted away and the POWs found themselves on their own. A number of them decided to set off to find the front line, but Geoff and Rupert Davies came across a Mercedes staff car which was parked outside a vacated enemy HQ. The key was in the ignition, so they requisitioned it and headed West. They first came across the Americans, who gleefully waved them on their way, even providing fuel for their onward journey. Eventually, they got to the British line, only to be stopped by British military police. "Oy! What do you think you're doin'? You aren't entitled to a staff car. Get out!" It was nice to be back in the land of sanity again! Eventually, they were flown to Antwerp and then home, where Geoff was sent to the Midlands. Judith, meanwhile, had had a very busy war and, in the spring of 1945, she was serving at Eastern Command HQ, near Maidstone, in Kent. She had been hoping to hear that Geoff was safe and, when the telephone rang on 2nd May, she leapt for joy.

"Hello, darling," he said. "I'm back."

"Oh, gosh! Where are you?"

"I'm at RAF Cosford."

"Right," said Judith. "I'll come up and see you straight away."

"I'm afraid they won't allow you anywhere near us. We've all got to be debriefed and so on. But I'll come up to London and see you at the weekend."

"Where shall we meet, darling?" she asked.

"Oh," said Geoff. "In the usual place."

"Where on earth is that?" she asked.

"Under the clock at Victoria." He must have been dreaming of that moment for years and, every time I tell that story, I get tingles at the back of my neck. Real *Morning Departure* stuff.

There is a footnote to this story. It is with much sadness that I have to report the removal of the clock at Victoria. Have they no sense of history? Where do people meet nowadays?

I met this lovely chap who was an artist. John painted postage stamps for any nation who wanted them. Apparently, he had a worldwide reputation, and one day he had a phone call from a firm called Microsoft. They asked if he could send them some samples of his work. John duly did and was then surprised to receive a letter from Microsoft saying, 'Thank you very much. We would like to order eighty paintings.'

John was a bit of a Luddite and did everything by snail mail; so, in order to find out what was going on, he went to see his friend, who was a bit more worldly-wise, and said, "Have you heard of a firm called Microsoft? Are they good for the money?"

His friend managed to reassure him that all was well, so John duly completed his order. He then wrote to Microsoft and told them that his paintings were ready. They asked him if he could kindly bring the paintings over to them. Happily, they also sent him the air tickets, which surprised him.

When he got to the United States, John was taken to the Microsoft headquarters. They wined and dined him and said that they thought his paintings were wonderful. During lunch, John confessed his ignorance about Microsoft and told his story about how he had checked out the company with his friend to see whether they were good for the money. The chairman nearly fell off her seat laughing and said, "Oh, how wonderful! Just wait till I tell Bill."

And John said, "Bill who?"

Susan was a lovely lady who lived in our village. She had an amazing story. She went to the Godolphin School in Salisbury and, when she was revising for the School Certificate, she used to lie out on the grass and watch the Battle of Britain being fought in the sky above. She decided that she didn't want to go to university, and opted instead to go to Secretarial College, where she did the two-year course in about nine months. She joined the ATS and was sent for a job interview in London. She could speak French quite well, but she said that she had no other particularly outstanding attributes. She had to report to the Passport Office and was then escorted up many flights of stairs by the porter, right up into the roof. They went over many buildings until she thinks she was over the Foreign Office. She was then interviewed in French by a major. Eventually, he asked how old she was and, when told that she was only seventeen, he said, "Oh, my dear, you are too young! Please go away and don't tell anyone about this." She was being interviewed as a possible Resistance worker, and was rather glad she didn't get involved in that.

In the ATS she had various jobs before she was sent to London to work at Eisenhower's headquarters, which were then at Bushey Park in West London. They lived in huts which were right across the other side of the camp from the headquarters, so she had a long walk to work. This was at the time of the buzz bombs, and it was by far the most frightening time she had. They were all very worried, being exposed for so long. But the best part was that she was now working in an American headquarters, so she had good food for the first time in ages! She then went down to Portsmouth to work at Eisenhower's new headquarters at Southwick House, high on the cliffs overlooking the sea. Glenn Miller was there then, and she spent the summer evenings listening to his band, before he was sadly killed. One good thing about being in Portsmouth was that she could quite easily hitch a lift home to Guildford. In those days, of course, young girls were quite safe doing that sort of thing, which, alas, is not the case today.

And then the time came to go over to France. She flew from Hayling Island in a Dakota which had no seats as such. On the way over, they apparently saw a Messerschmitt and were told to lie down on the floor of the aircraft – though what good that would have done if they'd been attacked she hadn't a clue!

In Normandy, she worked in the operations and plans branch and was responsible for producing the daily Sitreps (the situation reports) to keep everyone in touch with what was happening. She then moved on to Paris and then to Versailles, to where Eisenhower had moved his headquarters, and lived in the stables. She worked for a brigadier who was the Chief Planning Officer. He called her in one day to take some dictation and startled her by saying that he was going to outline the 'Plan for the retreat to England'! Susan was a bit taken aback by this news, but he explained that plans had to be written for every eventuality – just in case...

Susan then moved on to Rheims, where she lived in a school house. It was by then becoming obvious that they were close to the end and, on 6th May 1945, she was on duty. She was called to a room where there was a lot of coming and going. She was then told to type the German Surrender Document. She did the English and German versions, and there were French and Russian ones as well. The main document was actually very short, but there were lots of attachments. Of course, in those days they didn't have computers, but had to bash out the typing on those old, upright Imperial typewriters. Naturally, if a mistake was made, the whole document had to be started again. There was a great performance setting out the tables measuring exactly where the papers should be. And, because Susan had written the thing, she was then invited in and allowed to stand in the corner to watch while all the surrender documents were signed. She typed out the signal to say that the war was at an end, and then they all drank champagne out of mess tins! She had been on duty for twenty hours non-stop and so slept like a log afterwards. I expect the champagne helped as well.

She moved on to Frankfurt, to work at the Control Commission, where she worked in the Public Relations Information Services Control, which gave licences to newspapers and information services. You could only broadcast with a licence, and everything had to be de-Nazified. She shared a desk with a chap called Robert Maxwell, who she said was horrible even in those days! He was responsible for giving licences for publishing, and he worked on the principle that, "You may publish your book, but only with my firm in England." Despite her gentle nature, Susan was glad that Maxwell got his eventual comeuppance.

Susan then went to Berlin through the Russian zone. There were very few soldiers around before they actually got to Berlin, which was in a dreadful state. She worked in part of the university and they were welcomed by the

Berliners, who regarded the British as having saved them from the Russians. In fact, one Russian had been shot and was buried outside her door. There were terrible stories of what they had done. For example, they got all the people out of an area, made the women and children stand beside the road and forced all the men to lie down in the road. They then drove tanks over the men while their families watched.

It was in Berlin that she met Basil (who worked for the Head of the Economic Division), and they got married. Her parents wanted her to get married in England, but all their friends were in Berlin, so they got married there. The Americans gave them some food, so they bartered some of it for flowers for the wedding. A friend had given them a Volkswagen (which you could get for £160 in those days), and so they had the problem of getting it home. The Berlin Airlift had started by then, so they were lucky to get an aircraft to take the car to Hamburg. They got it into the aircraft after a lot of pushing and shoving, but it took about four hours to get it out again at the other end – which did nothing for the smooth running of the Berlin Airlift.

Susan was a lovely, gracious lady with no airs and graces at all, but what a fascinating story.

In 2011, I was speaking on a cruise ship going up to North Cape. Also on board were Peregrine Worsthorne and his fabulous, mad wife, Lucinda Lambton. They were a lovely couple and the greatest fun, and we spent quite a bit of time laughing with them. At one stage, I had a fascinating chat with Peregrine, who told me a wonderful story about when he was a junior reporter with *The Times*. He was in America, covering Eisenhower's Presidential election trail. In those days, the electioneering was done by train, so Perry travelled in the Press car. Every day, Ike came back to talk to the Press boys, and one day he wound up at Peregrine's table. One of the chaps said, "General, this is Peringrin Worsthorne of *The Times* of England."

They had a terrible time trying to say his name, but eventually Perry told him in his cut-glass accent. Ike just looked at him and said, "What did you say?"

So Perry leapt in again and repeated it. He then said, "You may be interested to know, General, that one of the founding fathers who came over on the Mayflower was called Peregrine."

There was a long pause, and then Ike said, "Well, I have to tell you, young man, that that name did not catch on over here!"

In 1960, Air Vice-Marshal Sid Hughes was our Group Commander. He was a friend of Francis Chichester, who, at the time, was attempting his first solo crossing of the Atlantic. There was concern that Chichester had not been seen or heard from for some time, so my squadron was tasked with finding him to see if he was all right. I took off with Baz, our wonderful squadron commander, to see what we could find. We plotted an area where we thought he should be and set off for it. As was usual in those days, the first thing we did on arrival was to try to establish what the local wind was, so we did a series of turns to check our drift, and then off we set. We searched the whole area, which took some time, and then, with nothing better to do, we went back to the beginning and started again. Amazingly, there was *Gypsy Moth III*, happily sailing along. We had flown round and missed her when we were doing our wind check!

In the usual fashion, we went down to low level and were surprised to see nobody actually sailing her – so we buzzed her, or Baz did. After a short while, Francis Chichester emerged and waved to us. We then sent him his position using the Aldis light, and set off home to tell the AOC that all was well. I thought no more about it.

In 1969, when I was instructing on Varsity aircraft at Oakington, they wanted volunteers to be ushers at the memorial service for Lord Douglas of Kirtleside. Apart from being a Baron, as Sholto Douglas, he had also been C-in-C Fighter Command and C-in-C Coastal Command during the war, so I offered my services to help see off this great man. Thus, I reported to Westminster Abbey at the appointed time and set about organising the Great and the Good into their seats. It was an all-ticket affair, so it was hardly stressful; and, shortly before the service, I set off for my seat in the choir stalls. Imagine my surprise to see the now-knighted Sir Francis Chichester coming up the aisle, looking for a seat. Alas, there wasn't one, so I gave him mine, for which he was most grateful.

We had a lovely chat after the service and he told me that he was making another *Gypsy Moth*, but he was very concerned that his wife was demanding some control over the design. "She wants to put a bloody kitchen in it," he said, much to his disgust. I then reminded him of our finding him during his first Atlantic crossing in 1960, and he got a bit worked up. "Oh, it was *you*, was it? I had just managed to get into dry clothes for the first time in a week, and then you turned up – so I had to go out and get soaked again! Incidentally, I knew exactly where I was, so I didn't need your fix, thank you very much!" He was a delightful man.

I have been so lucky to meet so many fascinating people in my life.